A few meters past the dead enemy soldier, we entered the killing ground. Most of the bamboo and saplings had been cut knee high by bullets, and many of the great trees had been snapped and stripped of their leaves and much of their bark. The still, hot air was filled with the smell of cordite and the roar of automatic-rifle fire. With rivulets of sweat stinging my eyes and blurring my vision, I slipped past a giant cypress. Glancing to my left over the top of a waist-high fern, I spotted the back of an enemy soldier less than ten feet away. He was wearing black pajamas and a camouflaged soft hat. A split second later, he sensed my presence and turned.

Chunk-chunk-chunk. A burst from my silencer-equipped Sten tore into his face and blew the contents of his skull against a nearby tree. Quickly stepping over shattered saplings and bamboo, I caught glimpses of men in khaki on our left flank.

Whack-whack-whack. Whump-whump-whump. A firefight erupted a short distance to my rear. . . .

By James C. Donahue:

MOBILE GUERRILLA FORCE: *With the Special Forces in War Zone D*
BLACKJACK-33: *With Special Forces in the Viet Cong Forbidden Zone*
BLACKJACK-34: *No Greater Love*

BLACKJACK-33

With Special Forces in the Viet Cong Forbidden Zone

James C. Donahue

PRESIDIO
PRESS

BALLANTINE BOOKS · NEW YORK

A Presidio Press Book
Published by The Random House Publishing Group

Published in the United States by Presidio Press, an imprint of The Random House Publishing Group, a division of Random House, Inc., New York, and simultaneously in Canada by Random House of Canada Limited, Toronto.

Presidio Press and colophon are trademarks of Random House, Inc.

www.presidiopress.com

Library of Congress Catalog Card Number: 99-90451

ISBN 0-8041-1764-0

Manufactured in the United States of America

First Edition: September 1999

20 19 18 17 16 15 14 13 12 11

To those Americans and Cambodians
who fought with the Mobile Guerrilla Force,
5th Special Forces Group (Airborne)

ACKNOWLEDGMENTS

Blackjack-33 was a team effort. It would not have been possible without the assistance of the following individuals:

Roy Barley   Sergeant, E Company, 50th Infantry (Airborne) LRP, 9th Infantry Division

James Battle   Staff Sergeant, Mobile Guerrilla Force, 5th Special Forces Group (Airborne)

Glen Bevans   Sergeant First Class, Mobile Guerrilla Force, 5th Special Forces Group (Airborne)

Paul Brubaker   Captain, Special Operations Augmentation, 5th Special Forces Group (Airborne)

Robert Cole   Sergeant First Class, Mobile Guerrilla Force, 5th Special Forces Group (Airborne)

Sandi Donahue

Philip Downey   Specialist Fourth Class, Detachment B-36, 3d Mobile Strike Force, 5th Special Forces Group (Airborne)

Dale England   Staff Sergeant, Mobile Guerrilla Force, 5th Special Forces Group (Airborne)

Thomas Gould   Lieutenant Colonel, 4th Brigade, New York Guard

James Gritz   Captain, Mobile Guerrilla Force, 5th Special Forces Group (Airborne)

Son Thai Hien   Machine Gunner, Mobile Guerrilla Force, 5th Special Forces Group (Airborne)

Bert Hoak

Thomas Horn   Staff Sergeant, Mobile Guerrilla Force, 5th
     Special Forces Group (Airborne)

James Howard   Master Sergeant, Mobile Guerrilla Force,
     5th Special Forces Group (Airborne)

Henry Humphreys   Specialist Fifth Class, 519th Military
     Intelligence Battalion, Gia Dinh

Becky Jo Johnson

Thomas Johnson   Captain, Mobile Guerrilla Force, 5th
     Special Forces Group (Airborne)

Steven Kedski

Francis Kelly   Colonel, 5th Special Forces Group (Air-
     borne)

Thang Kieng   Rifleman, Mobile Guerrilla Force, 5th Spe-
     cial Forces Group (Airborne)

Donald Koch   Sergeant, Detachment A-732, Kham Duc,
     7th Special Forces Group (Airborne)

Rob Krott   First Lieutenant, 10th Special Forces Group
     (Airborne)

Kim Lai   Platoon Sergeant, Mobile Guerrilla Force, 5th
     Special Forces Group (Airborne)

Forest Lindley   Captain, Detachment A-231, Tieu Atar, 5th
     Special Forces Group (Airborne)

Peter Linkowski   Sergeant, F Company, 2d Battalion, 3d
     Marines, 3d Marine Division

Donald Melvin   Sergeant First Class, Mobile Guerrilla
     Force, 5th Special Forces Group (Airborne)

Rex Newell   Specialist Fifth Class, Advisory Team 1, G-2
     Section, Da Nang

Bernie Newman   Master Sergeant, Detachment B-36, Pro-
     ject Rapid Fire, 5th Special Forces Group (Airborne)

Jake O'Connor   Airman, USS *Ranger*

Alan Pritchard   Sergeant, O Company, 75th Rangers, 82d
     Airborne Division

Kien Rinh   Senior Medic, Mobile Guerrilla Force, 5th Spe-
     cial Forces Group (Airborne)

David Rose   Staff Sergeant, Mobile Guerrilla Force, 5th
     Special Forces Group (Airborne)

Harve Saal   Staff Sergeant, Special Operations Augmentation, 5th Special Forces Group (Airborne)

Steve Sherman   First Lieutenant, Detachment C-2, 5th Special Forces Group (Airborne)

Hal Slusher   Sergeant, Mobile Guerrilla Force, 5th Special Forces Group (Airborne)

Ernest Snider   Sergeant First Class, Mobile Guerrilla Force, 5th Special Forces Group (Airborne)

Peter Stark   Sergeant, Detachment B-36, Project Rapid Fire, 5th Special Forces Group (Airborne)

Tan Dara Thach   Khmer Serei Representative

Dr. John Truax

Jamie Saal Van Eaton

Scott Whitting   Staff Sergeant, Detachment A-503, Mike Force, 5th Special Forces Group (Airborne)

Steven Yedinak   Captain, Mobile Guerrilla Force, 5th Special Forces Group (Airborne). Author, *Hard To Forget*

FOREWORD

Jim Donahue's book *Blackjack-33* is an account of a United States Army Special Forces operation of the same name. It was a joint operation conducted by the Mobile Guerrilla Force and Project Sigma, both then elements of the 5th Special Forces Group (Airborne), between 24 April and 24 May 1967, in the III Corps Tactical Zone. It took place in War Zone D, a military subsection of that zone. The Mobile Guerrilla Force was commanded by Capt. James G. Gritz; Project Sigma, as well as operational control of the mission, was under the command of Lt. Col. Clarence T. Hewgley.

This is a true story, not a fictional account. Jim was a participant in the operation, serving as a medic as well as deputy commander of one of the platoons involved.

There is nothing new about the concept of special operations. From the epic account of the Trojan horse in Homer's *Odyssey* down to more modern times and the early days of America, innovative and daring military men have left their mark on history, captured our imagination, and continue to inspire us: George Washington's surprise attack across the Delaware River against Hessian mercenaries on Christmas Eve; the exploits of Maj. Robert Rogers and his famous Rogers's Rangers; Francis Marion, the "Swamp Fox"; John Mosby, the Confederate cavalry colonel who became known as the "Gray Ghost" to the Union army during the Civil War; Darby's Rangers; Merrill's Marauders; and the Office of Strategic Services (OSS) Jedburgh Teams of World War II, as well as the 8240th Army Unit of the Korean War, were all contributors to, and molders of, our special operations tradition leading up to the Vietnam War.

Despite the wide divergence of time, weaponry, terrain, and goals of their conflicts, certain attributes were constants: unconventional leadership, daring tactics, and men willing to take great risks to achieve their objectives. Given these, along with the proper training, planning, and execution, it was and is possible for a smaller force to wreak havoc upon a force many times its size. So it was with the United States Army Special Forces in general and the Mobile Guerrilla Force in particular.

Encouraged by the suspension of Operation Rolling Thunder (December 1965–January 1966), the bombing campaign against the north, the North Vietnamese Army stepped up its infiltration of South Vietnam, augmenting units of its southern Communist allies, the Viet Cong. Certain enclaves or "secret zones," one of them being War Zone D, were used as launch sites for attacks against targets in South Vietnam. This zone in particular was referred to by the Viet Cong as "The Forbidden Zone" since they had almost complete control of and freedom of movement within it. Despite the fact that such areas were known enemy refuges, almost no reconnaissance or clearing operations had been conducted in them. As a result, limited hard intelligence was available on enemy units, base camps, and infiltration routes within them. Something needed to be done, and that fact was not lost upon Col. Francis J. Kelly, who assumed command of the 5th Special Forces Group (Airborne) in June 1966.

Kelly was an irascible individual, quick to relieve a man of command when he felt his performance was not adequate. Referred to by subordinates as "Blackjack" or "Saint Francis," the Blackjack operations were named for him, the first digit of the operation indicating the corps-area of execution, and the second the sequence; e.g., Blackjack-33 was the third Mobile Guerrilla Force mission to take place in the III Corps Tactical Zone.

After Kelly secured approval from Gen. William C. Westmoreland, COMUSMACV, he summoned Capt. James Gritz to his office. Gritz was the executive officer and chief instructor at the MACV Recondo School in Nha Trang and had seen prior service with Project Delta.

At their meeting Kelly detailed what he had in mind: a company-size force capable of conducting guerrilla operations in War Zone D for periods ranging from thirty to sixty days. This light-infantry company would have to operate without artillery support or chance of reinforcement. The unit's sole support would consist of a single forward air control aircraft, tactical air strikes, and parachute drops of food, supplies, and ammunition every four days. It sounded more like a suicide mission than a legitimate operational proposal.

Gritz promptly told the colonel that, based on his experience, it would be impossible for a company-size unit to conduct operations in War Zone D for more than a few days at best; as soon as the men were inserted they would be found, fixed, fought, and finished by much larger Viet Cong and North Vietnamese Army forces. Gritz didn't think that the idea was practical, but the boldness of it intrigued him and he informed Kelly that if the colonel was determined to proceed, then he was volunteering to be its on-the-ground commander. Ten days later, Captain Gritz was tasked to organize, train, and command a Mobile Guerrilla Force company that would commence guerrilla operations in War Zone D as soon as possible.

The American contingent came quickly. Among the volunteers was the author, Jim Donahue, then serving as a medic and an adviser to a Montagnard light-infantry company at Duc Phong Special Forces Camp.

But what of the indigenous personnel who would comprise the bulk of the fighting manpower for the Mobile Guerrilla Force? The answer lay with the Cambodians, already members of the Civilian Irregular Defense Group (CIDG) companies in service to Special Forces and its operations. They were ideally suited to the mission. Well-disciplined, good-natured, ferocious fighters, they were willing to sacrifice themselves for what they understood to be a greater cause. They were also familiar with the territory and the people and, by virtue of their own inherent distrust of the Vietnamese, were less susceptible to infiltration by Communist elements sympathetic to the Viet Cong.

Capt. Steven M. Yedinak, the deputy commander of Mobile Guerrilla Force, and recent author of *Hard to Forget*,* led the recruitment effort. Initial contact was made with representatives of the Khmer Serei through its headquarters on Trung Minh Gian Street in Saigon, and recruiting took place at the Special Forces Camp at Bu Dop, a transient point for the Cambodians. On 10 November 1966, two hundred and fifty volunteers were assembled in Bien Hoa and trucked to Ho Ngoc Tao Special Forces Camp, the home of Project Sigma, where four weeks of intensive training followed.

From 13 November to 15 December a weeding-out process took place. The regimen consisted of sixteen-hour days and included conventional military subjects as well as all aspects of guerrilla warfare: silent and special weapons, mining and booby-trapping, raids and ambushes, and aerial resupply drops.

On 15 December 1966, the Mobile Guerrilla Force completed training and was flown to Duc Phong Special Forces Camp, eighty miles north of Saigon on the northern edge of War Zone D, in preparation for its first mission, designated Blackjack-31. Only one day after arrival, the mission was put on hold; a U-2 spy plane returning from a signal intelligence (SIGINT) mission over North Vietnam experienced severe buffeting during its descent into Bien Hoa and broke up at an altitude of 26,000 feet. The pilot, Maj. Leo Stewart, safely ejected and was picked up by a rescue helicopter; the U-2 crashed somewhere in the enemy-controlled jungle south of Song Be.

On board the "Dragon Lady," CIA designation for the U-2, was a state-of-the-art Electronic Countermeasure (ECM)

*Ivy Books, 1998.

System 13A device that fooled enemy radar as to the plane's location. Its recovery by the enemy would have grave consequences for the national security interests of the United States. Although the black box was equipped with a self-destruct device, the air force technicians from the Strategic Air Command's 100th Strategic Reconnaissance Wing in Bien Hoa had not received instructional manuals on how to connect it before the mission on which it was lost.

The Air Force calculated that the aircraft had crashed in a fan-shaped area of triple-canopy jungle that encompassed 440 square miles. Numerous photoreconnaissance flights in search of the U-2's wreckage followed, all to no avail; the plane could not be located. A ground search had to be instituted, and that job fell to Special Forces. After reviewing his assets, Colonel Kelly assigned the mission to the Mobile Guerrilla Force.

The search that followed has been equated to looking for a very small needle in a very large haystack. Despite enormous odds against a successful conclusion, the Dragon Lady was located on the third day out. The black box itself was located on the fourth day by one of the Cambodians assigned to the Second Platoon. His identity remains unknown to this day.

President Lyndon Johnson was informed of the recovery of the black box, and on 8 January 1967, the Mobile Guerrilla Force began its ground infiltration of War Zone D. During the month-long Blackjack-31 operation, it fought fifty-one engagements and raided fifteen company- and battalion-size base camps. Just as in the black-box mission, it was the Cambodians who were instrumental in so many of Special Forces' operations in the III and IV Corps Tactical Zones, and yet the average American knows little or nothing of their contributions to such great successes.

Kampuchea is the ancient name of "the peaceful kingdom," that country that we Americans came to know as Cambodia. However incorrect the terms Cambodia and Cambodians may now be, they are used here and in the book for the sake of clarity. That is whom we understood them to be at the time.

The Khmers are the ethnic majority people of Cambodia, representing ninety-five percent of that nation's population. The term Kampuchea Krom means Lower Cambodia or, more properly, Cambodia Below, that segment of South Vietnam that had previously been a part of the Khmer empire. It extended from a point slightly north of Tay Ninh (known as Raung Damrei to the Khmer) down through the delta region of the Mekong River, the southernmost point of the country, those areas best known to veterans as the III and IV Corps Tactical Zones.

The Khmer Kampuchea Krom (KKK) are the indigenous people of that area, having occupied it prior to and during the reign of various Khmer kings, who ruled from the ninth through the thirteenth century. This territory was taken from them in warfare in 1632 by their far more numerous expansionist neighbors to the north, the Viets. For the sake of a comparative time line, it may be helpful for the reader to remember that the Pilgrims first set foot on Plymouth Rock in Massachusetts in 1620, only twelve years earlier. In short, far from being outsiders, these Cambodians knew the area best.

The term Khmer Serei means Free Cambodians and refers to an underground nationalist movement that existed within both Kampuchea (Cambodia) and Kampuchea Krom (Cambodia Below, i.e., southern South Vietnam) at the time of America's entry into the conflict. They were committed anticommunists who were devoted to the ideal of Cambodian autonomy and had a deep and abiding distrust of Vietnamese North and South. The issue of Communism aside, they made no distinction between the two. The Khmer Serei were becoming disillusioned with the policies being pursued by Norodom Sihanouk, crown prince of Cambodia. An astute politician, he had successfully negotiated Cambodia's independence from the French Union in 1953, prior to the French defeat at Dien Bien Phu and the Geneva Accords in 1954. Sihanouk, in their view, was courting disaster by allowing North Vietnamese Army and Main Force Viet Cong units to occupy Cambodia's eastern provinces, using them as staging areas to carry on the war in South Vietnam. The history of the Vietnamese was one of continuous territorial expansion and the Khmer Krom, victims of it, were hypervigilant on the issue.

The Khmer Serei were members of the organization that had a spontaneous birth in 1958 and was led by an elusive figure named Dr. Son Ngoc Thanh, himself a Khmer Krom, and later a key figure in the coup d'etat that deposed Sihanouk in March 1970. Their direct opposition were the Khmer Rouge, the Cambodian Communists who, even then, were a rising threat in the countryside, specifically the areas west of Tonle Sap, the inland lake, well out of the path of government forces and the Vietnamese invaders. Led by Saloth Sar, better known to the world as Pol Pot, theirs was a mindless and uncontrolled fury that would lead to the decimation of their own people, dictated by their ideology to return to what they termed "Year Zero."

History being what it is, there is a terrible irony here. Norodom Sihanouk and Pol Pot, both educated men, were actually very distantly related by marriage through the Sisowath family, who had ruled the country for generations. One of the accusations being leveled at Sihanouk was that he was digressing; during that time of great national strife, he was actually starring in movies extolling the glories of the old Khmer empire. Pol Pot, on the other hand, sought to return his people to the beginning of time. Their very different philosophies seem to point to a defect in the Cambodian royal character, a driving desire to shut out the reality of current events, to return to the more glorious times of yesteryear.

To those who served with them, it is always irritating to read accounts of the Khmer Kampuchea Krom and Khmer Serei that describe them as bandits and mercenaries. This is simply not true. While itinerant opportunistic bands of Khmer Kampuchea Krom did exist, they were no more representative of their people than those individuals who participated in the My Lai atrocities were representative of the average American soldier. Ethnic Cambodians in South

Vietnam were soldiers in service to that country of which they were citizens and residents, South Vietnam.

They enlisted under the umbrella of the CIDG program, that conglomeration of dispossessed and disenfranchised indigenous peoples who served with Special Forces. Numbered among them were ethnic Vietnamese from the Cao Dai and Hoa Hao religious sects, Montagnard tribesmen, Chinese Nungs, and these Cambodians. That is precisely why the CIDG program was created—to utilize the services of those peoples who, despite their differences with the government, could be persuaded to fight on its behalf.

In April 1967, the CIDG contingent numbered 37,850 men, the equivalent of two or three American divisions, and in conjunction with U.S. Army Special Forces, which was commanded only by a colonel, it operated throughout the whole of South Vietnam.

No greater adhesive exists between men than the crucible of combat: it creates a bond that is difficult to understand for those who have not had that experience. I freely admit my own bias on the subject of the Cambodians. Having served with them, I know them to be brave and loyal men who proved their mettle in battle time and again. Theravada Buddhists, they were, on the one hand, warm, gentle, and loving, quick to smile and befriend another, and, on the other hand, absolutely ferocious warriors. They were known, on occasion, while in the midst of a firefight, to pause, present their middle finger to the enemy, and launch into loud discourse concerning their negative view of him, his ancestry, Ho Chi Minh, and Communism, and then resume firing. I never saw an American do that. Perhaps being twelve thousand miles from home accentuated our sense of self-preservation.

This is not a scholarly historical treatise, nor is it meant to be. Jim Donahue does not profess to be a historian and neither do I. What little history is provided here is intended simply to enable the reader to understand just who the Cambodians mentioned in the book were and how they came to serve with Special Forces on the operation known as Blackjack-33. It is not a story of great historic insight or hindsight; rather, it is a human one, the story of the men, American and Cambodian, who stood shoulder to shoulder in the thick of battle—good men, loyal and true, committed to their cause and one another, who threw in their lot together, the story of those who lived and those who died.

Come along now reader, as the author takes you into that enemy sanctuary known as War Zone D in pursuit of a wily and determined adversary, where every step might be the last. Meet our Cambodian brothers and experience the sights, sounds, smells, and emotions of combat, and the camaraderie of the men who waged guerrilla warfare in "The Forbidden Zone."

> Philip M. Downey*
> Upton, Massachusetts
> February 1999

*Phil Downey served two tours in Vietnam. When he arrived at the 1st Division's base camp at Lai Khe in May 1968, he was assigned to a Long Range Reconnaissance Patrol (LRRP) team with F Company, 52d Infantry. One month into his tour, he was transferred to the 5th Special Forces Group's 3d Mobile Strike Force at Long Hai where he served as a recon team leader. As an eighteen-year-old specialist-4, he was the unit's youngest member. Following his tour in Vietnam, Phil received orders to Fort Bragg, North Carolina, and in January 1970, he volunteered to return to Vietnam. When he arrived in Nha Trang, he was assigned as a light weapons leader with Special Forces Detachment B-33 at Hon Quan.—Author

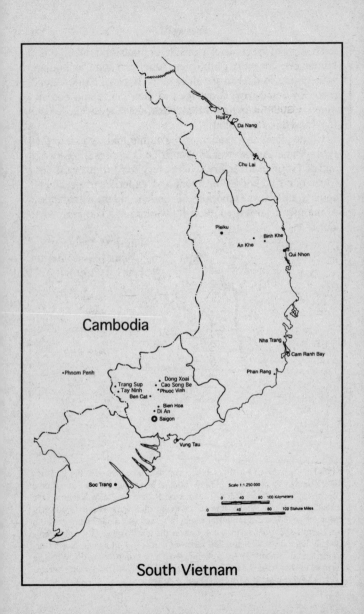

Cambodia

Phnom Penh

Hué
Da Nang

Chu Lai

Pleiku
An Khe
Binh Khe
Qui Nhon

Nha Trang
Cam Ranh Bay

Phan Rang

Trang Sup
Dong Xoai
Tay Ninh
Cao Song Be
Ben Cat
Phuoc Vinh
Bien Hoa
Di An
Saigon

Vung Tau

Soc Trang

Scale 1:1,250,000

0   40   80   100 Kilometers

0   40   80   100 Statute Miles

South Vietnam

GUERRILLA WARFARE OPERATIONAL AREA

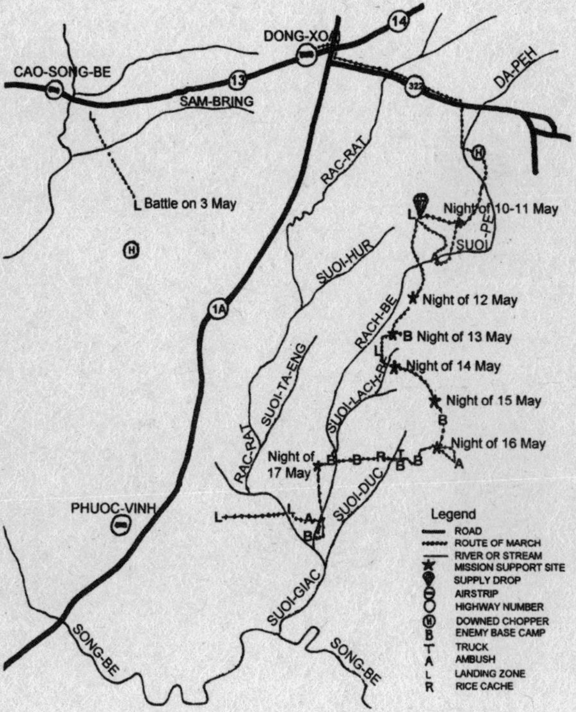

CAO-SONG-BE

DONG-XOA

SAM-BRING

DA-PEH

RAC-RAT

L Battle on 3 May

L Night of 10-11 May

SUOI

SUOI-HUR

Night of 12 May

RACH-BE

B Night of 13 May

SUOI-TA-ENG

Night of 14 May

SUOI-LACH

Night of 15 May

B

Night of 16 May

RAC-RAT

Night of 17 May

E B R T B B
A

SUOI-DUC

PHUOC-VINH

L A

B

SUOI-GIAC

SONG-BE

SONG-BE

Legend

ROAD
ROUTE OF MARCH
RIVER OR STREAM
MISSION SUPPORT SITE
SUPPLY DROP
AIRSTRIP
HIGHWAY NUMBER
DOWNED CHOPPER
ENEMY BASE CAMP
TRUCK
AMBUSH
LANDING ZONE
RICE CACHE

1

0750 HOURS, 3 MAY 1967

With seventy-pound rucksacks on our backs, our column threaded its way through thick undergrowth and triple-canopy jungle. In our shadowy world, the still morning air was heavy with the smells of humus and mold. High in the trees, the morning mist was beginning to burn off, and a few rays of sunlight glowed a translucent white as they penetrated to the soft, moist earth. The jungle was alive with buzzing and chirping, and to the southeast, I could hear the faint hum of the forward air controller's single-engine observation aircraft.

Ten meters to my front, SFC Bob Cole led silently on point. Bob was an operations sergeant who had come to the Mobile Guerrilla Force after SFC George Ovsak was killed at Trang Sup Special Forces Camp. To the Cambodians, Bob was known as *Trung si Khmao*. They were awed by the fact that his skin was darker than theirs, and they held him in great esteem. With his silencer-equipped, nine-millimeter, MK-II British Sten gun at the ready, Bob slipped through the wet foliage with feline grace. A seasoned point man, he paused every few steps while his brain sorted every shred of stimulus for possible danger—the rustling of leaves, a color that didn't fit, the smell of a Vietnamese cigarette.

With every step, my boots sank into creamy black mud, and from the jungle floor, twisting trails of steam slowly worked their way skyward. As the navigator, I used a map and compass to keep Bob on a zigzag course to the southeast.

Every few minutes, he looked to the rear, and I used hand-and-arm signals to adjust his course to the left or right.

Two paces behind me, Ly, our seventeen-year-old Cambodian radio operator, walked with our PRC-25 radio handset pressed to his ear. Ly was well built, had straight black hair, and friendly brown eyes. He didn't speak much English but was very reliable. Ly was followed by Luc, our Cambodian platoon sergeant. Luc was a quiet, no-nonsense professional who had been fighting the Communists for nearly twenty years. Rumor had it that he was wanted for the murder of a South Vietnamese Army officer. Next in line was our three-man machine-gun section and the remaining thirty-five Khmer-Serei Cambodians of the 3d Platoon.

Following our bootprints through the mud were Capt. Jim Gritz, the Mobile Guerrilla Force commander, S.Sgt. Tom Horn, the headquarters-section radio operator, and the fourteen Cambodians of the headquarters section. Bringing up the rear were SFC Glen Bevans, S.Sgt. Roy Sparks, and the thirty-nine Cambodians of the 2d Platoon. The Recon Platoon—S.Sgt. Dale England, S.Sgt. Jim Williams, S.Sgt. Hal Slusher, and forty Cambodians—was five kilometers to the southeast. Our 1st Platoon remained at Trang Sup Special Forces Camp—the home of the Mobile Guerrilla Force—because we didn't have the necessary helicopter support to airlift the entire company into the area of operations.

Since January 1967, there had been extensive enemy sightings in the Viet Cong Secret Zone southeast of Cau Song Be Special Forces Camp, and intelligence suspected that the 271st and 273d Main Force Viet Cong regiments had moved into the area. Intelligence also believed that elements of the 84th and 141st North Vietnamese Army regiments were operating in the enemy Secret Zone. In addition to Viet Cong and North Vietnamese Army regiments, guerrilla bands from the 81st Rear Service Unit were also known to be operating throughout the area. Our mission had been code-named Blackjack-33, and our objective was to draw the enemy regiments into a decisive engagement so that they could be fought and destroyed by the 1st Infantry Division. I didn't like the idea of being used as bait, but Col. Francis "Blackjack" Kelly, commanding officer, 5th Special Forces Group (Airborne), had received assurances from Maj. Gen. John Hay, commanding general, 1st Infantry Division, that units of his division would immediately move to reinforce the Mobile Guerrilla Force if we made contact with a large enemy unit. It was a dangerous game—like hunting a three-hundred-pound tiger with a jackknife.

Kaw, kaw, kaw. A crow interrupted my thoughts. Looking up through a few holes in the canopy, I saw patches of blue sky. Our world beneath the canopy would soon become a steam bath.

Whack-whack-whack! Whump-whump-whump! A distant firefight erupted to the southeast, and a surge of adrenaline shot into my system. As I closed the gap with Bob, I took a compass direction on the firing.

"Sixteens and AKs," Bob whispered.

"Yeah, 160 degrees," I said as we pushed silently through large, heart-shaped leaves.

"Gotta be Recon," Bob said.

"Bac-si." Ly handed me the radio handset.

"Say again, Fox Four," Captain Gritz radioed the Recon Platoon with a calm Oklahoma twang. "I'm only reading you two by two. Over."

"Fox Control, this is Fox Four," Staff Sergeant England responded in his West Virginia drawl. "RT (Recon Team) Delta made contact with a VC platoon on our back trail. I'm moving to the POC (point of contact) with RT Bravo. Over."

"Roger, Four. What's your location and distance to the POC? Over."

"From the RP (a reference point on our maps), I'm at right 1.2, up 2.3. Delta's two hundred meters northwest. Over."

I looked closely at my acetate-covered map and saw that he was at the northern edge of a large clearing called Bau Chu.

"Got a fix on 'im?" Bob whispered as we moved together.

"Yeah." I used a twig to point to the location on the map. "He's at 951 669."

As Bob looked at my map, I grew concerned about the distance to the Recon Platoon. If England got into trouble, it could take hours for us to close the gap.

"Gonna be a long day," Bob predicted as the firing continued. "Intel intercepted AM radio signals from that area."

"That's what Horn was tellin' me," I said.

The enemy used long-range AM radios for communications between their regiments. For tactical operations, they used short-range FM radios. The fact that there were AM radio transmissions coming from the area of the Bau Chu clearing was a good indication that at least one regiment was operating in that area.

We continued southeast through a thicket of green, tan, and brown clumps of bamboo. Near the ground, the fifty-foot stalks were bundled together, but at the higher elevations, the weight of their long narrow leaves bowed them over. High in the bamboo, small green birds chirped as they fluttered from stalk to stalk.

"Memphis, this is Fox Four-Bravo. Over." S.Sgt. Hal Slusher, a recon section leader, was calling the forward air controller.

"Fox Four-Bravo, this is Memphis. Over," the FAC responded.

"Memphis, this is Bravo. We need gunships. Over."

"Roger, Bravo. Memphis, out," the FAC responded as we slipped between tall stalks of lime green bamboo. To the southeast, the exchange of small-arms fire and explosions intensified.

"Fox Control, this is Fox Four. Over," England gasped for air.

"Four, this is Control. Over," Gritz responded.

"Control, I've linked up with Delta. We're in contact with an undetermined number of VC. Mixed black-and-green uniforms. Got movement on both flanks."

Whoomph, whoomph. What sounded like two claymore mines exploded.

"Four, this is Control. Break contact. Over," Gritz ordered.

"Roger, Control. We've broken contact," England yelled.

When a Viet Cong unit made contact with what they thought was a recon team, they would generally lay down a base of fire, move quickly on both flanks, and try to encircle it. If the team was to survive, it had to move to the rear before the encirclement was complete.

"Fox Three, this is Fox Control. Over," Gritz radioed the 3d Platoon.

"Control, this is Three. Over," I whispered into the handset.

"Three, this is Control. Pick it up. Straight line to the POC. Over."

"Roger, Control. Three, out."

"Psst." I closed the gap with Bob. "Move it out," I whispered. "Straight to the POC."

"Right." Bob had a green triangular bandanna tied around his neck and used it to wipe his face. He didn't say anything, but I sensed he didn't like the idea of moving in a straight line. It was dangerous because it provided the enemy with the opportunity to predict our route of march. Setting a pattern was an invitation to sudden death, and Bob knew that if we were ambushed, he would be the first to die.

As the sun rose higher in the sky, we moved quickly through an area of dead and dying bamboo. The ground was littered with broken sections of mold-covered bamboo and brittle leaves.

"Memphis, this is Fox Four-Bravo. Over," Slusher radioed the FAC.

"Bravo, this is Memphis. Over," the FAC responded.

"Memphis, got a Bode down with a gut wound. Need an immediate medevac. Over."

"Roger, Bravo. I'll have a Dustoff on the ground in one-zero minutes. Memphis, out."

The temperature must have been close to a hundred, and

my black-green-and-brown tiger-stripe fatigues were soaked with sweat. With my finger on the trigger and my thumb on the selector switch, I watched for movement on both flanks and tried not to step on the decaying sections of bamboo—a *crunch* could be heard for a hundred meters.

Whack-whack-whack. Whump-whump-whump. The stutter of M-16s and AK-47s broke the silence.

"Fox Control, this is Fox Four. Over." England was still short of breath.

"Four, this is Control. Over," Gritz responded.

"Control, made it back to our patrol base. Heavy fire on both flanks. Need gunships, now. Over," he reported with a sense of urgency.

"Fox Control, this is Memphis. Over," the FAC broke in.

"This is Control. Over," Gritz responded.

"Control, I've got a message from Hustler. Over."

"Roger, Memphis. What d'ya got? Over."

"Control, Hustler advises that Americans will not—I say again—will not be committed. Hustler also advises that Fox One is being airlifted to the POC, over."

The FAC's message scared the hell out of me. Without the support of the 1st Infantry Division, we would be lucky if anyone survived the day.

"Memphis, this is bullshit," Gritz responded. "Pass the word to the FOB that we're gonna need TAC air and gunships. Over."

"Roger, Control. Memphis, out."

I caught up with Bob on the four-foot bank of a slow-moving stream called the Sam Bring. It measured three meters across and flowed west to the Song Be (the Be River). Both banks were crowded with large, oblong, green-and-white leaves, and hungry red dragonflies cruised its surface, hunting for mosquitoes. On the far bank, large black birds with yellow heads paced back and forth, stabbing at insects. Upstream from the crossing point, the tops of a few palm trees were silhouetted against a blue sky. To the southeast, I detected the faint *wap, wap, wap* of helicopters.

"Big Red One ain't comin'," I whispered to Bob as we watched for movement on the far bank. "They're liftin' in the 1st Platoon."

Bob's jaw muscles tightened, and his nostrils flared with anger.

"Fuck 'em." Bob was a man of few words.

With our M-16s at the ready Ly, Luc, and I continued to watch for movement as Bob slid down the muddy bank into the clear, knee-deep water. Downstream from the crossing point, I caught glimpses of shadows moving through the higher elevations of the canopy and heard the familiar *ka, ka, ka* of monkeys.

Ta-tow-tow-tow. Whoomph, whoomph. It sounded like helicopter gunships were working the area around England's position. It was a comforting sound. Airpower was the great equalizer.

"Many VC this area," Luc whispered as his piercing black eyes flashed back and forth under the rim of his soft hat.

"Think you're right, partner," I said as I looked closely at my map. To the southeast of the point of contact there was a stream called the Suoi Nuoc Trong. With good overhead cover and a year-round water supply, it provided the ideal location for a Viet Cong or North Vietnamese Army regimental headquarters. It was also within striking distance of 1st Infantry Division units at Phuoc Vinh and the Special Forces Camps at Cau Song Be and Dong Xoai.

"If Americans not come, many Cambodian die," Luc predicted.

I could feel my anger building and took in a deep breath.

"They'll send in the Mike Force," I said, hoping to convince him.

Bob gave us a thumbs-up—the all clear signal—from the far bank before continuing to the southeast. I reached down, grabbed a root that was growing out of the bank, and slid into the cool water. In the distance, helicopters continued to work England's perimeter. When I reached the far bank, I dug the toes of my boots into the soft mud and used a few saplings to pull myself to the top. A few meters ahead, Bob's pace slowed to a crawl as he hacked a tunnel through a wall of thorn-covered vines. We called them wait-a-minute vines because every time one of their thorns hooked your skin, you had to stop to pull it out. I removed a canteen from my BAR belt and, while swallowing a couple of salt tablets, detected the faint odor of wood smoke. I worried that the enemy would hear Bob's chopping but knew that England's contact required that we trade silence for speed. To the southeast, the shooting stopped, and only the *wap, wap, wap* of the helicopters remained.

"*Trung si* Slusher say one platoon come Trang Sup," Ly told me as he handed me the radio handset. "One Khmer go Bien Hoa."

"Good," I nodded. I was glad to hear that our 1st Platoon was on the ground and that Slusher was able to medevac the wounded Cambodian.

"One, this is Four," England radioed SFC Donald "Ranger" Melvin—the 1st Platoon commander. "Come to the red smoke. Watch for movement on your left flank. Over."

"Roger, Four. Spotted khaki in the tree line. One, out," Melvin responded.

As Bob continued to hack through the tangle, water dripped from the ends of dangling vines, and beads of sweat rolled down my face. To the north, an animal screeched and then cried. Death was everywhere.

Whack-whack-whack. Whump-whump-whump. Whoomph, whoomph. A cacophony of automatic-rifle fire and explosions erupted to the southeast.

"Control, this is Four," England radioed Gritz with a renewed sense of urgency. "We're in heavy contact—I say again—heavy contact. Khaki uniforms. Over."

Adrenaline surged into my system, and my heart pounded like a bass drum.

"Four, this is Control. Break contact! Over," Gritz ordered.

"Control, we can't move. We're pinned down and taking casualties. Over."

"Roger, Four," Gritz responded. "Tie it in tight with One."

"Shit," I mumbled. Mobility was one of the keys to our survival. I feared the enemy would now move quickly to wipe out Recon and the 1st Platoon. As we continued to the southeast, I watched for movement on our flanks but couldn't see beyond a few meters.

"Control, this is Four," England radioed. "Fox Four-Alpha's hit . . ."

With the radio handset pressed to my left ear, I used my M-16 to push aside a half dozen dangling vines. A few meters ahead, Bob continued his frenzied chopping.

"Fox Four, are you there? Over," Gritz radioed with concern in his voice.

"Roger, Control. Somethin' hit me in the forehead. Got blood in my eyes . . ." There was another pause. "Christ, Alpha's hit again . . ."

"Control, this is One," Melvin broke in. "We're up to our ass in alligators on the west side of the perimeter. We're being hit by khaki-uniformed troops. The Bodes say they're Chinese. Over."

"One, this is Control. Did you say Chinese? Over."

"Fuckin' Chinese," Melvin yelled.

"Roger, One. Are you tied in tight with Four? Over."

"That's a negative," Melvin responded. "Can't get to Four. Anything more than a foot off the ground is dead meat. Over."

"Control, this is Four," England broke in. "I'm hit bad. Except for Quan, everyone I can see is dead or wounded . . ." There was a pause. "Fox Four-Alpha's dead," he said with great sadness. "We're stackin' magazines. This may be my last transmission. Over."

The news of Williams's death left me with a sick feeling.

"Roger, Four . . ." Gritz paused. "Memphis, this is Fox Control," he radioed the FAC with renewed anger in his voice.

"Fox Control, this is Memphis. Go ahead. Over."

"Memphis, pass the word to Hustler that I want every god-damned gunship and tactical aircraft in III Corps deployed to the POC, over."

"Roger, Control. Memphis, out."

Our shadowy world beneath the canopy suddenly turned dark as we entered an area of four-story cypress trees with mottled gray-and-white trunks. Ten to fifteen feet off the ground, their roots buttressed out and gripped the moist earth an equal distance from the trunk. The areas between the great trees were packed tight with smaller trees and the dreaded thorn-covered vines.

Whoomph, whoomph. Whack-whack-whack. Whoomph, whoomph. A string of explosions followed by small-arms fire and more explosions.

"Memphis, this is Fox One-Alpha." I recognized SFC Alvin Rouley, the 1st Platoon's deputy platoon commander, by his Cajun accent. "We got a long line of blue uniformed Victor Charlie comin' our way. These boys do know their shit. Over."

"Roger Alpha. I see 'em," the FAC responded.

"Alpha, this is Control," Gritz broke in. "Pull 'em in tight. If Charlie gets inside your perimeter you can kiss your ass good-bye. Over."

"Roger—" Rouley's radio went dead.

Whumph-whumph-whumph. What sounded like a heavy machine gun joined in the exchange of fire.

The moisture-laden air was suffocating. As I watched Bob hack through the steaming tangle, I thought about Rouley's radio transmission. My best guess was that they were in contact with at least three different enemy units. The black-and-green uniformed troops that England first made contact with were likely a local Viet Cong security unit. The khaki-uniformed troops were probably members of the 271st Main Force Viet Cong Regiment. In our pre-mission intelligence briefing, we were told that there were Chinese mercenaries fighting with the 271st. The blue uniformed troops that Rouley reported had to be from another Main

Force Viet Cong or North Vietnamese Army unit. If my assessment was accurate . . .

Ta-tow-tow-tow. The firing from helicopter gunships interrupted my thoughts.

"Memphis, this is One. Over," Sergeant First Class Melvin radioed the FAC. "Fox Four-Bravo, Fox One-Bravo, and I are hit. We've got VC closing from the northwest and a fifty-one (heavy machine gun) tearing us up from the far side of the clearing, over."

"Fox One, this is Memphis," the FAC responded. "Give me an azimuth on the fifty-one. Over."

"Roger, Memphis . . ." There was a pause. "Two hundred and fifty degrees from the yellow smoke. We need heavy ordnance—I say again—heavy ordnance. Gunships ain't gonna do it, over."

"Roger, One. That's a can do. I'm in contact with a flight of fast movers. Estimate their TOT (time on target) in zero-five minutes. Memphis, out."

I was stunned by the news that Crighton, Slusher, and Melvin had been wounded. Crighton had arrived at the Mobile Guerrilla Force as a specialist four and had only recently been promoted to captain. Prior to Special Forces and the Mobile Guerrilla Force, he had served as the commander of a Canadian Airborne company. There was something very British about him, so we nicknamed him Critchley. Slusher was a talented medic and small-unit leader who had served with me at Duc Phong Special Forces Camp, and I now felt bad that I had encouraged him to volunteer for the Mobile Guerrilla Force. Melvin—we called him Ranger Melvin— was an experienced team sergeant who had also only recently joined the team. When he arrived in Vietnam, he received orders to report to MACV-SOG, but Captain Gritz somehow managed to shanghai him to the Mobile Guerrilla Force.

Whoomph, whoomph, whoomph. Rockets from helicopter gunships exploded to the southeast.

A blazing sun filtered through the overhead canopy, and in the higher elevations, the leaves shimmered in the heat. A few meters ahead, the pace of Bob's relentless hacking was slowing. I closed the gap and saw that his camouflaged fatigues were streaked white with salt.

"Bob," I hissed. When he turned I saw that his eyes were glazed and that he appeared close to collapse.

"Yeah."

"Let me take over," I said.

"I'm okay." He used his scarf to wipe his dripping face.

Bob was as bullheaded as they came. I knew that he would continue until he dropped and that dehydration would affect his judgment and ability to react quickly.

"A few minutes," I pleaded. "Get some salt into your system."

"Okay," he relented.

I gave him my M-16, and he passed me the silencer-equipped Sten and a few extra magazines, an M-18A1 claymore mine, and a razor-sharp, twenty-three-inch machete that was sticky with sap. If I came face-to-face with an enemy soldier, I would kill him with the silenced Sten before he could alert his comrades. The claymore came in a green cloth carrying case with its retractable steel legs extending through the bottom of the case. If we made point contact with a large enemy force, I would use it to blow a hole through their ranks. It wouldn't necessarily stop them, but it would slow them down.

I rolled down my sleeves and slipped on a pair of leather work gloves. With the Sten in my left hand and machete in my right, I stepped in front of Bob. A point man was never more than a heartbeat from sudden death, and my body immediately adjusted to a heightened level of danger. I was suddenly charged with electricity and full of energy. Since the difference between life and death was often measured in fractions of a second, a point man had to react instantly. If you had to think about what you were going to do, you wouldn't live long enough to become an experienced point man.

With moss-covered tree trunks to my left and right, I cut through an almost impenetrable wall of thorn-covered vines.

With every swing of the machete, needle-sharp thorns tore at my glove and sleeve. Occasionally, one of them hooked an ear, and I had to stop to remove it.

Karoumph, karoumph, karoumph. A string of bombs exploded to the southeast. Seconds later, a jet screeched over our column like a banshee. And, after an agonizing hour of relentless chopping, we put the thorn-covered vines behind us, and I was able to pick up the pace. An unyielding sun tortured the jungle, and with the taste of salt on my lips, we moved through an area where everything was dressed in shades of green. The trunks of the four-story cypress trees were covered with moss, and the areas between the great trees were crowded with dripping leaves and chest-high ferns. In the jungle, everything seemed to sweat.

Slipping silently through the foliage, I watched for the enemy to my front, on both flanks, and high in the trees. On point, nothing could be overlooked, and only the fortunate lived to talk about his mistakes. After moving through leaves and giant ferns for fifteen minutes, I came upon a massive cypress lying across our path. Its trunk measured a good eight feet in diameter, and what remained of its broken branches were as sharp as spears. With Bob's help I climbed atop the mossy hulk and saw that we had entered an area where hundreds of cypress trees had been uprooted like a box of toothpicks spilled on a kitchen table. Years earlier, the area must have been devastated by a tropical storm.

"Jim," Bob whispered from the ground. "England's alive."

"Great." I smiled as I used my scarf to wipe the stinging salt from my eyes. England and I had been together since we formed the Mobile Guerrilla Force in October 1966, and were good friends.

Karoumph, karoumph, karoumph. As more bombs exploded to the southeast, I reached down to pull Bob to the top of the trunk. Being careful not to slip on the moss, I took a few steps. *Crunch!* The trunk caved in, and I found myself standing up to my armpits inside the rotted trunk. When Bob reached me, he extended a helping hand.

"What the hell are you doing?" He laughed as he pulled me out. I quickly brushed hundreds of white termites from my trousers and jumped to the ground. For what seemed like hours, we crawled over, under, and around the great trees. I carried six quarts of water, and with a relentless sun beating down on us, I found myself drinking close to a quart an hour.

Once past the fallen trees, we entered an area of fifty-foot palm trees. Their bowed trunks were wrapped tight with vines and supported clumps of coconuts and large, feather-like fronds. Between the tall trees grew clumps of green bamboo and drooping banana plants. I stopped when I saw that a few of the bamboo stalks had been shattered by bullets.

"What is it?" Bob whispered as a jet screeched in low from the west.

Burrrrr. The jet's twenty-millimeter cannons roared as they pounded enemy positions around Recon and the 1st Platoon.

"Must be where Recon first made contact," I whispered while looking at my map. "Two hundred meters to go."

When I bent over to stretch the muscles in my lower back, a wild pig crashed through the brush a few meters in front of me. The sudden movement scared the hell out me and left my heart racing in my chest.

"I'll radio Melvin that we're closin' from the northwest," Bob said as a few stray rounds cut through the overhead foliage.

Entering a defensive perimeter during a battle could be non-habit-forming. It was critical that Melvin notify every-one that we would be entering from the northwest. If he missed someone, that person might open fire as soon as he spotted or heard movement outside the perimeter.

While waiting for Bob to complete his radio contact, I saw something lying on the ground. When I picked it up, I saw that it was a human nose. It must have belonged to one of the Viet Cong who made contact with the Recon platoon. As I waited, another jet knifed in low from the west.

Kawhoosh. The familiar sound of liquid hell splashing through the canopy.

"Napalm," I whispered as large black butterflies drifted on waves of heat.

"Melvin's got the word," Bob told me. "Gritz says to go balls to the wall. Don't stop for nothin'."

My heart shifted into high gear.

"Let's do it." I took in a deep breath and moved out.

Ten meters from where I found the nose, I crossed a hard-packed, east-west trail. It measured a meter across, was littered with battle-dressing wrappers, and smelled of death. From a few of the shattered sections of bamboo hung pieces of half-dry intestine. The wild pig must have been feasting on what remained of enemy soldiers.

One hundred meters from the perimeter, the temperature shot up when we entered an area where only the charred trunks of cypress trees remained. Blankets of blue-gray smoke drifted above the ash-covered ground, and the odor of jellied gas and charred flesh permeated the area. Moving quickly through the smoke and ash, I passed a blackened corpse that reminded me of an overcooked hot dog. With his mouth agape, he lay in the ash with a blackened hand reaching toward the sky.

A few meters past the dead enemy soldier, we entered the killing ground. Most of the bamboo and saplings had been cut knee high by bullets, and many of the great trees had been snapped and stripped of their leaves and much of their bark. The still, hot air was filled with the smell of cordite and the roar of automatic-rifle fire. With rivulets of sweat stinging my eyes and blurring my vision, I slipped past a giant cypress. Glancing to my left over the top of a waist-high fern, I spotted the back of an enemy soldier less than ten feet away. He was wearing black pajamas and a camouflaged soft hat. A split second later, he sensed my movement and turned.

Chunk-chunk-chunk. A burst from my silencer-equipped Sten tore into his face and blew the contents of his skull against a nearby tree. Quickly stepping over shattered saplings and bamboo, I caught glimpses of men in khaki on our left flank.

Whack-whack-whack. Whump-whump-whump. A firefight erupted a short distance to my rear.

"Go!" Bob yelled from a few meters behind me.

Nearing a large fallen tree, I spotted a familiar Cambodian face staring at me over the top of the trunk. I yelled the password.

"Wetsu!"

Then I saw the Cambodian had a small round hole in the middle of his forehead. The back of his head was gone.

"Bac-si," three Bodes called from the far end of the tree.

"Chey-yo," I yelled the Cambodian battle cry.

I stepped over a dead Cambodian, and a few meters beyond the tree, I spotted Capt. Ken Crighton lying on his side in a shallow depression. The area was blanketed with a mantle of gray smoke and haze, and the ground was littered with discarded ammunition boxes and medical supply containers and wrappers. The smell of spent gunpowder hung heavy in the moisture-laden air—so hot and humid it seemed almost suffocating to breathe.

"Critchly," I called over a roar of automatic rifle fire and explosions.

"Get down," he motioned with his hand.

Next to Crighton, Huong—a rifleman from the 1st Platoon—lay dead with his intestines spilling from a gaping hole in his midsection.

I dropped my rucksack and knelt at Crighton's side. He had his nine-millimeter Swedish-K submachine gun at the ready and a nine-millimeter Browning automatic pistol lying on the ground next to him. A jagged, six-inch piece of shrapnel was sticking out of his upper back.

"Ah, Dunahoo me boy!" He smiled. "Good of you to drop in. It's been a bit sticky, you know."

"You okay?" I asked as I examined his wound.

"Slusher didn't find any internal bleeding. Said not to touch it."

"What hit you?" Glancing to my rear, I saw Bob and Luc

deploying the 3d Platoon along the eastern side of the perimeter.

"RPG or 106." Crighton pointed to a dead Cambodian lying on his back a few feet outside the depression. "Hout pulled me out of the line of fire," he paused. "Dunahoo, don't worry about me." He pointed toward the clearing. "Check old England."

"I'll be back," I said, picking up the Sten.

Running in a low crouch, I found England lying next to his dead radio operator. The Cambodian's face was black and torn, and his PRC-25 radio was pockmarked with bullet holes.

"You still kickin'?" I dropped to my knees and found his face streaked with dried blood and dirt.

"Yeah, I'll live," he said with a West Virginia drawl. "Williams died a hard soldier's death," he pointed. A few meters into the grass-covered clearing, I saw Williams lying with his knees drawn up to his chest.

"What hit your face?" I asked.

"Burst of machine-gun fire hit the bamboo and sprayed me with splinters. Nothin' serious."

"Let me check your butt," I said.

"Hit me up near the top of my right cheek. Can't find an exit wound."

"Let me take a look," I said as I used surgical scissors to enlarge a hole in his trousers.

"The only thing that saved me was the cover that termite mound gave me." He pointed to a foot-high hill that had been chewed up by bullets.

Karoumph, karoumph, karoumph. Exploding bombs shook the earth.

I looked up and saw Gritz kneeling over Williams. Bob was standing next to the captain with his M-16 at the ready.

"How's Critchley?" Dale asked.

"Got a nasty piece of shrapnel sticking out of his back," I told him.

"Saw the smoke trail from an RPG headin' his way," he said.

"Yeah, it killed old Huong."

With part of England's trousers cut away, I saw that a few sections of gauze had been taped over the wound. The entire right cheek of his buttocks had turned purple and black. After carefully peeling back some of the tape, I lifted the gauze and saw a small round black hole.

"No bleeding," I told him.

"When I got hit, my leg went numb," he said. "Thought I lost it."

I cut his pant leg down to his ankle and saw that his whole leg was swollen, like an overfilled balloon. I couldn't find an exit wound.

"Round's still in there," I told him. "How much morphine you had?"

"Hell," he said. "I didn't wanna deaden my senses."

"I'm surrounded by bullheads." I shook my head in disbelief. We both started laughing, and I noticed a battle dressing tied around his left wrist. "Let me see."

"It's nothin'. Just shrapnel," he said as he pulled it away. "Jim, the Bodes fought their hearts out. There were just too many."

Karoumph! Another explosion shook the earth. I glanced to my left and saw that Captain Gritz and Bob had moved Williams to a shaded area. With outstretched legs, he sat with his back against a large tree. I felt myself being overcome by emotion.

"Okay. Let me check Williams," I said.

I picked up the Sten and ran the short distance to where Williams was sitting. Kneeling at his side, I saw that the front of his uniform was caked with blood and dirt. His eyes were closed, and with a peaceful expression on his face, he appeared deep in sleep—a tragic end to a great soldier's life.

"I'm sorry, my friend," I squeezed his hand.

"Jimmy." I turned and saw Captain Gritz circle his hand over his head. He and S.Sgt. Tom Horn—the headquarters section radio operator—were standing near Captain Crighton, with their PRC-25 radio leaning against a tree. Gritz had an acetate-covered map in one hand and his radio handset pressed to his ear. I ran to where they were standing.

"Pop a smoke," Gritz told Horn as automatic-rifle fire and explosions erupted along the eastern half of the perimeter.

"I passed the word to bring the dead and wounded here," Gritz told me.

Horn removed a smoke grenade from his harness, pulled the pin, and tossed it in the direction of the clearing.

"Any chance of getting 'em out before dark?" I asked as thick yellow smoke billowed from the canister and slowly twisted skyward.

"FAC's got fast movers and gunships stacked up," he told me. "If we can break contact, we're only a few minutes flying time from Phuoc Vinh."

"Donahue." I turned and saw that it was Rinh, our chief Cambodian medic. Rinh and I had worked together for over a year and, during that time, had become good friends. He was the best indigenous medic I had ever known, and he spoke excellent English. "There are many wounded," he told me as a jet approached from the north.

"Get our M-5 kit and a few ponchos."

Karoumph, karoumph, karoumph. As bombs exploded along the western side of the perimeter, I turned and saw Hal Slusher limping toward me. His uniform was splattered with blood and dirt, and through a tear in his trousers, I spotted a battle dressing. He looked exhausted.

"You okay?" I asked.

"Yeah." He dropped a shot-up M-16 on the ground. "Would you believe the bastards shot the damned thing right out of my hands. I think it was the fifty-one that did it," he said as he used his sleeve to wipe the sweat from his eyes.

"Lucky to be alive."

"Yeah, it was the fifty-one that got Williams," he said with great sadness. "Hit 'im in the chest."

"And your leg?" I pointed.

"RPG. I saw it comin' a hundred meters away. Exploded

right over my head." He shook his head. "I don't know how it made it through the trees."

"What about Melvin and Rouley?" I asked.

"They're lucky to be alive."

"What happened?"

"VC overran 'em," he said. "I saw this VC standin' on Ranger Melvin's back with his AK pointed down at 'im. The instant the VC pulled the trigger, one of the Bodes fired a burst and took his head off."

"Melvin okay?"

"Yeah, just a flesh wound of the right shoulder. No bone involvement."

"That's good," I said as another string of bombs shook the earth. "And Rouley?"

"VC shot the flash suppressor off his rifle, and the damned thing stuck in his forehead."

"The flash suppressor?"

"Yeah," he smiled. "If you're gonna kill a Cajun you gotta hit 'im someplace other than the head."

"Got a count on the wounded?" I asked.

"God, I've lost count." He shook his head. "Got some nasty head wounds."

"How d'ya wanna handle it?" I asked.

"Why don't you take the eastern half. I'll take the west."

"Bac-si." It was Danh, our silent-weapons specialist. Danh was a well-built sixteen-year-old with straight black hair. He was also very intelligent and agile—two qualities which made him the best point man in the 3d Platoon. He handed me my M-16, and I returned his Sten and extra magazines.

"Ahhhh!" Someone screamed. We turned and saw Huong —the Cambodian I thought was dead—sitting in the depression with a grenade in his hand and his intestines lying on the ground at his side.

"I got it," Horn yelled as he pulled the live grenade from Huong's hand.

Slusher and I dropped to our knees at Huong's side and

slowly lowered him to the ground. The young Bode was shaking violently and appeared confused.

"I'll take care of him," Slusher said as Horn slipped a safety pin into the grenade.

"Okay," I agreed. "Let me get out to the perimeter."

Rinh had our M-5 kit over his shoulder and a half dozen ponchos under his arm. He, Danh, and I moved thirty meters east to where we found Bob and Ly crouched behind a large fallen cypress tree. Bob had his radio handset pressed to his ear and was directing an air strike.

Ta, tow, tow, tow. A couple of meters to Bob's left, Son, our cross-eyed machine gunner, had his M-60 resting atop the moss-covered hulk and was firing short bursts. Son was the most cross-eyed person I'd ever seen and yet was the best machine gunner I'd ever known.

"Get down," Bob yelled as we took up firing positions between him and Son.

I peered over the moss-covered trunk, and all across our front, I caught glimpses of khaki uniforms and muzzle flashes. The jungle had been ripped apart, and many of the massive cypress trees had been stripped bare of their leaves and splintered like matchsticks. Here and there, fires continued to burn, and blankets of blue-gray smoke thickened and thinned in wispy, ghostlike patterns. And over everything hung the acrid scent of burnt cordite and jellied gas.

High above the canopy, the whine of a jet engine rose to a scream as it approached from the south. Fifty meters out, I spotted the head and shoulders of a khaki-clad enemy soldier firing at us. I lined up the top of my front sight blade on his face and squeezed off a burst of three rounds. He disappeared beneath a sea of green, and to his rear, a daisy chain of orange-black fireballs flashed across our front. A split second later, shrapnel cut through the overhead foliage, and earth-rending concussions pounded my eardrums.

"Jim, got wounded down to the left," Bob yelled over the firing and pointed.

Rinh, Danh, and I moved along the fallen tree in a low

crouch. Just beyond the end of the cypress we found Tang, a member of England's platoon, firing from a standing position behind a large rotting stump. Tang was a poet who one day hoped to write a book about the war. When the tall skinny Bode turned toward us, his left arm dangled at his side. No flesh remained between his wrist and shoulder—only bones streaked with blood and dirt. He had an empty morphine syrette attached to the collar of his fatigue jacket.

"Bac-si," he forced a smile. Beads of sweat coursed down his ashen face and he appeared close to passing out. "We kill beaucoup VC."

"Chheu reu te?" I asked if he was in pain. My Cambodian was limited, but the Bodes generally understood what I was trying to say.

"Bat, chheu nars." He said that he was.

I grabbed his good arm and lowered him into a sitting position with his back against the stump. A couple of inches down from his shoulder, I found a battle dressing and a tourniquet tied tight around his arm. Both were soaked with blood and covered with dirt, but I didn't see any fresh bleeding.

"Let's get an Ace on that arm," I told Rinh. Just the sight of it would be enough to send Tang into shock.

"Okay, Donahue," he said as he searched through our M-5 medical kit.

As I held Tang's cold stiff hand Rinh quickly wrapped the exposed bones with an Ace bandage.

"I soldier no more," Tang said with great sadness.

"Bullshit," I said. "You'll always be a soldier. You'll always be Special Forces."

Rinh explained what I had said, but I sensed that I hadn't convinced him.

"Tang, my friend," I said slowly. "It'll be through your writing that the dead will live on in the minds of their sons and daughters."

Rinh again translated my words, and Tang's eyes welled with tears.

"Okay, *Bac-si,*" he nodded.

"Bac-si." I turned and saw that it was Luc, our platoon sergeant. "More wounded. Come, I show you."

"Wait one," I told him as I checked Tang's pulse.

"Should we start an IV?" Rinh asked as more bombs exploded across our front.

"Yeah, he's in shock," I said. "If we can restore his blood volume and get the pain under control, he'll make it. How long has it been since he had morphine?"

"Five hour, *Bac-si,*" Tang responded.

Rinh removed a bottle of normal saline from our M-5 kit and extended its plastic tubing. While he taped the bottle to a sapling, I worked the needle at the end of the tubing into a vein on the inside of Tang's lower arm. I then taped the needle in place and opened the regulator on the tubing.

"There we go," I said as the lifesaving liquid flowed into his vein.

"Should I give him penicillin and streptomycin?" Rinh asked as he injected a syrette of morphine into the tubing.

"No, let's keep moving. If we get stuck here overnight, we'll load 'em all up with antibiotics," I said. "Danh, get Tang up to the *bo-chi-huy,*" I said as another jet screeched in low from the south. "Make sure ya keep the bottle over his head."

"Okay, *Bac-si.*"

There was a dull thud and a sickening *kawhoosh* as orange, yellow, and black globs of liquid fire splashed through the jungle to our front. Even at one hundred meters, I could feel the napalm's heat.

"Let's go," I said to Luc as a pungent petroleum smell permeated the air.

Rinh and I followed him along the perimeter, and every few meters passed Bodes who had set up fighting positions in groups of two or three. As we passed behind their positions, they waved and joked, and shouted obscenities at the Viet Cong.

"Fuck Ho Chi Minh," one of them yelled to me. Luc stopped when he came to two Bodes who were lying in prone positions on the rim of an old bomb crater that measured a good ten meters across.

"Bac-si," they greeted me and pointed into the hole.

In the shadows at the bottom of the depression Lu, a young rifleman, was lying on his side on a poncho. The poncho was wet with blood and vomit. Rinh and I slid down the side of the crater and knelt at his side.

"Knhum slarb reu te?" He moaned as I lifted his torn fatigue jacket and found a six-inch section of green bamboo sticking out of his stomach.

"He thinks he will die," Rinh told me.

"Moen ei te, kom barom oy sos." I told him that he wasn't going to die. Looking further, we found three inches of the same piece of bamboo sticking out of his back.

"What do you think?" Rinh asked as he checked his pulse.

"If it severed anything important, he'd already be dead," I said. "If we get him to a good surgeon within five or six hours, he should make it."

"His pulse is fast and weak," Rinh told me.

Examining him further, I found that his belly had a blue-gray tint to it and felt like a slippery bowling ball. There wasn't any serious bleeding. At least nothing external.

"He get morphine?"

"I have, *Bac-si,*" Lu moaned.

"How long's it been?"

He said a few words to Rinh.

"One or two hours," Rinh told me.

"That should hold him for a while," I told Rinh as I removed a bottle of normal saline from our M-5 kit. "Tell 'im he's going to a hospital, and we'd better not get any complaints about him chasing the nurses."

Rinh translated my words, and a smile appeared on Lu's face.

"Do you think he will go to an American hospital?" Rinh asked.

"I hope so," I said. "Tell him about the one you went to."

A few weeks earlier, Rinh had been shot in the leg during a raid on a suspected Viet Cong prisoner of war camp north of

Cau Song Be Special Forces Camp. An ear-to-ear smile appeared on Rinh's face as he told Lu about his stay at the 196th Light Infantry Brigade's Mobile Army Surgical Hospital in Tay Ninh. For over a week, he was the only patient on the ward and had a team of American nurses caring for him. I sensed that Rinh's story relieved some of Lu's anxiety.

"Go ahead and rig a stretcher," I told Rinh. "I'll get the IV goin'."

Rinh crawled out of the crater, and I searched Lu's left arm for a good vein. I found one on the back of his hand, and much to my relief, the needle slipped right into it. By the time I had the IV flowing, Rinh had an improvised litter—a poncho and two eight-foot sections of green bamboo—ready to go.

With everything in place, we carefully placed Lu on the improvised stretcher, and his comrades carried him to the *bo-chi-huy*. While sitting on the rim of the crater, Rinh and I removed canteens from our BAR belts and took a long drink. The relentless sun had lost much of its intensity, but the burnt-over expanse to our front was still steaming from the day's bake. Here and there, sunlight angled through holes in the canopy, creating a mesmerizing effect as dust and smoke drifted through the light. A few meters away lay a man in blood-soaked khakis who had no head or legs.

"Get down," I yelled to Rinh as a jet screamed in low from the south.

Karoumph! The earth shook; we were showered with dirt, and my ears were left ringing.

"That was close." I smiled as we sat brushing ourselves off.

"Jim." I turned and saw Bob moving toward us in a low crouch. To the east I could hear the *wap, wap, wap* of approaching helicopters. "VC broke contact. Choppers comin' in."

"Yahoo!" I yelled. "How much time we got?"

"Not much. Wounded on the first lift."

"Where they taking 'em?"

"CIDG hospital in Bien Hoa."

"Good, I was worried we wouldn't get 'em out." I wiped my face with my sleeve. "What about the dead?"

"To Phuoc Vinh with the rest of the company."

"If Charlie's got a couple automatic weapons on that clearin', he's gonna kick our ass."

"We've got every gunship in III Corps standing by to pound it," Bob smiled. "Here, rig these on your way out." He handed me two claymore mines, a demolition bag, and a box of blasting caps.

"Don't leave without me," I yelled as he moved down the line. "It's a long walk."

I found it hard to believe that the Viet Cong had broken contact. If they had remained on the offensive, none of us would have lived to see the sun come up again. I could only assume that when we broke into the perimeter, the enemy commander must have thought that we were the Mike Force battalion from Bien Hoa. It was probably a conclusion based on years of experience. No one in his right mind would send in only two platoons.

"How many more wounded we got?" I asked Luc.

"One, *Bac-si*."

"Let's get to 'im," I said.

As Luc led Rinh and me down the line, another jet streaked in with its rasping twenty-millimeter cannons blasting away. Then, with the roar of jet engines fading to the north, Luc stopped and said something to Rinh.

"Donahue," Rinh said. "Do you remember the Set who was with the 3d Platoon at Ho Ngoc Tao?"

"Yeah, the young curly-haired guy."

"He is in the crater," Rinh pointed twenty meters in front of our lines. "An RPG exploded and cut the spinal cord in the back of his neck."

"Damn." The news left me shaken. It had only been a few weeks since he married a beautiful girl from Tay Ninh.

"It paralyzed him," Rinh said with great sadness. "His

friend gave him an overdose of morphine. I do not know if he is alive."

I didn't know what to say.

"Shit!" It was a no-win situation. Facilities to treat paraplegic casualties were nonexistent. Even if he made it to Saigon, he would suffer and die. If I were in his situation, I could only hope that my friends would do the same for me. "Let's get 'im outta there."

Rinh and I crawled to the rim of the crater. A tree had fallen across the depression, and in the shadows at its bottom, I saw Set lying on his back. As we slid into the crater, my hands started to shake.

"Set," I said as I knelt at his side and held his cold hand.

"Bac-si." He appeared very drowsy, his pupils were constricted, and he was having difficulty breathing. He was close to death.

"My friend," I trembled. *"Chheu reu te?"* I asked if he was in pain.

"No, *Bac-si,*" he said as a tear coursed down his cheek. "I die."

I felt myself being overcome by grief and took in a deep breath.

"You will be remembered as a man of honor and a great soldier." My lips quivered, and my eyes pooled with tears.

Rinh held his other hand and explained what I had said.

"Thank you, *Bac-si.*"

We carried Set to the top of the crater and placed him on a poncho. With the *wap, wap, wap* of helicopters pulsating above the canopy, we each grabbed a corner of the poncho, and on our hands and knees, dragged Set through the underbrush. When we reached the perimeter, we found Danh waiting.

"Get 'im up to the *bo-chi-huy,*" I told Rinh as thousands of leaves drifted to the ground around us. "I'm gonna rig a couple of claymores. Danh, you stay with me."

"Okay, Donahue," Rinh said.

Danh and I moved twenty meters north to where we found

two fallen cypress trees. They formed a large *V* and would funnel the advancing enemy to a narrow gap at its base.

"I'll rig it," I told Danh as I knelt in knee-high grass in the gap between the trees. With Danh standing guard over me, I removed the olive drab Fiberglas mine from its cloth bandolier. After spreading the mine's scissors-type folding legs, I slowly pushed them into the soft earth. The front section of the mine held spherical steel balls embedded in plastic. When detonated, its exploding C-4 would propel a pattern of steel shot, which—at fifty meters' distance—would cover an area fifty meters wide and two meters high.

With the *wap, wap, wap* of helicopter gunships and the roar of their machine guns drowning out all other sound, I moved forward a few meters and knelt in the grass next to a sapling. I removed a trip wire from the demolition bag and, three inches above the ground, tied one end to the sapling. Five meters to the right of the sapling, I selected a stalk of green bamboo to connect the other end of the trip wire to. While sitting on the ground, I used pliers to crimp a nonelectric blasting cap to a pull-type firing device. I then used green tape to attach the firing device to the stalk of the bamboo.

With the firing device and blasting cap in place, I pulled the trip wire until it ran shin-high through the grass and tied it to the firing device. On my hands and knees, I positioned individual blades of grass and leaves around the trip wire so that it wouldn't be spotted by the enemy. Thinking again about the enemy as I worked, I worried that their commander—at some point—would realize that we were only two platoons, not a Mike Force battalion. If he resumed his attack during our pullout, it could be disastrous for us.

Whoomph, whoomph, whoomph. Gunship rockets exploded to my front. Moving back to the firing device, I tore off another piece of green tape and used it to secure the end of a thirty-foot section of white detonating cord to the blasting cap. With everything in place, I walked backward toward the claymore, dragging my heel and unraveling the detonating cord as I walked. My heel left a shallow trench in the soft earth, and after placing the milky white cord in it, I covered it with dirt and leaves.

A gunship was hovering above the canopy, its pulsating downdraft filling the air with the smell of burned aviation fuel. While the gunship pounded suspected enemy positions to the east, I used the pliers to crimp a second blasting cap onto the end of the detonating cord. The blasting cap firmly attached, I inserted it into the detonating well on the mine. With the claymore armed, I covered it with leaves and twigs.

"One more," I told Danh as I used my sleeve to wipe sweat from my eyes.

"Jim!" I turned and saw Bob. "Let's move it. Last lift's comin' in."

I picked up my M-16, and Danh and I followed him toward the center of our perimeter.

"Got a count on the dead and wounded?" I asked as we approached the *bo-chi-huy*.

"Ten to twenty killed," he said. "Fifty to sixty wounded."

"Not a good day." I shook my head.

At the center of what was the *bo-chi-huy*, we found Kien standing guard over our rucksacks. Kien was a short stocky Bode with a clump of hair growing from his chin. During the Black Box Mission, he lost part of his ear to an exploding mortar round, and during Blackjack-31, he lost three toes to an M-14 toe popper mine.

"We go." He grinned while chomping on an unlit cigar.

"Kien, you're not wounded?" I joked as I picked up my rucksack and swung it around to my back.

"No, *Bac-si*." He smiled and pulled a Chinese Type-59 nine-millimeter pistol from his belt. "I take from China man."

As the four of us ran toward the clearing, I noticed that most of the small trees and bamboo had been cut knee-high by small-arms fire. The whole area was strewn with empty ammunition boxes and plastic and cardboard medical containers. A half dozen empty normal saline bottles remained attached to saplings with white surgical tape. At the edge of the clearing, we found Captain Gritz, S.Sgt. Tom Horn, and Dien, a tall headquarters-section interpreter. Gritz had his radio handset pressed to his ear and bent over to pick something up.

"Don't leave anything for the sons of bitches," the captain yelled while holding a Mobile Guerrilla Force patch.

A short distance into the clearing, a line of Hueys sat in the foot-high grass with their pulsating rotors slapping the humid air. Streams of hot, black exhaust poured from their Avco-Lycoming T-53 engines, as men in camouflage uniforms moved to the waiting choppers. Just above the tree line, the red tongues of gunship tracer rounds probed the tree lines on both sides of the clearing. Darting in and out, the gunships looked like angry dragonflies as they raked the jungle's fringe. High above the landing zone, the FAC drifted in a lazy circle in a steel gray sky streaked with red.

"That's everyone, sir," Bob yelled.

"Let's get outta Dodge," Gritz ordered.

We covered our eyes with our arms to protect against the pieces of grass kicked up by the prop wash, and followed the captain. With my first steps into the clearing, my heart shifted into high gear. I suddenly felt very vulnerable, imagining a long line of khaki uniforms streaming from the wood line. When we reached the helicopter, we found three Bodes sitting with their backs to the fire wall. A door gunner sat in the jump seat, his finger on the trigger of his M-60.

"Phuoc Vinh?" I yelled to the Bodes.

"Phuoc Vinh, *Bac-si,*" they grinned and flashed me a thumbs-up.

Bob, Tom, Dien, Kien, and Danh scrambled aboard and took up seats on the chopper's honeycombed floor. Gritz and I squeezed in with our feet dangling out over the skid. With the main rotors slapping the humid air at over three hundred RPM, the pilot increased the pitch on the blades, and the shaking Huey slowly lifted a few feet off the ground.

"Yahoo," I yelled as the chopper tilted forward, transitioned to forward flight, and climbed across the clearing and over the trees.

"We made it, buddy," Bob shouted from behind me. I turned and shook his hand.

As we rose high above the broccoli-topped jungle, a cool rotor wash blew through the cabin and tugged at my fatigues. To the west, the last light of day had turned the sky a fiery crimson. To my left, the captain sat with his bloodshot blue eyes fixed on the horizon and his sandy brown hair blowing in the wind. He appeared deep in thought.

"Sir," I yelled. "What's the plan?"

He leaned toward me.

"We'll redeploy as soon as we replace the dead and wounded," he said.

"Where we gonna get the replacements?" I asked.

"Capt. Tom Johnson and A-304 are at Trang Sup. They just got back from an operation in the Seven Mountains area," he hollered over the noise of the engine and rotors. "I'm gonna suggest to Colonel Kelly that we absorb the Americans and Cambodians from A-304. We'll be ready to return to the AO in a week to ten days."

"The same AO?" I asked.

He smiled and placed his hand on my shoulder.

"Next time, we'll do it the Special Forces way."

2

1130 HOURS, 4 MAY 1967

At three thousand feet, our twin-engine C-123 aircraft cruised beneath white cloud formations that billowed like towering mountains into the blue sky. I was the only American in the cabin and sat in one of the web seats that lined both sides of the aircraft. The rest of the Mobile Guerilla Force had been transported back to Trang Sup Special Forces Camp by CH-47 Chinook helicopter. The floor in front of me was crammed with dead Cambodians, and as they lay in silence, I could feel the pain that was forever etched on their faces. There were no body bags, and the smell of death was suffocating.

The plane banked, and I lifted my feet when a pool of blood flowed to the right side of the aircraft. Glancing out the window, I saw the dry rice paddies of Tay Ninh Province. Seconds later, the landing gear whined down, and looking out the window again, I saw the muddy waters of the Tay Ninh River three hundred feet below. Just past the river's edge, the wheels thumped down, the pilot reversed the pitch on the propellers, and we slowed to a crawl. I stood up and, moving down the line of bodies, said what would likely be my last good-bye to each of the dead. I had known them all and would always remember them as good friends and brave soldiers. When we finally came to a full stop, the ramp slowly cranked down, and the cabin filled with sunlight and fresh air. I walked down the ramp into the torrid sun and found a half dozen Cambodians and three three-quarter-ton trucks waiting to pick up their lifeless cargo.

With the dead lined up on ponchos in the beds of the trucks, we slowly drove over the Tay Ninh bridge and through the business section of town. Dingy storefronts with colorful signs lined both sides of the street, and Vietnamese music blared from a few of the shops. The stagnant air was thick with the smells of spicy Oriental cooking and human waste, and a red Vespa motor scooter belched black smoke as it sputtered down the street.

When we hit the outskirts of town, we picked up speed, and a plume of sand-colored dust followed us down the road. Under a blazing sun, we sped past dry rice paddies and an occasional thatch-roofed house with woven bamboo sides. Ten kilometers to the east, Nui Ba Den—an extinct volcano—rose three thousand feet above the flatlands to brush the clouds.

Five kilometers north of town, we pulled in the front gate of the crumbling Mobile Guerrilla Force compound, a former French complex adjacent to Trang Sup Special Forces Camp. The compound was surrounded by strands of rusted barbed wire and three coils of concertina wire, all overgrown with tall grass and weeds. Thirty meters inside the gate, we passed two of the camp's half dozen dirty white stucco structures. Their walls were pockmarked by bullets and streaked with mold and rust. A few had holes big enough for a man to walk through. Also scattered around the compound were seven general-purpose tents.

"Yaaaah!" A high-pitched scream broke the silence, and a dozen wailing women in black pajamas and sandals ran from the tents. We stopped at a tent near the rear of the camp and were immediately surrounded by the grieving women. With tears running down their cheeks, they swarmed over the trucks, and the wife of England's radio operator fainted when she saw her husband's burnt and torn face. I waited in silence as the women held, kissed, and caressed their loved ones. Then, one by one, we carried the dead into the shade of the

tent and placed them on camouflage poncho liners that had
been spread on the ground. A colorful Buddhist altar, crowded
with candles and photographs, had been set up at one end of
the tent, and smoke from coils of incense drifted close to the
ceiling.

On the way to a small stucco building where Bob and I
shared a room, I passed another tent where members of the 3d
Platoon were cleaning their weapons.

"Bac-si," Thang, a rifleman from the 3d Squad, yelled.
Inside the tent, the men were gathered around two fifty-
five-gallon drums that had been cut in half and filled with
a fifty-fifty mixture of gas and oil. After stripping their
weapons, they took turns scrubbing each part with the oily
mixture.

When I arrived at my room, I dropped my rucksack onto
the floor and leaned my M-16 against the wall. Bob and I each
had a cot, two footlockers, and a wall locker. I removed a
pistol belt and holster from my wall locker and strapped it on
my hip. The holster contained a nine-millimeter Browning
automatic pistol that Captain Crighton had given to me when
he was commissioned. Just as I walked back out into the sunlight, Bob and Rinh drove up in a truck loaded with coffins.

"Son of a bitch doubled the price," Bob yelled as he
jumped to the ground. "Fifteen hundred piasters each."

"What?" I found it hard to believe.

"Sergeant Cole did not pay him," Rinh smiled from the
driver's seat.

"Fuck 'im," Bob scowled.

Rinh pulled away, and Bob and I went into our room to
square away our gear. As we sat on our footlockers cleaning
our M-16s, he gave me an update on the wounded.

"That round that hit England in the butt exited next to his
right testicle," Bob told me as he scrubbed the face of his bolt
with Hoppes #9 cleaning solvent. "They're gonna send him
and Crighton to Japan."

"What about the others?" I asked as I ran a patch down
the bore of my rifle.

"As far as I know, England and Crighton are the only ones goin' outta country."

"What about the Bodes?"

"Most of 'em went to the CIDG hospital in Bien Hoa," he said.

Having cleaned our weapons, Bob and I walked back to the tent where I had taken the dead. The sides of the tent were rolled up tight, and the coffins were lined up on the camouflage poncho liners. The air was filled with the smell of incense and a thin layer of smoke from the nearby mess tent drifted a few feet above the ground. Standing next to the tent, we found Dien, the headquarters section interpreter, restraining a beautiful young woman. She had long black hair, large, tear-filled, almond-shaped eyes, and wore a black *ao dai* and sandals. It was Linh, Set's wife.

"She want to open," Dien pointed to one of the coffins.

"She's Set's wife," Bob said. "It's her right."

"Okay, *Trung si,* I help her."

Dien pulled a knife from its sheath, and he and Linh entered the tent.

"It's her call," Bob said as we watched Dien use his knife to pry open the coffin.

"Yaaaah!" Linh screamed and covered her eyes with her hands. With a terrified expression on her face, she bolted from the tent and ran in the direction of the front gate.

"Go get her," I told Dien as I pointed to a nearby jeep.

He jumped into the jeep and tore away in a cloud of dust. When Bob and I entered the tent, we found that the heat was beginning to take its toll on Set. Both eyes were open and bulging from their sockets, and his swollen tongue was sticking out of his mouth.

"Let's get over to the team house," Bob said as we resealed the coffin. "Gonna be late for the meetin'."

We walked the short distance to the adjacent Special Forces compound and found the team house filled with Americans. With the Beatles' "Yesterday" playing on the speaker system, some of the guys stood talking at the bar while others sat reading mail or playing pool.

"Let me have your attention," Captain Gritz yelled from behind a small table.

Everyone stopped what they were doing and pulled up a chair.

The captain explained that Colonel Kelly had approved combining Detachments A-303 and A-304 and that Capt. Tom Johnson would be serving as the deputy Mobile Guerrilla Force commander. The new headquarters section would consist of himself, Captain Johnson, and S.Sgt. Tom Horn. The Recon Platoon would be led by S.Sgt. Ray Fratus and his deputy, S.Sgt. Larry "Stik" Rader. The 1st Platoon would be commanded by SFC Ernie "Duke" Snider. His deputy, S.Sgt. Dave Rose, would also serve as our second medic. SFC Bill Ferguson and S.Sgt. Jim Battle would take the 2d Platoon, and Bob and I would remain with the 3d Herd. SFC Glen Bevans and S.Sgt. Roy Sparks would command the 4th Platoon.

Captain Gritz also informed us that we would be airlifted to Dong Xoai Special Forces Camp at 1200 hours (noon) on 9 May and that we would make a night ground infiltration of the guerrilla warfare operational area. Captain Johnson then assigned a long list of tasks that had to be accomplished before our departure on the ninth. As he was speaking, Dien walked into the team house and whispered something to Captain Gritz.

"They're ready to start the funeral fires," Gritz told us.

When we walked out of the team house, we found the last light of day quickly fading. The horizon was painted in shades of red and yellow, and directly overhead, a few stars appeared in a gray sky.

"Jimmy," Captain Gritz said as we walked. "The cook tells me we're almost out of meat, beer, and soft drinks. You wanna make a run down to Saigon?"

"Yes, sir," I said. "First thing in the mornin'. Be back on the sixth."

"I'll check with the B-Team," S.Sgt. Tom Horn offered. "Might have a flight goin' down."

"Don't worry about the M-3 and M-5 kits," S.Sgt. Dave Rose told me. "I'll make sure they're ready to go."

"Thanks," I said. "Rinh's got everything secured in the dispensary."

We found the Cambodians of Detachments A-303 and A-304 and the families of the dead gathered in a large circle near the rear of the Mobile Guerrilla Force compound. At the center of the circle, the coffins were perched atop a chest-high pile of gasoline-soaked wood. The still night air was filled with incense, and a monk wrapped in saffron robes was chanting scripture. Next to the monk, Thang stood with a burning torch in his hand. I found Rinh standing with Hien, the 2d Platoon's machine gunner, and a few members of the 3d Platoon.

"What does the monk pray for?" I whispered to Rinh.

"That they will be reborn in a peaceful place," he said.

"A good prayer for men who died in battle."

"Buddhists believe that they will be rewarded or punished for their behavior in this life," Rinh whispered as the monk continued to chant.

"Like heaven and hell?"

"No, we do not believe in heaven and hell," he said. "We believe that death is the end of one life and the beginning of another. It is not to be feared. If you live a good life, you will be reborn a better person. Life is a continuous cycle—a circle."

The monk nodded, and Thang ignited the wood beneath the coffins.

"Ooohhh," the women moaned—some falling to the ground. Within seconds, thick black smoke billowed skyward, and I could feel the intense heat of the flames.

Hien said something that I didn't understand.

"Say again," I said.

"He said that the fire will burn for nine hours," Rinh said.

"What then?"

"In the morning, only ashes and small pieces of bone will remain," he said. "We will collect a piece of bone from each soldier and take it to the pagoda in Saigon."

As we stood in silence, the wood popped and cracked, and the chanting and wailing continued. With the coffins engulfed in flames, sparks disappeared into a sky that was white with stars. Around midnight, I returned to my room, and by the time my head hit the pillow, I was deep in sleep.

Hours later, I awoke to the crow of a rooster and the smell of bacon. I could have slept for a few more hours, but knew that I had to get moving if I was going to catch a flight down to Saigon. Bob and I got dressed, grabbed our toilet articles, and with the horizon glowing with the first light of day, we headed for the showers in the adjacent compound. After showering and shaving, we walked to the nearby mess hall where we found S.Sgt. Tom Horn sitting at one of the tables, eating scrambled eggs.

"Mornin', Tom," I said as Bob and I pulled up chairs across from him.

"Jim, Bob," he said as he sipped his coffee.

"Anything goin' down to Saigon?" Bob asked.

"No, I checked with the B-Team," Tom responded.

"Hell, I'll hitchhike down," I said.

"Would you like eggs?" asked a beautiful young Indian girl wearing a white blouse and black silk pants.

"Just toast and coffee," Bob told her.

"Same here," I smiled.

"I'll drive ya into town," Bob said as the girl brought us cups of steaming coffee and a plate piled high with toast.

"Cam on, co," I thanked her.

After breakfast, I returned to our room to pack my rucksack, and Bob went to get a jeep. Minutes later, he picked me up, and as we drove out the gate, the morning air was cool and filled with the smells of Cambodian cooking. To the east, Nui Ba Den was shrouded in mist and appeared black against a rose-colored sky. Mornings were always the best time of day.

We pulled into Tay Ninh just as it was coming to life, and

as we drove down the main street, I waved to a Cao Dai monk wrapped in a blue robe. Near the center of town, a bearded Indian was busy displaying python skins in front of his shop, and Bob beeped the horn and waved to the Frenchman who owned the coin store.

"Bac-si!" a young woman yelled from the sidewalk. "I *soc mau* you," she shook her fist and threatened to give me a bloody nose.

"It's Ha," Bob smiled.

"Don't stop," I begged him.

Ha was a pretty Cambodian girl with long, black hair, high cheekbones, and almond-shaped black eyes. She worked at the Bamboo Club, our favorite restaurant, and always served us the best buffalo steaks in the province. When we returned to Trang Sup from an operation code-named Liberty Blackjack, I took our squad leaders to the restaurant for dinner. While we were enjoying grilled buffalo steaks and cold *Biere "33,"* she told me that she needed a typewriter and that if I agreed to get her one, our dinner would be on the house. I cut the deal, but unfortunately the typewriter that I planned to give her was being used, and I didn't deliver.

"Ain't she the one who was chasin' ya down the street with the butcher knife?" He laughed.

"Yeah, that's her. Gotta find her a typewriter before she kills me."

"Told ya not to mess with Cambodian women," Bob said as we both broke into uncontrollable laughter.

Just past the Tay Ninh River bridge, Bob pulled off the road and stopped under a clump of palm trees.

"Thanks for the ride," I said as I climbed out of the jeep. "I'll see ya tomorrow night."

"Take care, Jim." He reached to shake my hand.

Bob pulled away and left me standing alone under the palms. Thirty minutes later, I stuck out my thumb as an ARVN jeep approached. When it slowed, I spotted a smiling Vietnamese lieutenant sitting in the passenger seat.

"Saigon," I yelled.

"Okay." The jeep stopped, and the lieutenant motioned for me to jump aboard.

I threw my rucksack and MAT-49 submachine gun into the backseat and climbed in. Highway 22's faded blacktop was in a poor state of repair, and as we picked up speed, I hung on for my life. It was going to be a bumpy ninety-six kilometers to Saigon.

As we sped down the road, we passed an occasional cluster of huts with thatch roofs. Most had been built in the shade of fifty-foot palm trees, and a few had banana plants and mango and guava trees growing around them. To the rear of the huts, women in conical hats and black pajamas tended their gardens, while pigs wallowed in their sties and chickens pecked at the ground. Fifteen minutes into my ride, the driver made an unexpected left on to a dirt road and stopped.

"Okay," the lieutenant smiled and motioned for me to get out.

"I go Saigon," I said slowly.

"Saigon," he smiled and pointed southeast down Highway 22.

"You gotta be shittin' me," I mumbled as I grabbed my rucksack and MAT-49 and jumped to the ground.

The jeep sped away in a cloud of dust, and I found myself alone in the middle of nowhere—nothing but rice paddies in every direction. Standing in total silence under large white clouds and a blue sky, I swung my rucksack around to my back and checked my weapon. As I walked down the road toward Saigon, I counted eleven men—in groups of two or three—working on the rice-paddy dikes. The closest was about two hundred meters away. I walked backward for a few minutes, hoping to see another vehicle coming down the road, but no such luck. When I glanced back to the paddies, I noticed that a few of the guys in the conical hats and black pajamas had stopped working and were moving in my direction.

"Shit," I mumbled as I picked up the pace.

They were most likely curious farmers, but there was also the possibility that they were Viet Cong who were hoping to cut my throat. I broke into a jog, and twenty minutes later, lost sight of them. Walking backward again, I wiped the sweat from my eyes and took a long drink from my canteen. In the distance, I saw a plume of sand-colored dust moving down the road in my direction.

"Yahoo!" I yelled.

Seconds later, I spotted a jeep followed by a three-quarter-ton truck filled with troops, and a thirty-ton flatbed truck carrying a bulldozer. When the jeep neared, I stuck out my thumb and smiled. The jeep slowed to a crawl.

"What the hell are you doing out here?" A Filipino sergeant yelled.

"Goin' to Saigon." I grinned.

"Get in." He shook his head. "We're going to Tan Son Nhut."

With a sense of relief, I climbed into the backseat of the jeep. In the truck behind us, eight Filipino soldiers sat with their weapons pointed outboard. If we were ambushed, they were ready to return fire immediately. As we drove down the bumpy road, the sergeant told me that they were with a Filipino engineer unit that had a compound inside the 196th Light Infantry Brigade's base camp in Tay Ninh.

When we pulled into Saigon, they dropped me off near the entrance to Tan Son Nhut Air Base. At the gate, streams of American military personnel and Vietnamese civilians were entering and leaving the base. The street outside the gate was jammed with Lambrettas, Vespas, and Hondas, and the still hot air was filled with exhaust fumes and the raucous sound of sputtering scooters. Across the street from the gate, three blue-and-yellow Renault taxicabs were parked at the curb.

"Cholon PX, fifty P," I told the driver of the nearest taxi.

He shot me a you-gotta-be-kidding expression. "Two hundred P."

"One hundred," I countered.

"Okay, *Trung si.*"

I tossed my rucksack and MAT-49 into the backseat and jumped in next to the driver. As soon as we pulled away from the curb, we were enmeshed in heavy traffic. Cong Ly Street was congested with jeeps, cyclos, bicycles, scooters, military trucks, and an occasional black Citroen, all jockeying for position. The sidewalks were lined with soldiers and civilians shopping at white stucco buildings with first-floor storefronts, and at each intersection, the blaring of impatient horns heralded our attempt to inch forward.

After making a right turn on Phan Thanh Gian Street, we were soon in Cholon, Saigon's Chinatown, and above many of the shops hung signs in Vietnamese and Chinese. At the second traffic circle, we turned off the main street and stopped at the entrance to the PX. After paying the driver, I stopped at a mobile soft-drink stand that was set up on the sidewalk in the shade of a large tree.

"Pepsi," I told an old woman with rotting teeth.

She handed me a cold can of Pepsi-Cola, and I stood in the shade sipping it. On the far side of the street, a half dozen American jeeps and trucks were parked along the curb while their drivers were inside shopping. Just as I finished my Pepsi, a two-and-a-half-ton truck from the 1st Logistical Command pulled up and parked. The truck was covered with dried mud but appeared to be relatively new and in good shape. As soon as the driver entered the PX to shop, I strolled across the street, climbed into the cab, and drove away.

I made a quick right on Hong Bang Street and, a few minutes later, made another turn into an alley—Cholon was the land of a thousand alleys. Both sides of the narrow dirt street were lined with small shanties made of flattened beer and soft-drink cans. Squatting next to charcoal grills in front of many of them were civilians in conical hats, dark pajamas, and shower shoes. Others were stretched out in nylon hammocks. I pulled up in front of an auto repair shop that was constructed of rusting sections of sheet metal attached to a wooden frame. Just as I jumped to the ground, a skinny old man with leathery skin walked out into the sun. He was the father of a Chinese Nung who was serving with the Mike Force in Bien Hoa.

"Trung si," he shook my hand. "What you need?"

"Clean it up and replace all of the numbers and letters with A-303 and CIDG," I told him as we walked around the truck. Vehicles with Civilian Irregular Defense Group markings were the property of the Vietnamese government and wouldn't be stopped by American military police. "Also, take off the frame and leave the canvas in the back of the truck."

"You write," he said as he handed me a pad and pencil.

I printed "A-303" and "CIDG," and after handing him the pad, again explained what I wanted.

"Okay, *Trung si,*" he smiled. "You want gas?"

"Yeah, fill it up and check the oil," I said. "I'm in a hurry."

He looked at his watch. "Maybe one hour."

"Okay, my friend."

I walked down the street to a tin-roofed restaurant with open sides and a hard-packed dirt floor. The rear of the building extended over a listless canal and was supported by long stilts. It didn't appear to be a place that catered to Americans. I lowered my rucksack to the floor and sat on a stool next to one of its four worn wooden tables. In the rear of the restaurant, singsong music blared from a record player while a pretty, middle-aged woman with long, tied-back hair stood at a charcoal grill, turning chicken. Strips of dried meat hung from the ceiling above her head, and on a table next to the grill were what appeared to be a half dozen spring rolls.

"Chao, ong," the woman said hello and smiled.

"Chao, ba. Ba co tra khong?" I returned her greeting and asked if she had tea.

"Tra," she nodded that she did.

"Bach gio," I pointed to the spring rolls and asked for three.

In the shadows behind the grill, I saw what appeared to be a man sitting on the floor. Minutes later, the woman brought out my spring rolls and an orange-colored Vietnamese soft drink. I cut open one of the rice-paper rolls and found it filled with pork, vegetables, and spices. It was excellent, but the soft drink smelled like perfume and didn't taste much better.

As I sat eating my spring rolls, a man emerged from the

shadows. He was a double amputee—only short stumps remained—wearing dark blue pajamas. To cushion the impact of moving on hard surfaces, he had a piece of automobile tire attached to the end of each stump. He moved by reaching forward and then swinging what remained of his body through his arms.

"*Trung si,* I am Le," he said as he reached to shake my hand. He had short black hair, leathery skin, and a few long gray hairs growing from his chin. "My wife is Ba," he pointed to the woman at work behind the grill.

"*Cho, ong.*" I smiled. "*Moi ong ngoi.*" I invited him to join me.

"Thank you, *Trung si.*"

As he positioned himself on the stool at the other side of the table, I noticed that he was also missing parts of his left hand and right cheekbone.

"You Airborne," he smiled.

"Yes, *Luc-Luong-Dac-Biet,*" I said. "I'm with the Mobile Guerrilla Force."

"Groupement Mobile Des Partisans?" His eyes lit up with excitement.

"No, a Cambodian guerrilla unit in Tay Ninh Province."

"Oh." I sensed his disappointment.

"I Airborne long time," he said with great pride. "I fight with 5th Vietnam Parachute Battalion at Dien Bien Phu." He yelled something to Ba.

"One of my Cambodian squad leaders jumped with the 5th at Dien Bien Phu. His name is Thach."

"Number two company?"

"I don't know." I shook my head as Ba placed cold bottles of *Biere la Rue* and a plate of grilled chicken on the table.

"*Cam on, ba,*" I thanked her.

"All my friend from Dien Bien Phu, they die now," he said with great sadness. "Maybe you tell Thach come see me."

"I'll do that." I took a long drink of cold beer and smacked my lips.

Le slid from the stool. "I come back," he told me.

Minutes later he returned wearing a camouflaged French fatigue jacket with silver parachute wings and three rows of colorful medals pinned to it. The only one I recognized was the Vietnamese Cross of Gallantry.

"Lookin' good," I smiled as he climbed back on his stool.

With his back now ramrod straight and authority in his voice, he yelled something to Ba.

"Did you lose your legs at Dien Bien Phu?"

"No, *Trung si,* Pleiku," he said as Ba placed two more bottles of *Biere la Rue* on the table.

"Cam on, ba," I again thanked her.

Le took a long drink and then unbuttoned his camouflaged jacket. As I bit into a piece of chicken, he pushed his jacket to the side and exposed a gaping scar on his shoulder. "This Dien Bien Phu . . . at Eliane." His eyes fixed and welled with tears as he drifted off to another time and place.

"You fought at Eliane?"

"Oui, the 5th Vietnam Parachute Battalion fight at Eliane."

He began to shake and again barked something to Ba. She said something I didn't understand and then placed another record on the turntable.

"At Eliane we sing the *'Marseillaise,' "* he said as he took a drink.

When the scratchy record started to play the *"Marseillaise,"* Le's face filled with emotion. He took another drink and started to sing softly. I found his emotion contagious and joined him. As we sang, he motioned to Ba to turn it up. The louder it got, the louder we got. Before long, a half dozen dirty-faced kids were standing in the alley staring at us. By the time we finished singing the *"Marseillaise"* for the fourth or fifth time, my head was spinning from the *Biere la Rue*.

"Don't you have a wheelchair?" I asked.

"I not know," he shook his head.

"A wheelchair," I said slowly as I made a pushing movement with my arms.

"Oh, no, *Trung si.* Too much money."

"Hey," I said. "I need some armed security. You got time?"

"Oui, Trung si."

"Shouldn't take more than two or three hours," I told him as I stood up and pulled a roll of piasters from my pocket.

Le reached up and put his hand over mine. "No, *Trung si.* You not pay."

"Thank you, my friend."

While Le briefed Ba, I headed for a rest room in the rear of the restaurant. Squatting over a round hole in the floor, I looked down and saw a piece of wood floating in the canal twenty feet below. I imagined myself a bombardier at thirty thousand feet as, a short distance away, I could hear someone washing clothing on the bank of the canal. When I finished, I found Le standing in the alley, wearing his camouflage jacket and a red beret.

"Airborne!" I gave him a thumbs-up.

Moving down the alley at a brisk pace, we returned to the auto repair shop. My truck was parked out front, and a woman was using a rag to put the finishing touches on a mirror. It looked new.

"Numba one," the old Chinese man grinned as he walked out into the alley.

He and I walked around the vehicle. "Lookin' good," I nodded my approval. The paint wasn't dry, and I hoped that the dust wouldn't stick to it. "What do I owe ya?"

"Two thousand P, *Trung si.*"

After paying the old man, he and I helped Le into the passenger seat of the truck. I climbed into the driver's seat, and Le's eyes lit up when I handed him my MAT-49.

"I use many year," he said as I started the truck. "Kill many Viet Minh."

"We're off," I said as we rolled down the alley.

After turning back into traffic, we drove the short distance to the beer and soft-drink distribution center. I hoped to pick up pallets—fifty cases each—of Budweiser and Coca-Cola. When we pulled up to the gate, a Vietnamese guard waved us through. The compound was as large as a city block, and stacked inside its barbed and concertina wire were pallets of every conceivable brand of beer and soft drink. Pallets were stacked everywhere, and in the passageways between the stacks, Vietnamese civilians drove back and forth on forklifts. Three trucks were being loaded by the forklift drivers, and another five were parked in front of the administration building.

"Be out in a few minutes," I told Le as I pulled into a space.

Inside the building, I found Americans standing in line waiting to place or pay for their orders. I was glad to see that it was busy. I went to the rest room to wash my hands and face and then strolled back to the truck. Le was sitting with the MAT-49 at the ready.

"We're all set," I told him as I pulled a metal box out of my rucksack, opened it on my lap, and removed an order form from a previous visit. The signed and stamped form indicated that I had paid for pallets of Budweiser and Coca-Cola in April 1966. It was over a year old but was still in mint condition. With the order form in my hand, I backed the truck up to the loading area and flagged down one of the forklift drivers.

"*Mot* Bud, *mot* Coke," I told him what I wanted as he stood on the running board examining the order form.

"Okay, *Trung si,*" he said before jumping to the ground.

While Le and I sat in the cab, he located pallets of Budweiser and Coca-Cola and loaded them on the truck.

"*Cam on, ong,*" I thanked him.

With my heart racing in my chest, I pulled the truck up to the gate. When the guard climbed to my running board, he saw the medals on Le's chest and snapped a salute.

"*Mot* Bud, *mot* Coke," I smiled and handed him the receipt. I prayed he wouldn't notice the April 1966 date. He glanced at the paper but couldn't take his eyes off Le. Finally, he handed me the paper, jumped to the ground, and proceeded to check my load.

"Okay," he yelled and waved us out the gate.

A few blocks from the compound, I stopped to slip the receipt back into the metal box and pull the canvas over the pallets.

"Off again," I grinned as we pulled back into traffic.

I didn't have a map but had a general idea of how the city was laid out. When we hit Cong Ly Street, I turned left and followed it to the 3d Field Hospital. With the late-day sun sinking slowly into Cambodia, I parked in front of the hospital and told Le that I'd only be a few minutes.

Just inside the entrance to the hospital, I spotted what appeared to be a brand-new wheelchair parked at the side of a wide walkway. I stood with my back to the wall and watched as American doctors, nurses, and enlisted personnel went about their business. After more than sixteen months on an A-Team, I felt like I was on another planet. The Americans appeared sterile—almost unreal—and as they passed, waves of Old Spice, Shalimar, and Aqua Velva began to nauseate me. When I was sure no one was looking, I wheeled the chair back down the walkway and out to the waiting truck.

"Got ya a wheelchair," I yelled as I climbed into the rear of the truck and positioned it next to the pallets.

"No, *Trung si*," he shook his head. "Too much money."

"It was on sale," I told him.

By the time we got back to Cholon, the last light of day was quickly fading. The streets were crowded with vehicles with their lights on, and the sidewalks and cafes were lit and filled with people. I pulled up in front of Le's restaurant and helped him to the ground. While he waited, I climbed into the rear of the truck and, with the wheelchair in hand, jumped to the ground.

"Give her a try," I said as I helped him into the seat.

With the MAT-49 on his lap, he wheeled fifty meters down the alley. When Ba walked out into the alley, she began weeping.

"This, very good," he grinned as he pulled up.

"Hey, thanks for your help," I said. "I gotta get goin'."

Le attempted to hand me the MAT-49.

"Keep it," I told him. "I got another one."

"Oh, *Trung si*," he shook his head. "I cannot."

"Hey, now you're armed, mobile, and dangerous."

He thought about it, and a mischievous smile appeared on his face.

"If VC come Cholon, I kill them," he smiled.

I hugged Ba and shook Le's hand before climbing back into the truck.

"I'll see ya next time I get down to Saigon," I said as I started the engine.

"Okay, *Trung si*. You tell Thach come see me."

I snapped him a salute and rolled back down the alley. Pulling back into traffic, I headed east toward downtown Saigon. When I hit Hong Bang Street, I made a quick left on Do Quang Dau and pulled up in front of the Ideal Hotel. It was a quiet, forty-room hotel, that I liked to stay at whenever I got down to Saigon. After chaining and padlocking the steering wheel, I walked into the lobby and told the clerk, a young woman wearing a peach *ao dai*, that I wanted a quiet room with a bathtub. She gave me the key to a room on the second floor and told me that she would have the truck unloaded and secure its cargo for the night. I gave her the combination to my lock and headed upstairs.

It was a small room with an overhead fan. Most of the floor space was taken up by a single bed with a mosquito net draped over it. There was a black lacquered dresser against the wall and a wicker chair in the corner. I placed my rucksack on the dresser and wedged the top of the chair under the doorknob. Walking into the bathroom, I found a full-size tub, a sink, and an American style toilet. It was a first-class operation.

I started the tub and emptied a small bottle of lilac bubble bath into its steaming water. After undressing, I brushed my teeth and shaved. I must have had a hundred scrapes and cuts on my body, and each of them stung as I eased into the hot water. For what seemed like an hour, I lay motionless watching a two-inch fuck-you lizard on the wall above the tub. I knew that I'd had enough when I noticed that my fingers looked like wrinkled white prunes.

I was tired and figured I'd take a short nap before driving

up to Bien Hoa to visit Ngoi. She was a beautiful eighteen-year-old Vietnamese girl I had met when SFC Warren Pochinski and I were teaching English to a group of civilians at Song Be. She later moved to Bien Hoa where she was studying to be a community health worker. Crawling under the mosquito net, I slipped between the sheets—they smelled of freshly washed linen—and quickly drifted off to sleep.

Hours later, I awoke to the sound of traffic. When I checked my Seiko, I saw that I had slept through the night. It only took me a few minutes to get dressed, and when I walked out the front door of the hotel, a thousand smells assaulted me. Groups of giggling, uniformed schoolgirls and women in colorful *ao dais* filled the sidewalk, and the street was crowded with bicycles, cyclos, and scooters. The curb was lined with mobile kitchens and other food vendors, and on the sidewalk, a woman sat behind a three-foot-high stack of French bread. In Saigon, almost everyone ate in the street.

"Pho?" yelled a woman from one of the mobile kitchens. The old lady had black teeth, red lips, and wore a conical hat and black pajamas.

"Okay," I said.

She handed me a steaming bowl and spit a wad of red betel-nut juice—an opiate—on the street behind her. I carried the soup, smelling of herbs, to a nearby bench. The bowl was filled with slices of rare beef, onions, and noodles floating in a clear broth. For close to an hour, I sat enjoying my breakfast and watching the passersby. When I finished, I returned to my room to pick up my rucksack. By the time I got back to the lobby, the clerk had my truck loaded and parked in front of the hotel. I thought again about making a quick trip up to Bien Hoa to see Ngoi but knew that it would take the better part of the day to pick up the meat and make it back to Trang Sup before dark.

Saigon's streets were congested with morning traffic, and it took me a good thirty minutes to get to the Saigon to Bien Hoa highway. The four-lane expressway was busy, but was moving along at over thirty miles an hour. Just before Ho

Ngoc Tao Special Forces Camp, I turned off the highway
and followed the road to Thu Duc. The town's main street
was crowded with Vietnamese Marines in starched utilities,
and civilians going to work or school. On the far side of
town, I continued on the bumpy dirt road until I came to a
sign that read:

1ST INFANTRY DIVISION
NO MISSION TOO DIFFICULT
NO SACRIFICE TOO GREAT
DUTY FIRST

The Big Red One's base camp was surrounded by rows of
barbed wire, concertina, tangle foot, and pungi stakes. Just
inside the wire, I was stopped by a helmeted military po-
liceman. He was backed up by two sandbagged machine-gun
bunkers and a .50-caliber machine gun mounted on an armored personnel carrier. After he waved me through the gate,
I passed thirty or forty Vietnamese girls standing next to a
bus. Before being cleared to work inside the complex, they
had to go through a body search in a nearby squad tent.

Once into the camp, I followed its crushed red-stone road
past rows of wood-frame structures whose tin roofs overhung
their sides. A few Americans were picking up cigarette butts
while Vietnamese in black pajamas used rakes and shovels to
clean debris from the deep drainage ditches that ran along
both sides of the road. After passing the post exchange, the
noncommissioned officer's club, and a prisoner of war compound, I entered the base's quartermaster area and spotted the
warehouse I was looking for—a large, wood-frame building
covered with sheet metal.

A thirty-ton flatbed truck was parked in front of the warehouse's large open entrance while a forklift loaded it with
pallets of food. I parked next to the flatbed and, inside the
building, found row after row of pallets stacked from floor to
ceiling. A couple of soldiers were cleaning up a box of
ketchup that had smashed on the hard dirt floor while others

were busy filling orders. The still air smelled of cardboard and reminded me of a supermarket.

"Hey, Sarge," a voice called.

I turned and saw the guy I was looking for. He was carrying a clipboard and wore a green T-shirt and a baseball hat. I didn't remember his name.

"Mornin'." I smiled.

"Good to see ya again, Sarge." He shook my hand and motioned with his head for me to follow him. "Don't say anything in front of the men," he whispered as we walked back into the sunlight.

"Got somethin' for ya." I climbed up on my running board, reached into my rucksack, and pulled out a nine-millimeter automatic pistol. When I jumped to the ground, he turned to make sure no one was looking.

"Wow, it's a beauty," he said as I handed it to him.

"The star on the grip identifies it as a Russian-made Makarov," I pointed out. "This one belonged to an officer from the 271st VC Regiment. Got eight rounds in the magazine."

"What d'ya need?" He slipped the pistol under his belt.

"Meat. About a dozen boxes."

"I'll get ya a good mix," he said as he removed a key ring from his belt. "Back her up to the first freezer."

I backed the truck up to a line of walk-in freezers that were shaded by a sheet metal roof and kept running by a nearby generator.

"Got a little of everything in this one," he said as he removed a padlock from the metal door and I jumped to the ground.

When we walked into the freezer my breath turned white. Both sides and the back wall were lined—floor to ceiling— with fifty-pound boxes of frozen meat.

"Could I get one of these to live in?" I laughed as he checked the labels on the boxes.

"How about bacon?" he asked.

"Yeah, gimme two."

He tossed the frost-covered boxes to the floor and moved on.

"Veal and porkchops," he said as he tossed four more to the floor. "Just got this chicken in yesterday," he pointed to a stack of boxes.

"How about eight?"

"Whatever ya need, Sarge."

We carried the boxes out of the freezer and tossed them into the back of the truck.

"Got somethin' else for ya," he said as he motioned for me to follow him.

"Appreciate it."

"This is the general's food locker," he told me as he removed the padlock from another freezer. "If we get caught, we'll end up in the stockade," he added with a nervous laugh.

"Don't sweat it," I told him. "General Hay owes us."

"Strip steak?" he asked as we entered.

"Can ya spare four?"

"You got it." He reached up and threw them to the floor.

"How about a couple of these filet mignons?" I pointed.

"I don't know, Sarge," he shook his head.

"Would ya consider two?"

"Hell, take 'em. They won't miss it."

We carried the boxes out to the truck.

"What about eggs?" he asked as I crawled into the back of the truck.

"Six crates," I said as I lifted the canvas and piled it on top of the Budweiser.

While I stacked the boxes of meat between the beer and the side of the truck he carried six crates of eggs out of another freezer. With the meat and eggs neatly stacked, I covered everything with the canvas and crawled into the driver's seat.

"Next time I get down to Saigon, I'll bring ya an M-1 sniper rifle with a side-mounted scope and a leather cheek pad," I told him. "Shoot a deer's eye out at a thousand meters."

"Can't get anything like that around here."

"That road through Thu Duc's gonna do a job on the eggs," I said. "There another way back to the highway?"

"Yeah, take the back gate." He pointed. "It'll take you into

Di An. When ya get to the square, turn right and follow the old plantation road back up to the highway."

"Thanks."

"Anytime." He waved as I backed out.

When I pulled into the town of Di An, I turned right when I hit its crowded market, and picked up speed as I headed out of town. With a cloud of dust following me down the sandy road, I sped past a large Buddhist pagoda and soon entered a rubber plantation. Both sides of the road were lined with evenly spaced rubber trees that had been bulldozed back a couple of hundred meters from the road. A short distance into the rubber, I was stopped at a roadblock manned by an infantry squad and an armored personnel carrier.

"Sniper activity up ahead," a young sergeant with a southern drawl let me know.

"I'm on a priority-one mission," I said with authority. "Gotta be in Saigon in thirty minutes."

"Hell, it's your ass," he shook his head. "Go ahead and kill yourself."

I pulled away and slid down as low as possible in the seat. If there was a sniper, his only target would be the top of my head. With the gas pedal to the floor the boxes began to bounce around under the canvas, and I worried about the eggs. A few minutes later I drove out of the rubber plantation and passed another armored personnel carrier parked at the side of the road. A short distance farther down the road, I hit the Saigon to Bien Hoa highway just south of the Dong Nai bridge.

Once back on the highway, I pulled over and stopped at one of the many flimsy sheet-metal shanties that had been thrown up along the expressway. I climbed into the back of the truck, and while I was checking the eggs, a middle-aged woman in black pajamas walked out into the sun.

"Numba one girl?" she asked.

"Just a cold Pepsi."

"Hey, GI, you want short time?" asked a young girl in skin-tight red shorts and a white T-shirt.

"No time, today." I smiled.

"Special Force numba ten." She shook her head in disgust.

As soon as the woman returned with my Pepsi-Cola, I pulled out and headed for Saigon. Once into the city, I down-shifted when I hit the bumper-to-bumper traffic of Phan Thanh Gian Street. The sidewalks were crowded with people and rows of parked bicycles, and at the intersections, lines of women waited to fill large metal cans at public water faucets. With my horn competing with those of jeeps, buses, and taxi-cabs, I made a right onto Le Van Duyet Street and within minutes began picking up speed.

When I hit Highway 22, I removed my nine-millimeter Browning automatic pistol from its holster and placed it on the seat next to me. It wasn't likely that the Viet Cong would ambush a convoy, but a single person could be easy pickings. To minimize the threat, I sat low in the seat and sped down the one-lane road in a cloud of dust. If the enemy had an ambush in place, I hoped to be in and out of its killing zone before they had a chance to figure out that I was alone.

The ride back to Trang Sup proved to be uneventful, and by the time I pulled in the main gate, I was covered with a layer of dust and could feel its grit in my eyes, nose, and mouth. With the late-day sun sinking slowly into Cambodia, I deliv-ered my cargo to the mess hall and sat enjoying a couple of cheeseburgers while it was being unloaded.

On 7 May, the 3d Platoon arrived at the nearby rifle range just as a large orange sun peeked over the top of the range's earthen berm. The berm was about fifty meters long and five meters high and had firing lines at twenty-five, fifty, and one hundred meters. Our first objective was to make sure that the sights on our M-16s were aligned with the barrels. Thach, our 3d Squad leader, had set up three sandbagged firing positions on the twenty-five-meter firing line and three twenty-five-meter "zero" targets at the base of the berm.

"First thing this mornin', we're gonna zero your weapons," Bob told the Bodes as they sat in a circle behind the firing line. "Almost all of our contacts with the enemy take place between 0 and 250 meters. Once your weapon is zeroed, you'll be able to hit anything you can see between those distances without changing your sights." He paused while Rinh translated his words. "Okay, everyone push your rear sight forward so you can see the *L* on it." Rinh again translated. "Everyone got it?" Bob asked.

Thang said something that I didn't understand.

"He wants to know why we are so close to the targets," Rinh told Bob. "Why don't we shoot from one hundred meters?"

"Good question. It has to do with the flight of the bullet," Bob explained. "Once you're on target at twenty-five meters, you'll flip your rear sight back to close range. Then your rounds will hit exactly where you aim at 40 and 250 meters. In between 40 and 250 meters, you'll hit a couple of inches high; but not enough to make a difference. So, if you squeeze off your rounds when the top of your front side blade is centered in the enemy's lower chest, you'll almost always get a kill."

Rinh repeated what had been said, and the men nodded that they understood.

"Using this system, you can hit anything you can see, and you never have to adjust your sights," I added. "Also, if you pick up someone else's zeroed weapon on the battlefield, you'll be able to fire it accurately."

Rinh again translated.

"Any questions?" Bob asked, and then paused. "Okay, let's do it," he told Luc. "One squad at each firing point."

With their weapons resting on the sandbags, the first three men squeezed off three rounds each. All nine rounds hit the targets close to dead center.

"Lookin' good. Now flip your rear sights back to close range," Bob told them. "Next three."

While the first three shooters were using tape to cover the holes in their targets, the next three positioned themselves behind the sandbags. While the squad leaders put them and the remainder of the platoon through the exercise, Bob, Luc, and I stood to the rear, discussing our plans for the day.

When all of the weapons were zeroed, we moved back to the fifty-meter line for controlled automatic fire. In the heat of battle, some of the men had a tendency to fire bursts of ten to twelve rounds, and we wanted to reduce their rates of fire to three-round bursts because when they fired on automatic, the first round was generally right on target, but each subsequent round hit farther and farther from the intended point of impact. Anything more than three rounds often missed the target and was a waste of ammunition.

"No sandbags this time," Bob told the three men lying in prone positions. "I want each of you to squeeze off a burst of three. Remember, proper trigger squeeze is the key. Let go of the trigger as soon as you feel that first round."

Rinh again translated what had been said, and on Luc's command, they each fired a short burst. All three had satisfactory groups on their targets. Bob, Luc, and I watched the squad leaders put the rest of the platoon through the exercise. Most of the men did well, but the squad leaders had to spend some extra time with a few of the new guys.

"On automatic you gotta keep a tight grip on your handguard and pull the butt into your shoulder," I advised them. "Hold your breath during each burst."

When everyone finished the controlled-automatic phase, we took a lunch break and then moved on to the quick-fire exercise.

"Okay, listen up," I yelled as Bob connected fifty-meter pieces of commo wire to two pop-up targets. "If you come face-to-face with an enemy soldier, you won't have time to use your sights. You have to react instinctively. In this game, there's no second place; only the quick and the dead."

While Rinh translated my words, Bob finished testing the targets and moved to where I was standing.

"Each of you will walk toward the target with your rifle on automatic," Bob explained. "Somewhere between fifteen and twenty-five meters from the target, it'll pop up, and you'll have one second to put a burst of three into it. One second, no more."

"Remember," I added. "If you use your sights you're gonna lose time. Keep the butt in your armpit, and point your rifle at the target. You'll lose a little on accuracy, but it'll give you the edge on time. The split second you save will be the difference between life and death."

We ran them through the quick-fire exercise in two-man teams. Most did well, but a few fired high or didn't get their burst off in the allotted time. After running them through a second time, everyone was on time and on target. When we finished the quick-fire exercise, we took a dinner break.

On previous missions, we discovered that some of the men had a tendency to fire high at night, and we wanted to give them the opportunity to improve their night-firing technique. When we returned to the range at 2100 hours (9:00 P.M.), the crickets were chirping, and most of the light from the stars was filtered out by a veil of clouds. Everything appeared in tones of gray, and the men appeared as shadows as they took up prone positions on the fifty-meter firing line.

"On my command, you will have one second to fire a three-round burst," Bob yelled as I moved down the line, handing each man a magazine loaded with three rounds. The Bodes didn't know that they were tracer rounds.

"Lock and load," Bob yelled, and they inserted their magazines and chambered a round.

"All ready on the right." Bob paused. "All ready on the left. All ready on the firing line. Watch your targets. Fire!"

Whack-whack-whack! The area between the firing line and the fifteen-foot-high berm filled with lines of red tracers. Most stopped at the berm, but a good twenty percent were fired high and streaked over the top.

"Cease fire," Bob yelled. "Clear all weapons." He paused. "If this had been a night attack, we'd be dead. Half of you fired high." Rinh again translated, and Luc shouted something that I didn't understand.

"There's a couple of secrets to shooting at night," Bob told them. "To see a target at night you don't look directly at it like you do during the day. You look a little to the left or right of it." Bob again waited for Rinh. "If you look downrange at your target, you'll see that you can barely make it out. However, if you look a little to the side it becomes much clearer. Take a couple of minutes to try it."

"Aaahhh," the men muttered in amazement.

"Okay, next point," Bob said. "When you shoot at night, you don't use your sights, because you can't see 'em." Rinh repeated his words. "Get back into the prone position, and we'll go through this one step at a time." Bob paused. "All right. At night you place the butt of your rifle in the middle of your chest, with your chin resting on top of your stock. Everyone got it?" he asked as Luc and I moved down the line checking and adjusting each shooter's position.

"They're good," I yelled to Bob.

"Okay, *Trung si,*" Luc hollered.

"Now, look out over the top of your sights and point your weapon at the target . . . Nothin' to it. Okay, let's do it."

I moved back down the line, handing each man another three-round magazine.

"Lock and load," Bob yelled. "All ready on the left. All ready on the right. Watch your targets. Fire!"

Whack-whack-whack. Red lines again filled the air, but this time none went over the top of the berm.

"Cease fire," Bob yelled. "Clear all weapons. Good shootin'."

"Chey-yo!" the Bodes yelled.

"Let's call it a night," Bob told Luc.

At 0700 hours (7:00 A.M.) on 8 May, Trang Sup's tall guard tower was silhouetted against a red-orange-and-yellow sun. A few hundred meters west of the camp, the 3d Platoon sat in a circle in a dry rice paddy. A soft breeze blew across the paddy, and the sky appeared as a thousand white-cotton balls on a blue blanket. It was a beautiful day.

"This morning we're gonna cover ambushes and counterambushes," I said as Bob and Rinh stood next to me. "The objective of an ambush is to kill or capture the enemy. If it's well planned and well executed, no one escapes." I paused while Rinh translated. "Okay. What are the keys to a well-executed ambush? First, you must have total concealment. Surprise is critical. Second, you must remain alert and totally silent. Again, surprise is critical."

Rinh translated what had been said.

"Before you settle into your ambush position, you gotta clear all of the bamboo, branches, and leaves from your position. It also means no talking, sneezing, coughing . . . or farting." Bob smiled, and the Bodes laughed. "If one man moves or makes a noise, we die."

"The next key to a well-executed ambush is springing it at the right time," I explained. "If it's early or late, the enemy lives, and you may die."

"On every ambush, we'll have a prearranged signal for springing it," Bob said. "Most of the time it'll be Luc or one of the squad leaders blowing a claymore. You don't open fire until the signal is given. The instant you hear the signal, you open up and put maximum fire on the enemy."

"Short and violent," I said.

"If Charlie springs an ambush on us, you immediately return fire and assault the ambush," Bob said. "It's assault or die. If you hit the ground, you die. If you run away, you die. If you immediately assault the enemy, you may live."

"You won't have time to think," I added. "You just do it."

Bob turned the training over to Luc, and as he and I sat watching on a nearby dike, the squads took turns ambushing each other. When we finished the exercise, we returned to the Mobile Guerrilla Force compound and gave the men the remainder of the day to prepare for our departure.

On 9 May, Bob and I were up well before first light. Under a star-filled sky, the charcoal fires of the mess tent glowed softly, and the air was filled with the smells of Cambodian cooking. After showering and shaving, we went to the mess hall and loaded up on French toast and coffee. When we walked back outside, a rooster was crowing, and a golden sun was just coming up over the horizon. As soon as we got back to our room, we laid out our gear on our bunks and divided it into three areas: equipment on our web gear, equipment in our rucksacks, and individual equipment.

The equipment on my web gear included twenty magazines of M-16 ammunition, one M-26 fragmentation hand grenade, one M-18 smoke grenade, one CS tear gas grenade, twelve M-14 toe popper mines, a navy survival knife, two plastic one-quart canteens, a metal canteen cup, four syrettes of morphine, an escape-and-evasion kit, a can of serum albumin, and four battle dressings.

My rucksack was lined with a waterproof nylon bag that could be tied off at the top. In it, I carried another twenty magazines of ammunition, two additional one-quart plastic canteens, a collapsible two-quart bladder canteen, a nylon Vietnamese hammock, a lightweight Australian poncho, a five-foot-by-eight-foot piece of camouflage parachute nylon, a rifle-cleaning kit, a pen flashlight with clear and red lenses, six bottles of insect repellent mixed with lanolin, a thirty-five millimeter Pen ee camera and six rolls of color film, four C-ration and four indigenous rice meals, my toilet articles, and a bottle of Tabasco sauce—my only luxury item.

My individual equipment included an air force "white dot" signal mirror, an M-186 flare-gun kit, an international-orange signal panel, a lensatic compass, an acetate-covered map of the guerrilla warfare operational area and grease pencil, an acetate-covered signal operating instructions, a Swiss army officer's pocketknife, leather work gloves, dapsone, salt, and halazone water purification tablets, a P-38 can opener, a roll of green tape, a pen and diary, a quarter-pound block of C-4 high explosive, a box of blasting caps, a pair of crimpers, and American and Khmer-Serei battle flags.

At 1100 hours (11:00 A.M.), Luc had the platoon standing by for a full-field inspection.

"Krump tee bei, damrang chua," he barked, and the platoon snapped to attention. Each man's gear was laid out on a poncho in front of him.

"All present, *Trung si,*" Luc said as he saluted Bob.

"Stand at ease," Bob ordered.

Bob, Luc, and I moved slowly from poncho to poncho, and as we examined each piece of equipment, the squad leaders corrected any discrepancies we found. We also checked the pin on every grenade to ensure it was secured with green tape. Following the inspection, each man packed his ruck-sack and bounced up and down a few times to make sure there would be no noise when he moved.

We completed our inspection at 1300 (1:00 P.M.), and by 1330, the company was lined up just inside the main gate. A dozen wives hugged and kissed their husbands and said what for some would be their last good-byes. The headquarters section was standing near the gate and would be the first to depart. Lined up behind it were the Recon, 4th, 1st, 2d, and 3d platoons. We would be the last to leave.

"Radio on our primary?" Bob asked Luc.

"Yes, *Trung si,* 77.95."

Bob signaled Luc and Rinh to join us.

"If Jim and I get killed, and you can't make commo on our primary, switch to 44.20—our emergency frequency," Bob said. "Everyone got that?"

"Yes, *Trung si,* 44.20," Luc responded. Rinh nodded.

"Our emergency call sign will be Ugly Spices One-niner," Bob added.

"I not know this word," Luc responded.

"Ugly Spices One-niner," Bob said slowly.

Luc tried but had trouble repeating it.

"I'll tape it to the radio," Bob smiled. "Okay, once you make commo on the emergency frequency, you identify yourself as Ugly Spices One-niner and tell 'em that Handbag and Notch [Bob's and my confidential secure words] are dead."

"Okay, *Trung si,*" Luc agreed.

I sensed that Bob didn't appreciate his confidential secure word.

"Handbag!" I laughed and shook my head.

"You're gonna pay for this." He smiled as a black bird with outstretched wings soared high above Trang Sup.

"The FOB at Phuoc Vinh gonna monitor our primary?" I asked.

"Yeah," Bob responded. "Single sideband, primary, and emergency."

Wap, wap, wap. Looking toward Nui Ba Den, I saw a line of UH-1 helicopters that shimmered in the heat and were black against the blue sky.

"Here we go," Bob said as we lifted our rucksacks to our backs and bounced a few times to settle our heavy loads.

At the head of the formation, Captain Gritz stood near the gate with his radio handset pressed to his ear. Captain Johnson tossed a smoke canister, and a trail of red smoke poured from it and slowly twisted skyward. With their rotors slapping the hot dry air, the choppers glided in over the rooftops. Seconds later, they lowered their noses and touched down on the road.

Through blowing dust and red smoke, lines of black-and-green uniforms poured into the choppers. Seconds later, the Hueys lifted to a five-foot hover with streams of black fumes pouring from their turbine engines. Then, with a surge of power, they tilted nose down, transitioned to forward flight, and climbed as they moved down the road.

Before the dust settled, a second flight of choppers was on the ground, and the air was permeated with the smell of burnt aviation fuel. When the third flight touched down, we covered our eyes with our arms and moved to the door of the lead chopper. Luc, Ly, Rinh, our machine-gun section, and a few other Bodes took up seats on the honeycomb aluminum floor while Bob and I sat with our feet dangling out over the skid. With the main rotors kicking up a cloud of dust, the pilot pulled back on the collective, and the chopper shook as it lifted to a few feet above the ground.

"Chey-yo!" the Bodes yelled as we picked up speed and a refreshing breeze blew through the cabin. Within minutes, we were cruising east at ninety knots. Five thousand feet below,

the paddies and dikes of Tay Ninh Province were a giant checkerboard that extended as far as the eye could see. As we flew east, the terrain changed to rubber plantations, scrub brush, and mangrove swamps. When we reached the rolling green hills and triple-canopy jungle of Phuoc Long Province, the pilot slightly raised the nose of the chopper.

"War Zone D." Bob pointed as we began our descent into Dong Xoai.

I leaned toward him.

"The Viet Cong call it the Forbidden Zone."

3

Under a star-filled sky, our column moved east down a narrow one-lane road. The still night air smelled of mold and rotting vegetation and was filled with the sound of chirping crickets and an occasional grunt or screech. To my front, a line of ghostlike figures moved silently through knee-high mist. Four-story trees grew to both sides of the road and left me with the feeling that I was at the bottom of a black-walled canyon.

We had slipped out of Dong Xoai at midnight and were moving at a blistering pace. SFC Duke Snider's 1st Platoon was on point and was followed by the headquarters section, then the 4th, 2d, and 3d platoons. S.Sgt. Ray Fratus's Recon Platoon had departed six hours prior to the main force and was to rendezvous with us ten kilometers east of Dong Xoai.

Bob was at the head of the 3d Platoon, and I was the last man in the column. A few paces in front of me, Thach moved with his HT-1 radio pressed to his ear. With a heavy rucksack on my back and my M-16 at the ready, I kept glancing to the rear to make sure that we hadn't picked up any enemy trackers. At a distance of fifty meters, everything disappeared into the night.

"Bac-si," Thach whispered and extended his hand.

"What is it?"

"My wife cook," he said as the pace suddenly slowed.

"Thanks, partner." I bit into a piece of chewy coconut-and-pineapple candy, and started walking backward.

The column suddenly stopped, and while standing in the shadows at the side of the road, I felt like I had just completed a hard ten-mile run. I could taste salt on my lips and feel its sting in my eyes. Without taking my eyes off the road, I took in a few deep breaths and leaned forward to relieve the strain of the rucksack straps on my shoulders.

"Luc say we RV Recon," Thach whispered. "We go south."

"Okay." I wiped the sweat from my eyes.

Two hundred meters down the road, we turned south and immediately entered thick jungle. It was as black as tar, so I grabbed a strap on the rear of Thach's rucksack and followed him in short three-inch steps. With each step, thorns tore at my ears, face, and neck.

Soon after we entered the jungle, it came to life with the predawn chirping of birds and the chattering of monkeys. By the time we were three hundred meters south of the road, the grays were turning to dull shades of green, yellow, and brown. On the lower branches, a few small, brown monkeys sat watching our every move while others scurried to the higher elevations where they disappeared into the mist.

"We stop," Thach whispered as he monitored radio communications.

"Good, I need a break," I told him.

Thirty meters ahead, the men were alternating ten meters to the left and right of our line of march before lowering their rucksacks to the ground. If we were attacked during our break, our cigar-shaped perimeter would be easier to defend than a single column spread out over two hundred meters.

"Get security in place," I whispered to Thach when we stopped. "Machine gun on our back trail. Teams to the left and right."

"Okay, *Bac-si.*"

I lowered my rucksack to the ground and waited with my rifle at the ready, while Son, our cross-eyed machine gunner, positioned his M-60. Thach also sent two-man flank-security teams fifty meters to the left and right of our route of march.

With security in place, I removed a canteen from the side pocket of my rucksack, and swallowed two salt tablets with a long drink of water. Kneeling next to my rucksack, I opened C-ration tins of bread and peanut butter.

"Jim." I turned and saw Bob approaching. "Horn's making commo with Phuoc Vinh. We'll be here for thirty minutes."

"Okay," I said as I spread peanut butter on my bread.

"What's the delay on your time pencils?"

"Eight hours," I said as Thach returned and squatted next to his rucksack.

"Good, Gritz wants a claymore left on our back trail," he said.

"I'll take care of it."

"Catch ya later." He headed back to his position at the head of the platoon.

"I do claymore," Thach volunteered.

"Go ahead," I said as I used my finger to scoop the last of the peanut butter from the tin. "I'll get ya a time pencil."

Thach removed a claymore mine and our demolition bag from his rucksack and moved ten meters down our back trail to where Son was lying behind his M-60. Kneeling next to my rucksack, I removed an M-7 nonelectric blasting cap from a small wooden box. I then reached into my rucksack and pulled out a time pencil. The copper and brass device was shaped like a pencil with a glass vial of acid and a fuse at one end. Once the vial was crushed—with five pounds of pressure—it would take eight hours for the acid to eat through the restraining wire. The striker would then hit and detonate the percussion cap and the mine.

Using crimping pliers, I carefully attached the blasting cap to the end of the time pencil. M-16 at the ready, I moved to where Son was lying silently with his finger on the trigger of his M-60.

"Bac-si." He smiled and handed me the claymore that Thach had left with him.

"Hey, partner. How ya doin'?" I said as I watched Thach.

Ten meters to our front, he was on his knees adjusting blades of grass around an ankle-high trip wire that ran across our back trail. Danh was standing guard over him with his silencer-equipped Sten at the ready. While waiting for Thach, I extended the claymore's scissor-type folding legs and looked for a good spot to position it. Glancing back to our front, I saw Thach unraveling a roll of milky white detonating cord as he and Danh moved slowly in my direction. Kneeling among large featherlike ferns, I pushed the claymore's legs into the soft earth so that, when detonated, its exploding one-and-a-half pounds of C-4 would propel a fan-shaped pattern of steel balls down our back trail.

When Thach reached where I was kneeling over the mine, he handed me the detonating cord and a blasting cap. While I crimped the blasting cap to the end of the detonating cord, he and Danh retraced their route back to the trip wire to make sure that the entire length of white cord was covered with leaves. They then returned to where I was waiting.

"Okay, *Bac-si*." Thach used his sleeve to wipe the sweat from his leathery, scarred face.

"For an old fart you do good work," I said. "Psst," I hissed to Son. When he turned, I raised my arm over my head and by rotating it in small circles signaled him to join us.

With Son behind us, Thach inserted the blasting cap into one of the claymore's two detonating wells. At that point, the mine was dangerous because if an animal or a falling branch hit the trip wire, the back blast would likely kill or wound the four of us.

Whoomph! A muffled explosion sounded far to the west.

"Here we go," I said as I crushed the time pencil's glass vial, pulled the safety tab from the device, and slipped its attached blasting cap into the claymore's second detonating well. The mine was dual primed: If nothing hit the trip wire within eight hours, the time pencil would detonate the mine.

Everything set, we covered the mine with leaves, returned to our rucksacks, and called in security. Minutes later, we were moving uphill past massive three-to-five-story cypress trees and clumps of green bamboo. Nearing the crest of the hill, the column slowed and then stopped.

"VC bunker," Thach whispered as he monitored radio transmissions.

"Strange place for a bunker," I said as I looked at my map. "They don't build base camps on high ground."

"Yes, *Bac-si,*" he agreed. "VC camp by water."

For close to five minutes, we waited at the base of a great cypress tree with our weapons pointed down our back trail. High above our heads, most of the mist had burned off, and a few patches of blue could be seen. It was going to be another hot day.

"Eight bunker," Thach told me as he monitored radio transmissions. "No VC."

At the crest of the hill, we passed a log-and-dirt bunker with a south-facing, ground-level firing port. It was well constructed and camouflaged with branches whose leaves were still green and soft.

Fifty meters farther south, we crossed a well-used, east-west trail.

"Aaah," Thach whispered. "Bunker ambush trail."

While Danh stood guard, Thach and I used branches to sweep away the footprints that our column had left in the soft earth at both sides of the trail. Fifty meters south of the trail, we passed another bunker with a north-facing firing port.

"An asskicker," I whispered to Thach. "Eight bunkers. Interlocking fields of fire. If they caught a company on that trail, they'd wipe 'em out."

At 1015 hours (10:15 A.M.), we crossed a muddy, knee-deep stream, called the Da Peh, and moved uphill through triple-canopy jungle and gnarled green-and-brown vines that twisted off in every direction. Near the top of the hill, the column slowed to a crawl.

"Helicopter," Thach whispered as he continued to monitor his HT-1 radio.

"What?"

At the crest, I found Bob deploying the platoon to the left and right of our route of march.

"Got a downed chopper up ahead," he said. "Settin' up a perimeter around it."

"Any survivors?"

"Check it out," he said. "I'll stay with the platoon."

Thirty meters past Bob, I found Captain Gritz standing with his acetate-covered map spread out on a fallen tree and his PRC-25 radio handset pressed to his ear.

"That's a Roger, Memphis," Gritz said to the FAC. "From the RP, I'm at right 2.1, down 1.3. Over."

A short distance past the captain, a leaf-and-vine-covered Huey rested on its skids on the jungle floor. High in the trees, a thin layer of mist glowed white, and a brilliant shaft of sunlight angled through the foliage to touch the chopper. Its two main rotor blades were missing, but other than that, there didn't appear to be any serious structural damage.

Nearing the chopper, I found SFC Duke Snider pushing aside leaves and vines as he examined the area around it. S.Sgt. Dave Rose was kneeling among waist-high ferns, checking the contents of the aircraft's medical kit.

"No booby traps," Duke announced as Capt. Tom Johnson appeared near the tail of the Huey.

"All clear on this side," the captain said.

Looking in the window, I was shocked to see the perfectly preserved skeletons of the pilot and copilot sitting in their armored seats. Both wore helmets and flight suits with their shoulder harnesses locked in place.

"Gritz thinks it's a Project Delta chopper," Dave Rose told me. "Probably ran out of fuel."

"Could be," I said. "If there was anything left in the tanks, there probably would have been a fire."

"Look at those branches." Dave pointed.

High above our heads, many of the branches had been snapped like twigs, but over time, much of the area had filled in with new growth.

"Been here a while," I said. "Six months or more."

"No booby traps, sir," Duke told Gritz from inside the cabin.

"Get the skulls," Gritz said as the FAC's O-1E aircraft neared our perimeter. "We'll take 'em out with us."

"They'll use their dental records to get positive IDs," Dave told me as Duke jumped to the ground holding a bulging sandbag.

"Here, put it in your ruck," Duke told a Bode as he handed him the sandbag.

"Klach na." The young soldier's face flushed. He didn't want anything to do with the skeletal remains.

"Goddamn it," Duke said, "I'll take it."

"Roger, Memphis," Captain Gritz said to the FAC. "Come five degrees to your right. Over."

Sitting on the chopper's honeycombed aluminum floor, Captain Johnson reached forward and pulled an olive drab helmet bag from between the seats.

"Oh my God," he gasped as he read the name on the bag.

"Somethin' wrong, sir?" Dave asked.

"Chuck Able," he said as he pointed to the C. S. Able stitched on the bag. "We were platoon leaders in the 101st. Becky and his wife were good friends." He shook his head. "He left Campbell in '64 to go to flight school."

"Probably had him listed as MIA," Duke commented.

"Well, at least his wife'll know what happened to 'im," Dave added as the FAC neared our perimeter.

"Now!" Captain Gritz said into his radio handset when the O-1E was directly overhead.

Whoomph! A distant explosion.

"Roger, Memphis," Gritz said as he used a grease pencil to record our coordinates on his map. "Appreciate your assistance. Fox Control, out."

"Get a fix?" Duke asked as he squeezed the skulls into his rucksack.

"Eight digit," Gritz responded.

I returned to the 3d Platoon and briefed Bob on what had

taken place. Ten minutes later, we moved downhill to the southeast and again crossed the muddy waters of the Da Peh.

"We're outta range of Dong Xoai's 105s," I whispered to Thach as we moved uphill past fifty-foot stalks of lime green bamboo.

"Before I come Mobile Guerrilla Force, I stay Dong Xoai two year." He wiped the sweat from his leathery face. "VC tell soldier at Dong Xoai this bad area. You come here, you die."

"Same thing on Blackjack-31," I said. "As soon as we got outside Duc Phong's artillery fan, we found base camps."

"VC know how far artillery shoot."

Whump-whump-whump. Whack-whack-whack. An exchange of AK-47 and M-16 fire, not more than two hundred meters ahead of us. A surge of adrenaline electrified my system.

"*Trung si* Snider make contact three VC," he told me as he monitored radio transmissions. "No one die." The bad news was that the three Viet Cong were probably on their way to report our location to their superiors.

Two hours later, the shadows were beginning to lengthen as we moved uphill past massive cypress trees. Their mottled gray-and-white trunks measured ten to twelve feet in diameter and were wrapped tight with green vines. The space between the great trees was packed with clumps of green-and-yellow bamboo and saplings. At the top of the hill, I found the headquarters section setting up an inner perimeter that measured fifteen meters across.

"Third Herd, 240 to 360 degrees," Capt. Tom Johnson told me as S.Sgt. Tom Horn knelt on the ground, setting up his PRC-74 radio. To Horn's left and right, Bodes used machetes to clear a fifty-foot path for his long-wire radio antenna.

Thirty meters past Tom, I found Bob and Luc positioning members of the 3d Platoon along our assigned segment of the perimeter. Just inside the perimeter, Rinh and Ly were busy stringing their hammocks between stalks of green bamboo.

"We made it," I whispered to Rinh as I lowered my rucksack to the ground next to his. It was a relief to have the weight off my back. "Everyone okay?"

"Two cases of heat exhaustion," he said. "I gave them each a canteen of salt water."

"Good," I said. "Any dehydration?"

"Yes, dehydration, cramps, and nausea."

"If they're not better in an hour, hook 'em both up to normal saline IVs."

"Okay, Donahue."

"Everyone's in position," Bob told me as he and Luc joined us and looked for a good place to string their hammocks.

"LP out?" I asked.

"Two men," Luc responded as he and Bob leaned their weapons against a tree and lowered their rucksacks to the ground. "They go seventy-five meter."

"First Platoon's on an overnight ambush." Bob used a scarf to wipe the sweat from his face. "Three klicks east."

"Ya know, we could use another radio," I said. "It's a pain in the ass not havin' one."

"Yeah, I know. Need one for each American." Bob looked at his watch. "Let's get up to the *bo-chi-huy*." We picked up our M-16s.

At the center of the perimeter, we found Captain Gritz sitting on a fallen tree. The team members were standing in front of him holding their maps. Bob and I were the last to arrive. To the captain's rear, Tom Horn was sitting on the ground writing in a Dianna one-time pad.

"Listen up," Gritz said. "I know Fergy went over this in our pre-mission intelligence briefing, but I wanna go over it one more time," he paused. "To no one's surprise, the Big Red One's G-2 has confirmed that our 3 May contact was with the 271st Main Force Viet Cong Regiment. They've also confirmed that the 271st does employ Chinese mercenaries."

"No shit!" Larry "Stik" Rader quipped. "Who else would be speakin' Chinese?"

"Since the 271st is subordinate to the 9th Viet Cong Division, MACV is also reporting the 273d in the area," Gritz added.

As Gritz spoke, Tom Horn was tapping out a coded message to the FOB at Phuoc Vinh.

"Sir, any intel on NVA forces?" Glen Bevans asked.

"CIC's latest order of battle has the 84th and the 141st NVA Regiments in War Zone D," Gritz responded.

"With local guides and high-speed trails, they can move thirty to forty klicks a day," Ray Fratus added.

"So what's the bad news, sir?" Bill Ferguson joked, and everyone laughed.

"Make no mistake about it," Gritz turned serious. "Clyde's here, and he's here in force. If we think and operate conventionally, we will be found, fixed, fought, and finished. The key to our survival is mobility," he added. "If we get tied down, his Main Force units will kick our ass."

"What if we take casualties?" Jim Battle asked.

"Jimmy," Gritz looked at me.

"Speed is the key to breaking contact," I said. "If your wounded are slowin' you down and preventing you from breaking contact, I'd suggest you hide 'em in the underbrush and get back to 'em as soon as you can. It's not an easy solution, but it provides everyone—including the wounded—with a chance to live."

"Make damned sure you draw a detailed map of the cache site," Glen Bevans added. "Finding 'em later could be a problem."

"Okay," Gritz said. "Captain Johnson will update you on friendly forces. Tom—"

"The good news is that we do have other friendly forces operating in the GWOA," Johnson smiled tightly as he moved to the front of the group. "Project Sigma has nine roadrunner and seven recon teams operating out of the FOB at Phuoc Vinh. We also have three Sigma commando companies and three Mike Force companies on standby."

"Sir, what's their anticipated reaction time?" Ray Fratus asked.

"CG, II Field Force, has assigned ten UH-1D slicks for Sigma scramble," Johnson responded. "If we get into trouble, they can put a force on the ground in two hours."

"Sir, any other rotary-wing assets?" Jim Battle asked.

"Four UH-1D slicks and two UH-1B gunships from the Big Red One." Johnson paused. "We also have the two O-1Es from the 184th Aviation Company. With two FACs, we'll have full-time coverage from first to last light. Colonel Kelly also got us top priority on all fixed-wing aircraft in III Corps."

"Does that mean we can divert 'em to our targets?" Jim Battle asked.

"You got it," Johnson responded. "If it's in the air, we can divert it."

"Thanks, Tom." Gritz stood up and smiled. "Now for the really good news."

"Sir, I can't take any more good news," Ferguson said, and everyone laughed.

"No, I'm serious." Gritz smiled. "We just received word from Colonel Kelly that Tom's wife Becky Jo has given birth to a baby boy. Thomas Rickman Johnson Junior and Becky Jo are both doing fine."

"No cigars?" Tom Horn asked from where he was sitting on the ground decoding a message.

"Hey," Johnson responded. "When we get back to Trang Sup, it's steak for everyone at the Bamboo Club."

"Okay, tomorrow's assignments." Gritz looked at his map. "Second Platoon. Fergy, you and Jim go south to the Suoi Pe. SLAR and Red Haze reports indicate activity all along the stream."

"Got it," Fergy responded as he marked his map.

"Bob, you and Jimmy go southwest to where the Suoi Pe intersects the trail at—" he again looked at his map "—140 642."

"Got a major trail, a year-round water supply, and overhead cover," I said.

"Everything ya need for a base camp," Bob added.

"Make sure you maintain contact with the FAC," Gritz cautioned.

"Don't forget that he can call in artillery from Phuoc Vinh," Johnson added.

"Okay, 4th Platoon," Gritz looked at Glen Bevans. "Perimeter security."

"Yes, sir," Bevans responded.

"Good hunting." Gritz ended the meeting.

4

1700 HOURS, 11 MAY 1967

The sun had lost some of its intensity, and the shadows were beginning to lengthen as the 3d Platoon moved west past clumps of dead bamboo. The once green-and-yellow stalks had turned brown and brittle and were bowed to the ground by the weight of their wilted leaves. Danh was on point and was followed by myself, Bob, Ly, Luc, our machine-gun section, and the rest of the platoon.

With my M-16 in one hand and my map in the other, I kept Danh moving in the right direction and, when necessary, used hand-and-arm signals to adjust his course to the left or right. The ground was littered with pieces of moldy bamboo, and we were careful not to step on them: a crunch could be heard for a hundred meters.

Kaw, kaw, kaw. High above the bamboo, a crow with outstretched wings drifted on the thermals. As I looked back to my front, I saw Danh drop to one knee. I froze in midstep with my fist clenched above my shoulder—the danger signal. A long minute passed before Danh turned and waved me forward.

"Trail, *Bac-si,*" he whispered.

Leaning forward through a tangle of leaves, I saw that we were at the edge of a well-used, north-south trail. With bamboo and brush growing on both sides, it looked like a tunnel that had been cut through the foliage. Fifty meters to the north and south, its hard-packed red-clay surface disappeared into the green.

"What is it?" Bob whispered as he and Luc joined us.

"The north-south trail."

"It's gettin' late," Bob said. "Let's cross the creek and head north."

"Okay."

Luc sent Kien and Hoa fifty meters south on the trail, and once they were in position, we skirted it north until we hit the Suoi Pe. At the stream's edge, a dirt bank dropped four feet into clear, slow-moving water. Both banks were lined with large cypress trees whose spreading leaves shaded the stream's mirrorlike surface. In the near darkness of the lower levels of the canopy, the great trunks were wrapped tight with vines and covered with bright green moss. A cloud of mosquitoes drifted in the still air between the banks, and hundreds of vines hung like limp tentacles to touch the water.

While we waited with our weapons at the ready, Thang and Dung gripped roots growing out of the bank and slipped into the knee-deep water. As they moved across the stream, their boots sank into its soft bottom, and the downstream flow turned mud brown. When they reached the far side, they used vines to pull themselves to the top of the bank and disappeared into the foliage. Minutes later, Thang appeared on the bank and gave us a thumbs-up—the signal that security was in position on the trail.

With security to the north and south, Danh and I slid down the bank. While standing near the center of the stream, we immersed our empty canteens, and they bubbled full of cool water. As Bob, Ly, and Luc followed us into the stream, Danh and I used the vines to climb to the top of the north bank.

"VC come," Kien whispered while standing on the south bank, shaking his fist—the signal that contact was imminent.

"How many?" Bob asked.

"I hear," Kien said softly. "Not see."

"Get 'em on line," Bob ordered.

Bob, Ly, and Luc quickly climbed the north bank, and as the rest of the platoon scurried across the stream, Luc directed them to ambush positions along the bank. Ten meters to the left of our crossing point, I found a large fallen tree lying along the bank. I dropped my rucksack and took up a firing position behind the decaying, moss-covered hulk. Danh positioned himself to my left, and Ly to my right.

"Gimme the claymore," I whispered to Danh.

With the mine in one hand and my M-16 in the other, I ran a few meters to my left. Directly across from where the Viet Cong would cross the stream, I dropped to my stomach, reached down, and pushed the mine's legs into the soft creek bank. Unraveling its S-rolled detonating wire as I ran, I returned to my position just as Bob took up a firing position to Ly's right.

"Get a FAC up," Bob whispered.

Ly handed me the radio handset, and I passed the claymore's electrical firing device to Bob.

"Fox Control, this is Fox Three. Over," I whispered as I looked at my map.

"Fox Three, this is Fox Control. Over," Captain Gritz responded.

"Control, we're at left 1.1, down 2.8. Got an undetermined number of VC movin' north in our direction. We may need the FAC. Over."

"Roger, Three. Control, out."

I passed the handset back to Ly.

"Don't fire until I blow the claymore," Bob passed the word.

Suddenly, I heard the singsong chatter of Vietnamese voices coming down the trail. To my left and right, a line of camouflage uniforms lay hidden in the leaves with their weapons at the ready. I wiped sweaty palms on my trousers, and as the voices grew louder, I glimpsed a face moving through the foliage. With my rifle resting on top of the tree, I followed the enemy soldier with my front sight blade. Twenty meters from the stream, the top half of his body came into view. He was wearing black pajamas with a yellow scarf tied around his neck. I glanced at Ly.

"VC," he whispered.

At fifteen meters, I spotted a 7.62mm AK-47 assault rifle

being carried, nonchalantly, over his shoulder. He had no idea we were in the area.

"Shit," I mumbled when I saw that the water downstream from the crossing point had turned the color of mud. It wasn't likely that the enemy would miss it.

When the enemy soldier reached the bank he looked to his rear, said something, and laughed. He had straight black hair and appeared to be in his late teens. In the foliage behind him, I detected more movement and worried that he might be the point of a large unit. With my heart racing and beads of sweat dripping from the tip of my nose, I suddenly heard the faint groan of the FAC's single-engine aircraft.

As the young soldier slid into the water, a gray-haired man appeared on the bank behind him. He too wore black pajamas and a yellow scarf. He had his finger on the trigger of a 7.62mm RPD light machine gun with a one-hundred-round drum-type magazine. Attached to his shirt was what appeared to be a red badge. It may have been a military decoration.

With my front sight blade centered on his chest, I took up the slack in my trigger. The old man was about to enter the water but stopped himself at the last possible moment. His facial muscles tensed, and he took a step back. He was a trigger pull from eternity.

Whoomph. *Whack-whack-whack*. Bob blew the claymore and our line erupted with the stutter of automatic fire. The young soldier was blown against the far bank like a large bug hitting a car's windshield and the old man's head exploded in a spray of bone, brain, and blood.

"Cease fire!" Bob yelled.

A headless corpse lay still on the bank, while the young soldier's torn body slid back into the water and bobbed like a cork. I slipped a fresh magazine into my M-16 and, while chambering a round, saw that one of the young soldier's hands remained embedded in the bank.

"Update Gritz," Bob said as ribbons of blood trailed lazily downstream.

Ly handed me the handset.

"Fox Control, this is Fox Three. Over," I said as I rose to my feet and continued to watch for movement.

"Three, this is Control. Over," Gritz responded.

Bob and Danh were on their feet and were about to retrieve the body that was floating downstream.

"Control, this —"

"Bac-si!" Ly screeched and pushed me.

Whump-whump-whump. Automatic fire erupted on the far bank.

Falling in what seemed like slow motion, I hit the ground just as Ly jerked violently and a three-foot stream of blood exploded from his back.

"No!" I yelled as he landed flat on his back. I crawled to his side and found him looking up at the sky with his mouth open and a shocked expression forever frozen on his face.

"Fuck!"

"He dead?" Bob yelled.

"Yeah," I hollered over the roar of the firing and explosions.

"I'm sorry, my friend," I said as I closed his eyes and pulled the radio handset from his grip.

"Fox Three, this is Memphis. Over," the FAC radioed as I crouched low behind the tree.

"Memphis this is Three," I responded. "We're in heavy contact. Over."

"Roger, Three. I got fast movers one minute out. Gimme a smoke. Over."

As the exchange of fire continued I yanked a yellow smoke grenade from Ly's harness, pulled the pin, and tossed it to the far bank. Rising to my knees, I fired three quick bursts, and again dropped to a low crouch behind the moss-covered trunk.

"Three, this is Memphis," the FAC radioed. "I got your smoke. Where do you want it? Over."

"Memphis, can you see the stream? Over."

"That's a Roger, Three. Over."

"We're on the north bank. Can you give us twenty Mike-Mike along the south bank? I say again, south bank. Over."

"That's a can-do. Over."

"Roger, Memphis. You're cleared hot. Three, out."

I rose to my knees and fired three more bursts at glimpses of enemy soldiers.

Whoomph! A deafening explosion on the far side of the fallen tree left my ears ringing.

"Bac-si." I felt a tap on my back as pieces of bark rained down on us.

It was Danh. His thumb had been shot off, and a stream of blood was pulsing from a vessel that extended a quarter inch from the oozing stump.

"Get down," I said as Rinh crawled up, dragging our M-5 medical kit. Lying on the ground next to Danh, I removed a forceps from my pocket, and clamped it to the end of the bleeding vessel. While I held the forceps still, Rinh tied the vessel off with a piece of surgical thread.

"Does it hurt?"

"No, *Bac-si,*" he said as Rinh used a scissors to cut away the excess thread.

Ta-tow-tow-tow. Son fired a burst from his M-60 machine gun.

"Get a dressing over it," I told Rinh.

"Okay, Donahue."

I picked up the handset and peered over the moss-covered trunk just as a jet screamed in low from the east.

Burrrrr. Its twenty-millimeter cannons tore into the foliage on the far bank.

"Memphis, this is Three," I said into the handset. "Lookin' good. Keep it comin'. Over."

"Roger, Three."

I looked to my rear and saw Rinh holding a few sections of gauze over Danh's stump.

"Let me help ya," I said as I crawled next to him.

Another jet screeched across our front with its rasping twenty-millimeter cannons blasting away. While Rinh held the gauze in place, I wrapped it with an Ace bandage and three-inch surgical tape.

Burrrrr. A third jet worked the far bank, and falling branches and vines splashed into the water.

"As soon as you get a chance, load 'im up with penicillin and streptomycin," I told Rinh.

As the jet faded to the west, another one streaked in low.

"Napalm!" Bob yelled while holding the handset.

With much of the foliage shot away, I saw napalm pods tumbling lazily end over end from the F-4 Phantom.

Kawhoosh! We hugged the ground as liquid fire splashed through the canopy on the far bank. When I peered over the trunk, a wave of intense heat hit my face.

"Bac-si." Another tap on my back.

Danh was pointing to his shoulder.

"Again?" I shook my head.

Rinh and I crouched at his side, and using a scissors, I expanded the hole in his uniform and cut away his sleeve. His shoulder looked like a raw steak with a chunk blown out of it. There was some oozing but no serious bleeding.

"No bone involvement," I said as the pungent petroleum smell of burning napalm filled the air. "You're lucky."

While I held a dozen pieces of gauze in place, Rinh wrapped the wound tight with a battle dressing and surgical tape.

"Jim," Bob yelled over the firing. "FAC says they're crossin' the stream on both flanks. Let's get the fuck outta here."

"Right," I responded as we finished taping Danh's wound.

Bob's news scared the hell out of me. If the enemy got behind us, they would pin us against the creek and wipe us out.

"Take the 3d Squad north on the trail," Bob yelled as we huddled behind the tree. "Once we break contact, shoot an azimuth to the northeast."

"Okay."

Karoumph, karoumph, karoumph. A string of bombs exploded to the east, and as their shock waves rushed over our position, Bob and I tossed CS gas grenades to the far bank.

"Bac-si," Kien called as I lifted my rucksack to my back.

I turned and saw him struggling to lift Ly's body.

"Let me help ya," I said as we positioned Ly over his shoulders in a fireman's carry.

"Got 'im?" I asked.

"Yes, *Bac-si*."

"Jim." Bob grabbed my arm. "Hoa's got the radio. Keep 'im with you."

"Okay," I yelled. "Stay with me, partner," I told Hoa as the creek bed filled with a noxious cloud of CS gas.

Karoumph! The earth shook, shrapnel cut through the overhead foliage, and leaves and pieces of branches rained down on us.

"Candoey ma via," Thach screamed at the enemy. I think he'd told them that their mothers were whores.

"Thach," I yelled. "Let's go."

While Bob and the 1st and 2d Squads lay down a base of fire, we rushed north with Thach on point. Moving on the trail was a risk, but we had to get out of the pocket before the enemy completed an encirclement.

"Memphis, this is Three. Over." I radioed as we moved.

"Three, this is Memphis. Over," the FAC responded.

"Memphis, we're breaking contact to the north," I said. "Keep the pressure on the crossing points, over."

"Roger, Three. I've got fast movers stacked up."

Kawhooosh! Napalm splashed through the canopy a hundred meters to the west.

A short distance north of the stream, the trail made a sudden turn to the southwest. If I followed it, we'd run into the Viet Cong who were crossing the stream to the west.

"Set up here," I yelled to Thach.

He positioned four men just inside the foliage at the edge of the trail. A few meters into the jungle, Kien laid Ly's body on the ground and caught his breath. The remainder of the squad formed a small defensive perimeter around us as fire and explosions continued to the south. Standing at the edge of the trail, I spotted Luc moving toward us. Seconds later, a line of Bodes appeared on the trail behind him.

"Forty degrees, fifty meters," I yelled and pointed when Luc arrived at our position.

"Okay, *Bac-si*." He continued to the northeast and quickly disappeared into thick foliage.

"Where the hell's Bob?" I yelled to Rinh as he passed.

"He is coming, Donahue."

Seconds later, I felt a great sense of relief when I saw Bob and two Bodes running toward us.

"Move it!" I yelled.

"Left two grenades," he panted. "Got everyone?"

"Yeah, twenty-six. Luc's fifty meters in at forty degrees."

"We'll change direction every fifty meters," he said as he wiped sweat from his eyes and handed me a fragmentation grenade with an attached time pencil. "It's got a fifteen-minute delay."

"Okay."

Bob continued to the northeast and I took a few steps into the foliage. With Hoa standing guard over me, I dropped to my knees and pulled an M-14 toe popper from my pocket.

"Hold this," I said as I handed the grenade to Hoa.

Whack-whack-whack. Whump-whump-whump. The four Bodes on the trail opened up and a few enemy rounds cut through the overhead foliage.

Using my knife, I scooped out a hole three inches wide and two inches deep and placed the olive drab plastic toe popper in it. It was a loose fit, so I stabilized the mine by using my fingers to pack some dirt in around it.

"*Bac-si,* we go," Thach told me. "VC come."

"Okay." I pulled the safety clip from the mine and covered the device with a thin layer of dirt and leaves. Twenty pounds of pressure would drive its firing pin into the detonator and set off the mine's one ounce of tetryl.

"Gimme the grenade," I told Hoa.

Whump-whump-whump. The stutter of enemy fire grew closer.

I crushed the glass vial on the grenade's time pencil, pulled the safety tab, and buried it in a pile of leaves near the edge of the trail.

"Bac-si." Danh tugged at my sleeve. "We go."

I removed a smoke grenade from my harness, pulled the pin, and tossed it out onto the trail.

"Let's go," I told them as red smoke billowed from the canister.

With Thach leading, we pushed through a tangle of leaves and vines. Hoa was in front of me with the radio, and a few paces to my rear, Danh walked backward with his Sten at the ready.

"Memphis, this is Three. Over," I radioed the FAC.

Chunk-chunk-chunk. Danh fired a burst from his Sten. I looked but didn't see any sign of the enemy.

"Three, this is Memphis. Over," the FAC responded.

"Memphis, we're off the trail and movin' on four-zero degrees. Could you put some ordnance on the trail south of the red smoke? Over."

"Roger, Three. Got a storm closin' in. This'll be it for the day. Over."

"Thanks, Memphis. We owe ya a cold one. Three, out."

With the last light of day quickly fading and thunder rumbling in the distance, a jet streaked in from the north.

Burrrrr. The Phantom roared over the trail, its twenty-millimeter cannons screeching like rusty hinges on a large door.

"Fox Control, this is Fox Three. Over," I radioed Captain Gritz as the sound of the jet faded to the south and a cool breeze blew through the foliage.

"Three, this is Control. Over."

"Control, we've broken contact and are movin' on four-zero with one indig KIA and one WIA. Over."

"Roger, Three. Wait one." Gritz paused. "Three, this is Control. Plan to RV at 1130 hours (11:30 A.M.) at left 1.6, down 2. Will have a Dustoff on the ground. Over."

"Roger, Control. Three, out."

I found Bob and the remainder of the platoon set up in a small defensive perimeter in thick bamboo. Above the thicket, a lead-gray mushroom-shaped cloud towered into a blood red sky.

"Gonna move north on three-six-zero," Bob whispered as Luc extended a trip wire across our back trail.

"Okay."

Bob, Hoa, and Luc moved north with the 1st Squad on point. The 2d Squad fell in behind them and Thach, Danh, and I brought up the rear. As our black-and-green column snaked through thick undergrowth, the wind suddenly turned cold, and the approaching rain sounded like Niagara Falls.

We had only moved a short distance when we were hit by a blinding downpour. As the rain beat down on us, a brilliant streak of lightning flashed and thunder cracked. I grabbed the strap on the back of Thach's rucksack and could feel Danh gripping mine. With every bolt of lightning, I could see the backs of the men in front of me, but between flashes, everything was as black as midnight.

After what seemed like hours, the column suddenly stopped, and a jagged silver ribbon of lightning lit our world beneath the canopy. A few meters ahead, I saw Bob, Hoa, and Luc standing in the pelting rain at the center of a small perimeter. The scene reminded me of something in a dream.

"Jim," Bob whispered when I closed the gap between us.

"Yeah."

"We'll set up here," he said as he lowered his rucksack to the ground.

"Okay."

I felt my way to his rucksack and placed mine on the ground next to it. Kneeling in the mud, I pulled out my poncho.

"Fifty percent security," Bob told Luc as thunder clapped. "Keep 'em in tight. I don't want any movement. And make damned sure they keep the blasting caps outta the claymores until the storm passes."

"Okay, *Trung si,*" Luc responded.

A flash of lightning with as many branches as an old oak tree lit the jungle like the noonday sun.

"Jim, see if ya can make commo with Gritz," Bob said as Luc whispered to the squad leaders over his radio. "If Horn can contact Phuoc Vinh with the seventy-four, we can use him as a relay to call in artillery. I'm gonna check the troops."

"Okay." I sat with my back against my rucksack and covered myself, head to toe, with my lightweight Australian poncho. "Hoa, gimme the handset," I whispered into the darkness.

With the poncho in position, I pulled out my red-tipped pen flashlight and map. After closely examining the map's contour lines, I used a grease pencil to fill in our route from the stream. I figured we were 200 to 250 meters north of the stream and 50 to 75 meters east of the trail. I pulled the waterproof plastic indigenous-meal bag from the handset and began shivering.

"Fox Control, this is Fox Three. Over," I whispered as rain drummed on my poncho.

"Three, this is Control. Over," Gritz responded.

"Control, we're at left 1.2, down 2.3. Will remain this location until first light. Can you relay a danger-close fire mission to the FOB? Over."

"Three, wait one."

As I waited, the space beneath the poncho glowed a dull red and was filled with the hiss of static. Again looking closely at my map, I figured I'd put the first round in three hundred meters south-southeast of where we made contact. I marked the spot with my grease pencil.

"Three, this is Control," Gritz radioed. "That's a can-do. Over."

Craaaack! Lightning exploded against a nearby tree.

"Roger, Control. Inform FDC that this will be a sound-adjust mission. Will adjust fire in fifty- and one-hundred-meter increments. Over."

"Roger, Three. Where do you want it? Over."

"Control." I looked at my map. "Put the first one in at left 1, down 3. Over."

"Roger, Three. That's left 1, down 3. I'll give you a heads-up, when it's on the way. Control, out."

I switched off my light and sat waiting as the rain continued its beat on my poncho.

"Jim?" Bob touched my head.

"Yeah."

He sat to my left, and we adjusted my poncho so that it covered both of us.

"Troops are locked in tight," he said as I switched on my flashlight. "Got the machine gun covering our back trail. As soon as the storm passes, they'll put the claymores out."

"Good. I made commo with Gritz. He's on the radio with Phuoc Vinh. First one's goin' in three hundred meters south of the creek."

Bob leaned back against his rucksack and looked at his map.

"Be careful," he said. "I don't trust those 175s. One short round, and it's all over."

"Right." I checked my Seiko. It was a few minutes past midnight. With Bob's added body heat in the space beneath the poncho, I stopped shivering.

"Three, this is Control. One on the way. Over," Gritz radioed.

"Roger, Control. One on the way. Three, out."

Bob opened his compass and held it at the ready.

Suddenly, the sound of the rain was drowned out by that of an approaching locomotive.

"The round," he whispered.

Karoumph! An earth-rending concussion sounded to the southeast.

"One-nine-zero degrees," Bob said as I looked at my map.

"Control, this is Three. Over," I radioed Gritz.

"Three, this is Control. Over."

"Control, lookin' good. From my position. I say again, from my position. Drop two-five-zero, over."

"Roger, Three. From your position. Drop two-five-zero."

"Should hit where the trail crosses the creek," Bob whispered.

Karoumph! Another explosion.

For close to three hours we huddled beneath my poncho bracketing the area with 175mm artillery fire. The rain stopped around 0400 (4:00 A.M.), but drops continued to drum on my poncho. When we pulled the poncho from our heads, we found the cool night air filled with the smells of decaying vegetation and the chirping of crickets.

"Did you see what happened to Ly?" I whispered as lightning flickered to the east.

"Outta the corner of my eye," Bob said. "Saw ya both goin' down."

Thunder rumbled in the distance.

"He musta saw somethin' on the far bank," I said. "He pushed me down and took the round. If it wasn't for him, I'd be dead."

"He was a good soldier."

"When we get back to Trang Sup I'm gonna write him up for a Bronze Star with *V*," I said.

"I'm sure Gritz'll approve it."

"Twenty or thirty years from now, it'll be important to his son," I said. "He'll understand who his father was and what he did."

"Ol' Ly was Special Forces."

"That he was."

As we sat waiting for the dawn, the jungle came alive with the chirping of birds. With thunder still rumbling in the distance, everything slowly turned to shades of gray, and a knee-high blanket of mist drifted in the still air.

"Get a claymore fifty meters down our back trail and two-man patrols a hundred meters north, east, south, and west," Bob told Luc.

"Okay, *Trung si.*"

"We'll move as soon as they get back," Bob said as I stuffed the wet poncho into my rucksack.

As we waited for the patrols to return, the grays turned to

dull shades of yellow, green, and brown, and in the higher elevations, everything disappeared into mist. I moved to the perimeter and found Rinh wrapping Danh's hand with a fresh Ace bandage.

"How's it goin'?" I asked as I squatted next to them.

"Very good, Donahue," Rinh responded. "I cleaned both wounds with pHisoHex and hydrogen peroxide."

"Good. You in any pain, buddy?" I asked Danh.

"No, *Bac-si*. I take APC."

"I gave him Demerol." Rinh smiled.

"We're gonna link up with the *bo-chi-huy*," I said. "Got a chopper comin' in. They'll take ya down to the CIDG hospital in Bien Hoa."

"What you do Ly?" Danh asked with concern.

"We'll send his body back to Trang Sup."

"*Bac-si,* his wife be too sad." Danh paused to gain control of his emotions. "*Bac-si*, maybe I go Trang Sup with Ly. I talk his wife."

"What about your wounds?"

"No problem, *Bac-si*. I go Tay Ninh hospital."

"It's your call," I said. "But don't go to the Vietnamese hospital. Tell the medic at Trang Sup I said to take ya to the American hospital."

"It's a good hospital," Rinh added.

"Thank you, *Bac-si*."

I removed my diary and pen from my pocket, tore out a page, and wrote down the combination to the lock on my footlocker.

"The combination to my footlocker," I said as I handed Danh the paper. "Take ten thousand P. Get Ly a good coffin and give what's left to his wife."

"I do, *Bac-si*."

"Okay, load 'im up with 600,000 units of procaine penicillin and a half gram of streptomycin," I told Rinh. "I'm gonna check on Ly."

I found Luc kneeling over Ly's body. He was using a wet

battle dressing to clean the dirt from Ly's face. When he finished, we placed Ly in his nylon hammock and tied it to a ten-foot section of green bamboo.

Whack-whack-whack. A burst of M-16 fire a short distance to the west.

Luc picked up his radio and held it to his ear.

"Three VC move south on trail," he told Bob. "They run. No one die."

"Get 'em ready to move," Bob told Luc. "Kien on point. Jim, you navigate."

By the time I had my rucksack on my back, Kien was ready to move. I pointed him to the east, and we moved slowly on an azimuth of ninety degrees. We didn't want to continue on the same northerly azimuth because enemy trackers might anticipate our route of march and set up an ambush.

Thirty meters to the east, we stopped and waited in the mist for the rest of the platoon. Five minutes passed before Bob flashed me a thumbs-up. Everyone was in line and ready to move. We continued east for three hundred meters and then stopped to set up another small perimeter. Once security was in position, I sat against my rucksack eating breakfast—instant rice with dried minnows and Tabasco sauce.

Following breakfast, half the platoon detail-stripped and cleaned and oiled their weapons while the other half stood guard; then they switched places. I was worried that the enemy might smell the oil and solvent but was more concerned that a combination of high-carbon-content ammunition and moisture would cause malfunctions.

When the squad leaders completed their weapons, ammunition, and equipment inspection, we headed north. Hidden by the mist, monkeys cried *ka, ka, ka* as we pushed through a clutter of dripping vines, leaves, and ferns. One hundred meters to the north, we changed direction and headed for the clearing where we planned to rendezvous with the rest of the company.

By 1115 hours (11:15 A.M.), most of the mist had burned off, and we were moving northwest through a mosquito-infested area of dead and decaying trees and ankle-deep mud. The mud was as black as pitch and smelled of mold. As we struggled through the foul-smelling paste, Bob radioed Gritz that we would be closing from the southeast. Minutes later, we hit dry ground and were moving past clumps of dead bamboo and large ferns.

"Dung-lai!" Someone challenged Kien.

He froze and said something I didn't understand. Twenty meters ahead, I spotted S.Sgt. Larry "Stik" Rader and three Bodes from the Recon Platoon. Stik was as skinny as a rail and as hard as woodpecker lips. He reminded me of a gunfighter from the old west.

"Hey, Stik," I said as I closed the gap between us. "Good to see ya."

"Mornin', Jim." He shook my hand. "DZ's a hundred meters ahead."

A short distance past the outpost, I found Duke Snider leaning into a freshly dug slit trench. It was filled with aluminum napalm containers. Each of the empty resupply pods had been packed with four hundred pounds of food, supplies, and ammunition prepackaged in man-portable sandbags.

"What the hell are you doin'?" I asked.

He raised his head, holding an M-26 fragmentation hand grenade with an M-5 pressure-release firing device attached to it.

"Jim," he said as I passed. "Lotta bad folks around here. Leavin' a little surprise for Mister Charles."

Just past the containers, Capt. Tom Johnson and S.Sgt. Tom Horn were passing out bulging burlap sandbags to a short line of Cambodians.

"Jim." Johnson motioned for me to fall in behind the last man. "Get 'em in line."

"Keep it movin'," Horn told Kien as he passed him a sandbag containing four indigenous rice and four C-ration meals—a four-day supply.

Johnson handed bags to Bob and me. "Position your platoon along the southern edge of the DZ," he told us as he glanced at his watch. "Wanna be outta here in no more than fifteen minutes."

"Got high-speed trails all over the place," Horn added as he passed a bag to Luc.

"Jim." Bob grabbed my arm. "You and Rinh stay here with Danh and Ly. I'll take care of the platoon."

"Right," I said as Bob slipped a sandbag into my rucksack, and I did the same for him.

Ten meters ahead, I saw Captain Gritz and Dien standing at the edge of a grass-covered clearing with their backs to me. Gritz had his radio handset pressed to his ear and was pointing to the north.

Rinh and I carried Ly's body to the edge of the DZ and placed him on the ground next to Gritz. The clearing measured less than a hundred meters wide and extended to the northwest for more than four hundred meters. It was covered with wheat-colored grass and was surrounded by massive cypress trees with dingy white trunks. Thirty meters into the clearing, SFC Glen Bevans and members of the ground reception committee had five international orange panels spread out in the shape of a T. When Gritz saw us, he passed his handset to Dien.

"Jimmy." Gritz shook my hand. "Your radio operator?" he asked with great sadness.

"Yes, sir. Ly's been with us since Ho Ngoc Tao."

The captain knelt on one knee, lifted the section of nylon hammock which covered Ly's face, and said a short prayer.

"God will be good to him," he said as he rose to his feet.

"Dai uy." Dien pointed to the northwest and handed him the radio handset.

Shimmering in the midday heat, a single-engine A-1E attack bomber appeared black against the pale blue sky. As it neared the release point, I saw that it was camouflaged in green, brown, and tan, with a gray underside. The pylons beneath its wings were loaded with six silver napalm containers.

"Now!" Gritz said into his handset.

The napalm containers tumbled from the wings, and a hundred feet off the ground were quickly slowed as the attached camouflaged T-7A reserve parachutes deployed.

"Outstanding," Gritz radioed as the A-1E roared overhead.

As the aluminum containers floated to earth, members of the ground reception committee ran to where the parachutes would collapse in the grass.

Whack-whack-whack. Whump-whump-whump. An exchange of M-16 and AK-47 fire to the northwest.

"Recon," Dien said to Gritz as the captain monitored radio transmissions.

"Fox Five, this is Fox Control. Over," Gritz said into the handset.

When I looked back to the clearing, I saw the Bodes moving toward the *bo-chi-huy* with the aluminum napalm containers on their shoulders.

"Roger, Five. One VC KIA," Gritz radioed. "Remain in position until we clear the DZ. Control, out."

To the west I detected the *wap, wap, wap* of an approaching chopper.

"Get 'em ready, Jimmy," Gritz said as Dien tossed a smoke grenade ten meters into the clearing. Under the blazing midday sun, a trail of purple smoke poured from the canister and slowly twisted across the clearing's bleached grass.

Gliding in over the trees, the green hull of the Huey was silhouetted against the sky. Rinh and I shouldered the bamboo attached to Ly's hammock and moved a few steps into the clearing.

With its rotor blades slapping the humid air at over three hundred revolutions a minute, the pilot slowed his forward speed, and at the last possible second, lowered his nose and sat down twenty meters into the clearing.

Karoumph, karoumph, karoumph. Bombs exploded to the northwest.

Carrying Ly through blowing grass and purple smoke, we reached the side door of the chopper. With each pass of the rotor blades overhead, rays of sunlight flickered across the anxious face of the waiting medic.

"Here ya go," I said as he grabbed one end of the bamboo pole and we slid Ly's body across the Huey's honeycombed aluminum floor.

"Cong Hoa hospital?" the medic yelled as Danh crawled into the cabin and sat next to Ly.

"No, take 'em both to Trang Sup," I hollered over the noise of the engine and rotors. The name didn't register. "The Special Forces Camp in Tay Ninh Province. Ten klicks west of Black Virgin Mountain."

"Got it." He nodded.

"Bac-si." Danh leaned to shake my hand.

"I'll see ya in a few days," I yelled.

I reached to touch Ly's face.

I would never forget.

5

Under the spreading leaves of towering cypress trees, we were moving south-southwest in two parallel columns. A blanket of leaves blocked out the light of the sun and left the jungle floor dark and free of vegetation. Bob was on the point of the column on the left and was followed by myself, Hoa, Luc, the machine-gun section, and the rest of the 3d Herd. Bill Ferguson's 2d Platoon and Glen Bevans's 4th Platoon followed the trail we were leaving in the soft earth.

Thirty meters to our right, Ray Fratus was on the point of the Recon Platoon. To Recon's rear were the headquarters section and the 1st Platoon. While Ray set the pace and determined our direction, Bob was responsible for maintaining visual contact between the two columns. When the vegetation thinned he increased the distance between the columns, and when it thickened, he narrowed the gap.

In areas where visibility was more than twenty meters, we preferred to move in two parallel columns because that better enabled us to react quickly to enemy contact. Our tactical philosophy at the squad, platoon, and company levels was to move fast and shoot first. If we made contact, we would quickly deploy on line, gain fire superiority, and assault. If we were spread out in a long single column, our reaction time would be considerably longer.

We continued downhill past mold-covered stalks of dead and dying bamboo and then stopped when we came to the bank of a narrow stream. The creek's three-meter-wide surface was covered with a crust of green algae, and between the banks a few colorful dragonflies skimmed the surface, hunting for mosquitoes. Bob crunched through the crusted surface and, after clearing the algae with his hands, decided not to fill an empty canteen. When I slipped into the knee-deep stream, my boots sank ankle deep in mud.

On the far side of the stream, I followed Bob uphill past clumps of bamboo and large ferns, and at the crest of the hill, we halted in a thicket of bright green bamboo to set up our mission support site (MSS). Once we had everyone in position, I dropped my rucksack to the ground and removed an indigenous ration—precooked rice in a clear plastic bag. I tore open the top of the bag and added some dried minnows, shaking it up before adding water and Tabasco sauce. It would take about fifteen minutes for the water to be absorbed, so I tied it off with a rubber band and laid it on top of my rucksack.

"Bac-si!" I turned as Hoa collapsed to the ground.

"What's wrong?" I knelt at his side and grabbed his sweaty forearm. His pulse was rapid and weak.

"I too sick, *Bac-si,*" the frail teenager said as he struggled to sit up.

It appeared to be heat exhaustion. He had suffered a chest wound a few months earlier, and I wasn't convinced that he had fully recovered from it.

"He is not strong enough to carry his gear and the radio," Rinh said as he squatted next to me with our M-5 medical kit.

"Oooaaahhh." Hoa belched and threw up on the ground between his legs.

"The heart of a lion but no upper body strength." I smiled. "Get 'im in a hammock and hook up a normal saline IV."

"I will take care of him," Rinh assured me.

"He okay?" Bob asked as he squatted next to us.

"Yeah, heat exhaustion," I said. "Rinh's gonna plug in an IV."

"You wanna set up the LP?" Bob asked.

"Sure." I picked up my rifle and found Binh, a squad leader, waiting with Nuong and Sarine.

"Binh, *soc si by?*" I greeted him and reached to shake his hand. Binh was an easygoing person with friendly brown eyes and a warm smile. He was also one of the most deadly individuals I had ever known.

"Good, *Bac-si*." He grinned.

"Pass the word that we're goin' out on three-hundred degrees," I told Luc. I didn't want someone opening up on us when they spotted our movement outside the perimeter.

"Okay, *Bac-si*."

With Binh leading on point, and Nuong and Sarine a few paces behind me, we headed northwest on an azimuth of three hundred degrees. On the perimeter, we passed three men who were busy preparing their night defensive position. One stood guard with his weapon at the ready while the other two were clearing brush so that they would have clear fields of fire.

As we moved downhill past clumps of thick bamboo and large ferns, I noticed that Binh was walking with a limp. During a Christmas morning mortar attack on our mission support site, he had been hit in the leg by a piece of shrapnel.

"Psst," I hissed and he turned. "Your leg okay?"

"No problem, *Bac-si*." He grinned.

When we were one hundred meters from the mission support site, I stopped Binh in a thicket of new growth bamboo.

"This is good," I whispered as black-headed red birds chirped in the leaves above our heads.

"Okay, *Bac-si*," Binh responded.

"Go another fifty meters," I told him. I wanted to make sure that we weren't close to a trail or enemy base.

Binh said a few words to Nuong and Sarine and then continued alone to the northwest. While I stood guard, the two men cleared a three-meter area of leaves, branches, and moldy decaying bamboo. Within the cleared area, they would be able to move around at night without making noise. By the time Binh got back, they had the area cleared and a poncho spread on the ground.

"No VC," Binh told me as he wiped sweat from his eyes.

"Two claymores." I pointed to our left and right front.

While Binh and I waited, Nuong and Sarine positioned their claymore mines fifty feet from the listening post.

"Okay, *Bac-si*." Binh smiled when they returned.

"Let's go over a few things," I whispered. Repetition was one of the keys to survival. You could never assume anything.

"Remember: no talking, no cooking, and no smoking," I said slowly. "You can smell a cigarette for a hundred meters. If you smoke, you die."

Binh translated and Nuong and Sarine nodded that they understood.

"One man sleeps, one man stands guard," I told them. "If you both sleep, you both die."

Binh again repeated my words and they nodded.

"You are here to listen." I pointed to my ear. "Not to shoot. If you hear something, you call Luc on the radio."

"Okay, *Bac-si*," Sarine smiled.

Whoomph! Something exploded far to the west.

"If many VC come during the night, use your claymores," I said slowly. "If you shoot, you will give away your position, and you will die."

Binh again translated.

"And don't throw any grenades."

"No grenade, *Bac-si*!" Nuong laughed and pointed to the almost impenetrable growth around us.

"Okay, let me see your weapons."

"I clean." Nuong smiled as he handed me his M-16. I found his rifle clean and well oiled, with a round in the chamber and the selector switch on safe.

"Lookin' good," I said as I handed it back to him.

When I inspected Sarine's M-79 grenade launcher, I found it clean and well oiled. However, when I opened the breech, I found it chambered with a high explosive round. When fired, a high explosive round had to travel a minimum of fifteen feet before it armed itself. In dense jungle, it was of little value.

"Get a canister round in there," I told him.

He changed the rounds, and after Binh said a few parting words, he and I retraced our path back to the support site. I got back to my rucksack just as Bob and Rinh were returning from the perimeter. Hoa was asleep in his hammock, a normal saline IV flowing into his arm. Sitting on the ground next to our PRC-25 radio was a short muscular Cambodian named Ly. He was one of three Ly's in the 3d Platoon.

"Ly's our new radio operator," Bob said as he and Rinh sat on a fallen tree, opening C-ration cans. "He carried a radio at Bu Dop."

"Good to have ya, Ly," I said as I shook out my eight-foot nylon hammock. "LP's out; one hundred meters at three hundred degrees," I said as I strung the hammock a few feet in front of where Bob and Rinh were sitting.

"Good," Bob responded. "One of Sigma's recon teams spotted two hundred VC movin' south."

"In this area?" I sat in my hammock with my bag of rice.

"Don't know. Horn picked it up on the radio," he said as he enjoyed a can of pears. "Johnson says the FAC caught fifty VC in the open and put TAC air on 'em. Sigma captured two of 'em."

"They ID the unit?" I sprinkled a few more drops of Tabasco sauce on my rice.

"The 273d Main Force Regiment," Bob said as Luc returned from the perimeter and knelt next to his rucksack.

"The 273d?" I choked. "The whole 9th Division's in War Zone D."

"No shit," Bob responded.

"Many VC this area," Luc said as he removed a small bottle of *nuoc mam* from his rucksack and sat in his hammock with a bag of rice.

"Every man in the platoon's gotta pay attention to detail," I told him. "Weapons clean and on safe, fields of fire cleared, claymores out, grenade pins taped down. One missed detail, and everyone dies."

"They check every day, *Bac-si*," Luc assured me.

"Gotta rely on the squad leaders," Bob said. "If there's any breakdown in our SOPs, you gotta kick ass."

"Yes, *Trung si*."

I knelt in front of my hammock and used my finger to dig a narrow six-inch slit trench in the soft earth. After breaking off a thumb-size piece of C-4 from my two-and-a-half-pound block, I placed it in the trench and lit it with a match. I then filled my metal canteen cup with water and placed it over the glowing explosive compound.

"What's the plan for tomorrow?" I asked Bob.

"Patrols," he said as he and Rinh sat on the tree, applying a fresh coat of mosquito repellent. "We're goin' two klicks west to a clearin'."

I dropped a tea bag into the now steaming water. With the last light of day quickly fading, I positioned my rucksack under my hammock, my ammunition harness on top of my rucksack, and my rifle on top of my ammunition harness. During the night, everything would be within easy reach.

By the time my tea was ready, only dull shades of gray remained of the day. With the first firefly of the night flashing above my head, I removed my boots and lay back in the hammock to enjoy my tea.

"That's strange," I said in the darkness.

"What's that?" Bob whispered.

"A couple of minutes ago there was only one firefly," I said. "Now we got about twenty of 'em, all flashing on and off at the same time."

"Yeah, that is strange. They're synchronized. One of 'em must be the officer in charge."

"Donahue," Rinh whispered. "Do you know what the soldiers call Sergeant Battle?"

"No." I sipped my tea.

"They call him the big Bode," Rinh laughed.

"His skin's about the same color," I said. "If he wasn't so tall he could pass for a Cambodian."

"Before he came to Trang Sup, he was a radio operator on Nui Ba Den," Bob said. "His wife just had a baby girl."

"Sergeant Donahue told me that you were born in New York City," Rinh said softly as hundreds of fireflies flashed in the darkness.

"I grew up in the city but I was born in Society Hill, South Carolina," Bob said. "In 1931."

"In 1931?" I questioned. "We'd better find you a quiet job in some Saigon warehouse."

"Those were hard times," Bob said. "My father was wounded in Cuba during the Spanish American War. We lived on his pension and what he could make layin' bricks. He died last year," he said with sadness. "Ninety-two years old."

"Bob, this may be a strange question, but I was wondering if you can trace your ancestors back to a specific country in Africa," I asked.

"No," he said. "As far as I know, everything was lost when we were slaves."

"My guess would be that they were Masai or South African Zulu," I said.

"The Masai and Zulu were great warriors," Rinh added.

"Someday I'd like to look into it," Bob said.

"When we were at Duc Phong I saw a movie about a school in New York City," Rinh said.

"Blackboard Jungle," I remembered.

"I graduated from George Westinghouse High School in Brooklyn," Bob said.

"What did you do before you joined the army?" Rinh asked.

"Well, I took the oath when I was seventeen," he said. "In high school, I worked part-time at a Woolworth's five and ten."

"Do you have a family?" Rinh asked.

"My wife, Savanna, and five kids," Bob said with pride. "Latisha's nine; she's my oldest. Then there's Joyce, Robert,

Darren, and Steven; he's seven months. When I left Bragg they went to live with their grandmother in South Carolina."

"Donahue, what did you do when you were a civilian?" Rinh asked.

"Civilian? I was never a sorry-ass civilian," I kidded. "I joined the Marines when I was seventeen and a senior in high school."

"Why did you leave the Marines?" Rinh asked.

"Back in '63, I was with the 2d Marine Division at Camp Lejeune," I told him. "Other than training, there wasn't much goin' on. One day, I read this magazine article about Special Forces. It caught my interest, and here I am."

Whoomph, whoomph, whoomph. A series of explosions far to the west. It sounded like artillery fire. Probably H & I fire from Dong Xoai.

"You never had a regular job?" Rinh asked.

"Back in Buffalo, I made fifty cents an hour working at the Butler Mitchell Boy's Club after school," I said. "On Saturdays, I went bar to bar shinin' shoes. On a good day, I could make ten bucks."

"I shined shoes," Bob said. "In a barber shop. The owner took half of what I made."

"Rinh, didn't you tell me you were born in the Delta?" I asked.

"Yes, on a farm in Hoa Thuan village. My father did not want me to be a farmer, so after high school, I studied to be a medic at Tra Vinh hospital. I was trained by a Vietnamese doctor."

Whoomph, whoomph. Two more rounds exploded to the west.

"How long you been in the military?" Bob asked as I finished my tea and placed the cup on top of my rucksack.

"I joined the CIDG at Loc Ninh Special Forces Camp in 1963. In 1965, I married Son Thi Cua and moved to Dong Xoai." He paused. "In April 1966, I met Sergeant Donahue when we were building the camp at Duc Phong."

"Why'd you volunteer for the Mobile Guerrilla Force?" Bob asked.

"Volunteer?" Rinh chuckled. "Sergeant Donahue came to Duc Phong from Ho Ngoc Tao and hid me on an Air America plane. I think you Americans would say I was shanghaied."

"Hey, we needed the best medic in Vietnam," I laughed.

"I am happy here," Rinh added.

"How come you didn't join ARVN?" Bob asked.

"The army and the government oppress us because they fear Cambodian nationalism," he said.

"I heard there's over three million Cambodians in Vietnam," I said.

"Yes," Rinh said. "At one time, the Mekong Delta was part of Cambodia. Three hundred years ago, the Vietnamese imperialists took it from us. Now they treat us badly because we want our land back."

As Bob and Rinh continued to whisper, I drifted off to a deep sleep.

Hours later, I felt a tug on my hammock.

"Jim," Bob whispered in the darkness.

"Yeah," I yawned. "I'm awake." I checked my watch and saw that it was time for me to begin my midnight to 0200 (2:00 A.M.) watch. Most of the fireflies had disappeared, and except for an occasional grunt or screech, the jungle was quiet.

I slipped into my cold, wet boots and sat in my hammock, M-16 in one hand and the radio handset in the other. As I watched the last of the fireflies, they reminded me that back at Trang Sup the sparks from Ly's funeral fire were drifting in the same night sky.

6

The 3d Platoon was moving downhill through an emerald forest and a pearl mist. In the branches high above our heads, invisible monkeys cried *ka, ka, ka* as we pushed through dripping leaves and thick green vines. Kien was on point and was followed by myself, Bob, Ly, Luc, the machine-gun section, and the rest of the platoon.

Bob required Son, our cross-eyed machine gunner, to always maintain visual contact with him. The M-60 was our most effective weapon, and when we made contact with the enemy, it was important that we immediately deploy it to the point of contact. As an offensive weapon, it enabled us to gain and maintain fire superiority. As a defensive weapon, the superior brush-cutting capabilities of its larger, heavier bullet enabled it to penetrate foliage well beyond the range of the M-16.

Five hundred meters from our mission support site, we crossed the Rach Be, a slow-moving, waist-deep stream, and continued west past towering black-brown trees. Packed between the trees, large heart-shaped leaves grew from red stems.

Two hours later, Kien dropped to one knee a few meters short of the southeast corner of the clearing we were looking for. From where I was standing, the open area appeared to measure a good five hundred meters across. It was covered with sun-bleached grass and was surrounded by the gray trunks of tall trees. Except for the *kaw, kaw, kaw* of a few crows, everything was silent.

"Bac-si." Kien chewed on his half-smoked, unlit cigar and pointed to a hole just inside the wood line to our right front. I moved to the hole and found it to be a recently dug spider hole. It was three feet deep and two feet across and had nothing growing in it. Some loose dirt remained on the ground around it.

"Spider hole," I whispered to Bob when he closed the gap.

Looking to our left we saw another hole twenty meters away. While we waited in a small defensive perimeter, Luc sent two-man patrols along the south and east edges of the clearing. When they returned, they reported their findings to Luc.

"Many hole," Luc told us. "Maybe one company stay here."

"An *L*-shaped ambush," Bob concluded.

If the enemy was able to find and fix the Mobile Guerrilla Force, the clearing would be a likely landing zone for Mike Force or Project Sigma reinforcements.

"They'd do a job on anyone landin' here," I said.

Bob reached for the radio handset.

"Fox Control, this is Fox Three. Over," he whispered into the radio handset, and then gripped the radio's AT-892 whip antenna at its base and tried to tighten it. "Somethin's wrong," he told me. "Fox Control, this is Fox Three. Over," he tried again. "Switch to the long antenna," he told Ly.

Ly lowered his rucksack and the radio to the ground, and as Bob unscrewed the short whip antenna, Ly assembled the sections of the ten-foot antenna and screwed it into the radio.

"Fox Control, this is Fox Three. Over." Bob tried again to make contact. "Get a motorboat sound every time I try to transmit," he told me. "Gotta be the battery."

"Should be good for sixty hours," I told him.

Ly pulled the radio from his rucksack, disconnected the battery box from the transmitter case, and removed the battery. It was about the size of a carton of cigarettes, and its sides were wet and bulging.

"Numba ten," Ly shook his head.

"It's close to exploding," I said. "Got it out just in time."

"Gotta check it every mornin'," Bob told Ly.

"Okay, *Trung si,*" he said as he slipped a new battery into the battery compartment.

"Make sure the squad leaders check the HT-1s every mornin'," I told Luc. "Loose antenna connectors, corroded antennas."

"Lay 'em out in the sun whenever they get a chance," Bob added. "Moisture can get to 'em."

"Okay, *Trung si,*" Luc responded.

"Let me show ya somethin'," I said to Ly as I picked up the radio handset. "Ya gotta check the moisture cover every day," I said slowly and pointed. "Also gotta keep the cable connector clean and dry," I again pointed.

"Okay, *Bac-si,*" he nodded, and I passed the handset to Bob.

"Fox Control, this is Fox Three. Over." After a brief pause, Bob gave me a thumbs-up.

When Bob finished briefing Captain Gritz, we continued just inside the wood line along the southern side of the open area. Five hundred meters farther west, Kien dropped to one knee at the edge of a small clearing where all of the lower levels of vegetation had been cut and cleared. It measured a good forty meters across, and at its center was a large fire pit and a pile of firewood.

"Way station," I whispered to Bob.

"Gotta be a high-speed trail in the area." He wiped the sweat from his eyes.

A way station was a temporary base camp. They were used as stopovers, usually at night, when an enemy unit was moving from one base camp to another or on its way to an objective. That one may also have been used whenever the enemy anticipated a helicopter landing on the nearby clearing. They would likely remain in the spider holes during the day and cook and sleep at the way station at night.

"Get security in place," Bob told Luc.

Binh's squad quickly deployed just inside the wood line on

the far side of the way station. Once they were in place, I moved to the fire pit. Its ashes were cold but didn't appear to have been rained on, so they were less than two days old.

"Bac-si," Thang hissed from the far side of the clearing. As I neared he pointed to three, foot-long twigs lying parallel on a trail that led west from the clearing.

"Good work, my friend." I smiled and gave him a thumbs-up.

The Viet Cong used three sticks, or three rocks, or three pieces of string to signal danger. There was a good possibility that the trail was booby-trapped. Looking down the trail, I didn't see anything suspicious.

"What is it?" Bob asked as he joined us.

"Booby trap," I whispered. "Somewhere on the trail."

"Let's get some more security in place," he said.

While Thang and I waited, Bob took Thach's squad and skirted the trail to the west. Bob returned a few minutes later.

"High-speed north-south trail thirty meters west," he told me. "I'm gonna booby-trap it. Do somethin' with the firewood," he said as he handed me a fragmentation hand grenade with a yellow safety lever.

"Right."

With Thang standing guard over me, I lay at the beginning of the trail and looked for anything that wasn't natural; a change of color in the soil, loose dirt, a trip wire, the three metal prongs of a bouncing-Betty mine. With my eyes just a few inches above the ground, I noticed what appeared to be an unnatural depression a few meters down the trail. In the brush beside the meter-wide area, I also spotted a clump of grass that had been tied together. It was another Viet Cong danger signal that generally pinpointed the location of a booby trap.

"That's gotta be it," I whispered to Thang.

I used my knife to probe the trail in front of me and when I reached the edge of the depression my blade slipped to its hilt.

Karoumph! An explosion far to the north. It sounded like a 175mm artillery round from Phuoc Vinh.

"Got it," I told Thang.

While kneeling next to the depressed area, I carefully brushed aside some of the dirt and found a tightly woven bamboo mat under a thin layer of soil. The mat was held up by pieces of bamboo and concealed a mantrap measuring a meter wide and a meter deep. At the bottom of the dark moldy pit were at least a dozen eighteen-inch pungi sticks with fire-hardened tips.

"Thang," I pointed. "Untie that clump of grass and pick up the sticks on the trail. Check the other end of the trail for more sticks."

"Okay, *Bac-si*."

I covered the exposed section of mat and smoothed the dirt with my hand. With the sticks removed and the clump of grass untied, a Viet Cong who wasn't familiar with the local area might fall into the trap.

"Looks good," I said to myself as I wiped my hands on my trousers and moved to the woodpile.

Kneeling next to the firewood, I placed the grenade on the ground. The yellow paint on its safety lever identified it as a grenade whose four-second time-delay element had been removed. After the safety pin was pulled, it would detonate the instant the safety lever was released. There would be no delay at all.

I looked up and saw Thang using a leafy branch to sweep our bootprints from the clearing. Our jungle boots left a distinct pattern that wouldn't be missed by the enemy. Also, American footprints were generally long and narrow, while those of Asians were short and wide. While Thang swept, I used my knife to dig a hole for the grenade. It was a perfect fit.

Karoumph! Another explosion to the north.

I removed the grenade from the hole, pulled the safety pin, and slipped it back in the hole with the safety lever facing up. While carefully maintaining pressure on the safety lever with one hand, I used the other to pack in as much dirt as possible around the sides of the grenade. When it was snug, I slid a piece of firewood over the safety lever and took in a deep breath.

"Whew." I wiped the sweat from my brow and moved to the wood line, where I found Bob and Luc waiting.

"All set?" Bob asked.

"Yeah," I said as we waited for Thang to finish sweeping away the last of our bootprints.

"Okay, *Bac-si,*" Thang said as he moved into the wood line.

With Bob leading, we moved back along the southern edge of the clearing.

"Gonna leave a little somethin' for Mr. Charles," he said when he reached the point where we first saw the spider holes.

While Kien sat on the back of Bob's legs, he leaned into a spider hole with his knife in one hand and an M-14 toe popper mine in the other. When he finished booby-trapping the hole, we headed south for a hundred meters and then shot an azimuth back to the mission support site.

We arrived at 1515 hours (3:15 P.M.), and thirty minutes later headed southwest along a ridgeline. Our order of march: Recon, the headquarters section, 4, 1, 2, and 3. Whenever possible, we followed the ridgelines because it was less tiring than moving across compartments. The vegetation growing along the ridges was also generally thinner than it was in the valleys.

Late in the day, we came to the bank of a spring-fed inch-deep stream. Both banks were crowded with shoulder-high ferns and drooping banana plants. So that we could fill our canteens, the lead platoon had dug a few foot-deep holes in its gravel bottom. When I reached one of them, I immersed my empty canteens and watched them bubble full of clear water.

With the last light of day quickly fading, we moved uphill and crossed a well-used trail. The hard-packed trail measured a meter across and had foot-long grass growing along both sides. Much of the grass had been flattened to the south and yet remained green. A good indication that a large enemy unit had recently traveled south on it.

A hundred meters past the trail, we stopped to set up our mission support site in a thicket of lime green bamboo. Growing in the areas between the stalks were large, dark green ferns. Once we had the troops and listening post in position, Bob and I strung our hammocks next to a large fallen tree.

"Don't like setting up this close to a trail," I told Bob as I wiped down my M-16 with a silicone cloth.

"Got two ambushes on it," he responded.

"Donahue," Rinh whispered.

"Yeah."

"I gave Hoi 2.4 million units of procaine penicillin G, and he fainted."

"Where is he?"

I followed Rinh a short distance and found Hoi lying unconscious on his back. When I checked his pulse, I found it rapid and weak. He was also wheezing.

"Anaphylactic shock," I told Rinh. "He's allergic to penicillin. He could be dead in five minutes. Gimme a cc of epinephrine."

While Rinh prepared the injection, I used Hoi's rucksack to elevate his feet.

"Here." Rinh handed me the syringe.

"What was the penicillin for?" I asked as I unbuttoned Hoi's sleeve to expose his lower arm.

"The bullheaded clap."

I wiped down the inside of his arm with a section of alcohol-soaked gauze and injected the epinephrine into the muscle.

"This is the fourth or fifth time he's had it," I said as I massaged his lower arm.

"The whorehouse in Tay Ninh." Rinh smiled.

"Must be in love. When we get back, we'll go into town and treat the girls. Go ahead and give 'im ten milligrams of Benadryl."

"He has shit in his pants," Rinh commented as he prepared the injection.

"Yeah, I noticed."

Rinh administered the injection, and within minutes, Hoi regained consciousness and mumbled something.

"He is embarrassed that he shit in his pants," Rinh told me.

"Tell 'im not to worry," I said. "It's a common reaction."

"Should I put him on tetracycline?" Rinh asked.

"Yeah, one gram in the morning and five hundred milligrams every six hours," I said. "See if ya can get 'im another pair of trousers."

Hoi and I waited in the darkness, and a few minutes later, Rinh returned with a clean pair of trousers. With Hoi in good shape, I felt my way back to my rucksack.

"Tea's ready," Bob whispered. "It's on the stump."

"Thanks."

I removed a C-ration can from my rucksack, found my cup of tea, and felt my way to my hammock. While sitting in my hammock, I opened the can and found that it smelled like beef with spiced sauce. I was pleased that it wasn't ham and lima beans. I quickly ate the beef, and then leaned back to enjoy my tea. Looking up through a few holes in the canopy, I saw that the sky was white with stars. It was going to be a nice night.

"Jim," Bob whispered.

"Yeah."

"Fergy's on the radio with Gritz. His LP's reportin' voices."

"How far?"

"Don't know. Somewhere to the east."

"They on the move?"

"No."

"Could be a way station or base camp."

"Luc," Bob whispered. "Get the word out to the squad leaders."

"Okay, *Trung si*."

"I want everyone up, packed, and ready to move an hour before first light," Bob added.

As Luc used his HT-1 radio to whisper instructions to the squad leaders, I sat sipping my tea and thinking about Fergy's report.

"If they knew we were in the area, they wouldn't be makin' noise," I whispered to Bob. "They're pretty good when it comes to noise discipline."

"Yeah," he agreed. "But I wanna be ready for the worst." Bob was right. Anytime you underestimated the enemy you were inviting certain death. If Mister Charles had a fix on our position, he would likely hit us at first light.

When I finished my tea, I applied a fresh coat of mosquito repellent and rubbed some army-issue foot powder between my toes. It was a cool night so I lay back in my hammock and wrapped myself in my piece of parachute nylon. In the warmth of my cocoon, I listened to the sounds of the jungle and quickly drifted off to sleep.

7

Bob, Luc, Ly, and I sat shoulder to shoulder at the base of a great cypress tree. The predawn air was filled with the chirping of crickets and the faint smells of woodsmoke and Vietnamese cooking. In scattered spots, the light from the stars penetrated to the jungle floor, and in those areas, everything appeared in tones of gray. Everything else remained as black as midnight.

"Anything more from the LP?" Bob asked Luc.

"No, *Trung si,*" he whispered.

"Charlie does most of his cookin' at night," I said. "If they cooked durin' the day, they'd attract air strikes."

The radio crackled to life. With the handset pressed to Bob's ear, I could only hear muffled sounds.

"Fox Control, this is Fox Three. Over." Bob responded to Captain Gritz.

Again, a muffled transmission.

"Roger, Control. Three, out," Bob said.

"What's up?" I asked.

"As soon as they can see, Fergy and Battle are gonna check the voices out," Bob said. "Gritz thinks it's a base camp."

While I sat eating C-ration tins of bread and peanut butter, the jungle came alive with the singing of birds and the grays turned slowly to dull shades of green, yellow, and brown.

"Goin' to the *bo-chi-huy,*" Bob said as he passed me the radio handset.

115

While I monitored radio transmissions, Luc left to check the perimeter.

"Fox Control, this is Fox Two. Over," Fergy's hushed voice suddenly broke the silence.

"Two, this is Control. Over," Gritz responded.

"Control, got a shitload of VC three hundred meters east of the MSS," he whispered with excitement. "At least thirty of 'em sittin' on benches with their weapons stacked to the rear."

A surge of adrenaline energized my system.

"Roger, One," Gritz responded. "Take 'em out."

I removed the silicone cloth from my rucksack and continued to monitor radio transmissions as I wiped the morning dew from my rifle.

Whack-whack-whack. Whoomph, whoomph. M-16 fire and explosions erupted to the east. I didn't hear any AK-47s returning fire. To the west I heard the faint hum of the forward air controller's single-engine O-1E aircraft.

"Thirty VC in a classroom," I told Luc as he returned and squatted next to his rucksack.

"Good," he nodded. "Kill them."

Whump-whump-whump. The familiar sound of AK-47s joined the firing to the east.

"Roger, Fox Control, the first team's back," I heard the FAC say over the radio. "I'll have fast movers on target in zero-five minutes. Need some smoke. Over."

It was the familiar voice of Capt. Norman "Ed" Gammons. He was one of Project Sigma's forward air controllers and was arguably one of the best in Vietnam.

"Roger, Memphis," Gritz responded. "Two, this is Control," Gritz radioed Fergy. "Give 'em a smoke. Over."

"Roger, Control." Fergy sounded winded. "We've broken contact. Negative casualties. Headin' your way. Over."

Bob returned and squatted next to Luc and me.

"This is the deal," he said as he used his hand to clear a patch of ground of leaves and twigs. "Got a base camp three hundred meters east," he said as he used a twig to scratch a circle in the dirt.

"Fox Control, this is Memphis," Captain Gammons said over the radio. "Got your smoke. Where do you want it? Over."

"Memphis, this is Control," Gritz responded. "Heavy ordnance east of the smoke. Suggest they approach the target from the north or south. Over."

"Roger, Control. That's a can-do," Gammons responded.

"We'll advance in four columns," Bob said as he scratched four lines to the circle. "Fergy and Duke's platoons in the center, Bevans on the right, and us on the left. Recon and the *bo-chi-huy* will serve as a reaction force and cover our six o'clock. When we reach the camp, we'll deploy on line and assault."

"They're gonna be in their bunkers waitin' ta kick our ass," I cautioned as a flight of jets arrived overhead and the FAC dropped down low. The thought of assaulting an alerted base camp scared the hell out of me. Surprise was one of the keys to a successful raid.

"If we get into trouble, we'll break contact," Bob said.

Whoomph . . . pop! Captain Gammons marked the base camp with a white phosphorous rocket round.

"Don't like it," I told Bob as a jet screeched in low from the south.

Karoumph, karoumph, karoumph. A string of bombs exploded to the east, the earth shook, and rivulets of morning dew rained from the leaves.

"If we overrun 'em, we'll set up security and do a quick search," Bob said.

"Got a rally point?" I asked.

"Yeah," he said as he looked at his map. "If we get separated, we'll RV at the northeast corner of the clearing we went to yesterday," he pointed. "Thirty-five hundred meters northwest."

"Let's do it," I said as Luc handed me one of the three claymore mines he was carrying and a second jet streaked in from the south.

Karoumph, karoumph, karoumph. Another string of bombs

shook the earth, and pieces of shrapnel cut through the foliage high above our heads.

We quickly hid our rucksacks in the underbrush and, with Bob on point, moved east through knee-high mist. Thirty meters to our right, Jim Battle was on the point of the 2d Platoon, and to their right, I caught a few glimpses of Dave Rose and the 1st Platoon. As we pushed through wet leaves and dripping vines, another jet knifed in from the south.

Kawhoosh! Napalm spilled through the trees to the east. As we neared the base camp, I thought about the enemy and what might be waiting for us. Three hundred meters east of our support site, Bob stopped in thick undergrowth and dropped to one knee.

"What is it?" I whispered.

"A gate." He pointed as another jet streaked low over the base camp. Twenty meters ahead, I saw the top half of a bamboo gate. Above the gate was a faded white banner with the words *Chien Thang* printed in bold red letters.

Kawhoosh! Napalm again spilled through the foliage.

"Get 'em on line," Bob whispered to Luc. "Jim, take the left flank," he said as a line of Bodes streamed to our left.

"Don't touch that gate or banner," I cautioned. "Probably booby-trapped."

I moved to our left and stopped when I found Thach at the end of the line.

"Keep 'em on line, partner," I said in hushed tones.

Whack-whack-whack. Whump-whump-whump. A heavy exchange of fire erupted on our right flank. I raised my hand over my head and by lowering it forward gave the signal to advance. After moving through thirty meters of thick undergrowth, we encountered a wall of thorn-covered vines that had been cut and laid out in the shape of an upside-down *V*. Rather than allow ourselves to be funneled together, we pushed through the thorns.

Twenty meters past the thorns, we came to a mostly collapsed earth-and-log bunker. A single strand of black communications wire led east from the bunker and was a good indication that the camp was occupied by Main Force troops. This wasn't going to be a walk in the park.

Just beyond the bunker, twisting trails of steam poured from a bomb crater. The trees around the depression had been blackened by the blast and stripped of their leaves. Peering into the collapsed bunker, I saw a bloody hand extending from between two logs.

"They're dead," I said to Thach as I looked for other bunkers to our left and right. The bunker was likely part of a line of bunkers with interlocking fields of fire—the enemy's main line of resistance (MLR). In other base camps, their main line of resistance was almost always backed up by smaller bunkers, trenches, and spider holes. We were lucky that the bomb had knocked it out.

"Keep 'em on line," I cautioned Thach again as we moved through the soft dirt around the rim of the steaming crater. Above our heads, a layer of thick black smoke was trapped beneath the canopy, and the pungent smell of burning gas left my eyes burning.

With mist swirling around our legs and firing continuing on our flank, we slipped past a dozen bamboo benches and a blackboard. Next to the blackboard, Thach tripped over a human leg. It had been neatly severed just below the hip and reminded me of something you'd see hanging in a butcher shop.

Ten meters past the outdoor classroom, we came to a clump of banana plants and a thatch-roof building. Its bamboo sides extended from the ground to the waist, while the top half was left open for ventilation. Outside the structure, a generator and a five-gallon gasoline can were sheltered under a piece of sheet metal. As a few stray rounds cut through the overhead foliage, I entered the building while Thach stood guard at the entrance.

Just inside the building, I found an improvised canvas operating table with three light bulbs strung above it. A nearby table was covered with surgical instruments, a tray of injectable drugs, syringes, and needles, and bottles labeled Adramoxol, Phenergine, and Aminagin.

Near the center of the building, a French-made autoclave sat on another table. Next to the autoclave, a pile of surgical masks, smocks, and towels waited to be sterilized. At the far end of the building, four American folding cots were draped with mosquito nets.

Karoumph, karoumph, karoumph. A string of bombs exploded to the south.

Thach entered the building carrying the gasoline can, and while I waited at the entrance, he walked backward, splashing everything with fuel. When he reached the entrance, he tossed in a piece of burning paper, and within seconds, the structure was engulfed in orange-and-yellow flames and thick black smoke.

Whumph-whumph-whumph. The measured staccato of an enemy fifty-one-caliber machine gun opened up on our right flank. The sound sent a chill up the length of my spine. The presence of a heavy machine gun was a good indication that the camp defenders included a heavy-weapons company.

A short distance past the dispensary, our line came to the edge of an area where the smoldering ground was covered with a layer of black ash, and what remained of the foliage hung in blackened shreds. Here and there, orange-and-yellow flames engulfed entire trees and, like giant incandescent pillars, appeared to support a ceiling of thick black smoke. On the far side of the blackened area, I could see parts of what appeared to be four large thatch structures.

Whump-whump-whump. The enemy's green tracers streaked across the smoldering ground and thumped into the trees around us. On the far side of the blackened area, a line of soldiers in khaki ran through the smoke and mist with their rifles flashing like strobe lights.

Whack-whack-whack. The Bodes returned fire, and over everything, the battle cry *"Chey-yo"* echoed beneath the canopy. As I ran for the cover of a nearby tree, I fired a sweeping burst in the direction of the enemy. Then, with my rifle resting against the side of the tree, I squeezed off three quick bursts, and three enemy soldiers dropped like rag dolls and disappeared beneath the mist.

My heart raced as I quickly changed magazines, chambered a round, and looked to fire again. The line of enemy soldiers had disappeared, but green tracers continued to cut through the camp.

Whoomph! A rifle grenade exploded to my right, and I fired four short bursts at suspected enemy locations.

Wzzzzzz. Another rifle grenade just missed the tree and left a smoke trail a few feet from my head. *Whoomph!* It exploded to my rear just as three blasts on a whistle—the signal to break contact—resounded through the base camp.

"Break contact!" I yelled to Thach as I pulled a grenade from my harness and threw it to the far side of the blackened area.

"Doc thai!" He hollered over the firing.

Whoomph! The grenade exploded.

I pulled a CS gas grenade from my BAR belt and tossed it as far as I could. As soon as it hit the ground, a twisting trail of gray gas billowed from the canister. On the far side of the blackened area, I saw glimpses of khaki running through the foliage.

Whack-whack-whack. Thach and a four-man fire team laid down a base of fire while I and another fire team ran ten meters to the rear, hit the ground, and resumed firing. While my fire team laid down a base of fire, Thach's team leapfrogged to the rear.

The enemy firing suddenly slowed. I looked for movement but saw no sign of them. Rather than assaulting over relatively open terrain, they appeared to be moving to where they could roll up one or both of our flanks.

"Go!" I yelled to Thach as I pointed to our rear.

Thach yelled instructions, and the Bodes sprang to their feet and followed him through the mist and smoke at a slow run. I fired quick bursts on both flanks and then ran to close the gap with the last man in the column.

Whoomph! A hot blast hit my back and knocked me off balance. I fell into a trench.

"Yaaaaah!" My feet landed on something soft, and a blood-curdling, high-pitched scream filled the trench. I fell to my knees, my face slammed into the far wall, and I turned to shoot. An unarmed Viet Cong sat against the end of the short trench with outstretched legs. She appeared to be about eighteen years old, wore short-sleeve black pajamas, and glared at me through a tangle of long black hair. The right side of her face was gone, most of her right knee had been blown away, and halfway between her wrist and elbow, bloody sections of bone extended from her right arm. She was losing a lot of blood from her knee and appeared to be close to passing out.

With the barrel of my M-16 a foot from her face she covered her eyes with her good arm and started to shake violently. She was convinced that she was about to die.

I was paralyzed with indecision. I thought about taking her prisoner but knew she would die if I tried to move her. I considered shooting her but knew I couldn't. I thought about leaving her but worried she might one day kill an American.

"I hope to hell you're a nurse!" I yelled as I leaned my M-16 against the wall at the opposite end of the short trench. I pulled the triangular scarf from around my neck and slipped it under her injured leg a couple of inches above her knee. She lowered her arm and again glared at me.

"Ooohhh," she moaned when I tied it tight.

"Day la thuoc morphine lam giam dau." Morphine for the pain I told her as I injected a syrette into her left leg.

From outside the trench I heard the singsong chatter of Vietnamese voices.

"Shit," I mumbled. "Gotta get outta here."

I picked up my rifle and, with it at the ready, slowly looked out over the top of the trench. The voices were only a short distance away, but I couldn't see a thing through the blanket of mist that drifted a couple of feet above the ground. I pulled the claymore mine's bandolier strap from my shoulder and extended its legs. With the voices growing louder I quickly unsnapped the bandolier flap and grabbed the M-57 electrical firing device. Reaching out over the top of the trench, I stretched forward as far as I could and pushed its legs into the dirt. Crouching low in the trench, I used my thumb to swing the firing device's safety bail to the armed position, glanced at the girl, and depressed its handle.

Whoomph! A deafening explosion showered me with dirt and filled the trench with dust. I leaped from the trench and fired a long burst to my rear as I ran.

"Bac-si!" Thach yelled from behind a tree and motioned for me to follow him. I followed him and three other Bodes back to the collapsed bunker where we linked up with the rest of the squad.

"Got everyone?" I asked.

"Yes, *Bac-si,*" he responded. "We go."

"Yeah, we've worn out our welcome," I said. "Let's go."

We worked our way back to the gate, where we found two members of Binh's squad. Automatic-rifle fire and explosions continued inside the base camp.

"Where's Bob?" I asked.

"Trung si Cole." One of them pointed into the camp.

I moved in the direction of the firing and, twenty meters past the gate, spotted Bob firing from a prone position from behind a three-foot-high mound of dirt. A few meters to his left, a faceless, khaki-clad enemy soldier lay flat on his back. I ran toward Bob and slid to the ground next to him.

"Watch it." He pushed my head down. "Machine gun ten meters ahead."

I peeked around the side of the mound.

Whump-whump-whump. Rounds slammed into the mound and showered me with dirt.

"Ground-level flash," I said.

"He's in a spider hole," Bob said. "Can't knock the son of a bitch out."

Whack-whack-whack. Bob fired a burst over the top of the mound, and his hat blew from his head like he had walked into a prop blast. He dropped low behind the mound with his hand on his head.

"You okay?" I crouched next to him.

"Think so." He looked for blood on his hand. "Felt like someone hit me with a baseball bat."

"Let me see."

Examining the top of his head, I found a three-inch raised welt. There was some oozing but no serious bleeding.

"You're lucky. A hair lower and you'd be dead," I said as we both spotted movement to our left front. In seconds they would be on our flank and have a clear shot at us.

Whack-whack-whack. We fired bursts at glimpses of khaki moving through the brush.

"It's move or die," Bob said. "Got a grenade?"

"I'm out." I shook my head.

He picked up two fist-size rocks and handed me one.

"On three," he said.

"Got it."

We hoped the guy in the spider hole would think they were grenades and would duck to escape the blast.

"One, two," Bob counted and we cocked our arms. "Three!" We lobbed the rocks in the direction of the spider hole. Over the roar of the firing, I heard them thump to the ground.

"Go!" Bob yelled.

We jumped to our feet and ran zigzag to the rear.

"Over here," someone yelled.

A few meters into a clump of bamboo we found Captain Gritz, Tom Horn, and Dien providing covering fire.

"Got everyone?" Gritz asked as Horn and Dien tossed CS grenades in the direction of the enemy.

"One dead," Bob told him as we pushed through wet leaves and vines.

"Who?" I asked.

"Nuong," Bob said. "They caught him in the open. Cut 'im to pieces."

"Where is he?" I asked as we approached Luc.

"Keep 'em on line and move to the rear," Bob told Luc.

"Okay, *Trung si.*"

"Couldn't get to his body," Bob explained. "Two machine guns caught 'im in the open. They were movin' on both flanks. It was break contact or lose everyone."

"Fuck!" I responded.

"I left the decision up to Luc," Bob said.

"It was the right decision," Gritz said. "Main Force or locals?"

"Main Force," Bob responded. "Khaki uniforms, green helmets. They had their shit together."

"Same on the left flank, sir," I said. "A well-built bunker, a first-class dispensary, and a classroom. Could be a 9th Division training camp."

Glancing to the rear, I saw the 3d Platoon spread out on line from left to right and walking backwards. As we moved, Gritz contacted the Recon and 4th Platoons and instructed them to move west for two hundred meters before shooting an azimuth to the south.

One hundred meters from the base camp, we spotted Duke Snider positioning his platoon on line. When he was without a hat, you couldn't miss his bald head. Duke was one of a kind. He had a hard-earned reputation for being a fearless soldier and an authority on booby traps. He was also a legendary barroom brawler who wouldn't hesitate to take on the entire bar.

Bob looked to our rear and signaled Luc to get the 3d Platoon in line. High above the canopy, I once again heard the whine of jet engines.

"Lotta bad guys in there," Duke said as Captain Gritz stopped to talk to him. "I ain't ever seen shit like that before. Hell, they had field phones in the bunkers."

"We blow bunker," Dang, the 1st Platoon sergeant, told Gritz. "Many rifle."

"Porked a mess of them boys," Duke grinned.

"Keep your platoon on line until we clear the MSS," Gritz ordered.

"Yes, sir," Duke responded. "We'll slow 'em down."

I felt confident that Duke's booby traps and stay-behind

ambushes would discourage any enemy trackers who might try to follow us.

"Any wounded?" I asked.

"Two of our guys and one of Fergy's were hit by frags," Duke said.

"Can they walk?" Gritz asked.

"Yes, sir. Dave and Rinh took 'em back to the MSS."

Karoumph, karoumph, karoumph. A string of bombs exploded as we continued to the west.

Whoomph! The shock waves from an earth-shaking secondary explosion resonated beneath the canopy.

"Ammunition bunker." Bob flashed me a thumbs-up.

When we reached the mission support site, we found Ferguson's 2d Platoon set up in a defensive perimeter and the last of Bevans's 4th Platoon moving west. With the morning sun low in the sky, the mist in the higher elevations glowed white.

"Ready to move?" Captain Gritz asked Jim Battle as a jet roared over the base camp with its twenty-millimeter cannons screeching.

"Yes, sir," he responded.

"Beaucoup VC, *Dai uy,*" Kim Lai, the 2d Platoon sergeant, told Gritz.

"Greased a bunch of the bastards," Bill Ferguson told Gritz with wild-eyed excitement. "They were in a map-readin' class. The look on their faces—fucking beautiful."

"Let's get outta Dodge," Gritz ordered.

"At least a company of 'em came right at us," Jim Battle told me as I passed. "The Bodes kicked ass."

At the center of the perimeter, we found Captain Johnson on the radio directing air strikes. Dave Rose and Rinh had the three wounded on their feet and ready to move.

"They gonna make it?" Gritz asked Dave.

"Yes, sir," Dave responded. "Soft-tissue wounds. Nothing serious."

"We'll get 'em out," Gritz assured him. "As soon as we clear the area, I'll have the FAC direct us to an LZ."

"Need any help?" I asked Dave.

"Thanks, Jim. They're in good shape."

We quickly recovered our rucksacks from the underbrush and fell in behind the 2d Platoon as its men waited to follow the headquarters section to the west.

"We goin' back for your hat?" I asked Bob as we waited. He didn't appreciate my humor.

With air strikes continuing to pound the base camp, Bob moved to the head of the platoon and followed the last man in Ferguson's platoon to the west. Kien and I fell in at the end of the line and walked backward with our weapons at the ready. Snider's platoon would remain in position until we cleared the area and then move quickly to catch up with us.

Two hundred meters to the west, we changed direction and headed south. As we threaded through dripping undergrowth, I thought about the enemy and how he would react to our attack on his base camp. My best guess was that the base commander would immediately assign three-man teams to track our route of withdrawal. If the teams were able to maintain a fix on us, he would deploy his Main Force units, and attempt to destroy us.

During the next few hours, there would be a lot riding on Duke's ability to kill or discourage the trackers. My skin feeling was that after a run-in or two with Duke's tail-gunner ambushes and booby traps, they would likely attempt to follow us by moving parallel to the trail we were leaving. To make sure they didn't lose us, they would cut across our trail every ten to fifteen minutes and then resume paralleling our route of march on the opposite flank. I hoped they would miss our change of direction to the south and concentrate their search to the west. By the time they discovered the truth, we could be well out of the area.

As we continued south through sweating leaves and vines, I noticed that our world beneath the canopy was unusually quiet. There were no animal or insect sounds—only the ringing in my ears and an occasional explosion or exchange of fire to our rear.

Later in the morning, we entered an area of massive cypress trees. Growing between the great trees were clumps of lime green bamboo and large ferns. In the higher elevations, the mist was beginning to burn off, and a few patches of blue sky appeared. Here and there, brilliant shafts of sunlight penetrated the foliage, and where they reached the jungle floor, twisting trails of steam worked their way skyward.

As we threaded left and right around mold-covered stalks of bamboo, the FAC arrived overhead. Minutes later, the column stopped, and Kien and I waited under thirty-foot stalks of dying bamboo that had been bowed to the ground by the weight of their wilted leaves.

"How's your foot?" I asked him as we both watched for movement to our rear. A few months earlier he had lost three of his toes to a booby trap.

"Foot good, *Bac-si,*" he said as he chewed on his unlit cigar. "Ear numba ten." He smiled and pointed. "I not hear." The top half of his ear had been sliced off by an exploding mortar round.

"When we get back to Trang Sup, I'll take ya to an American ear doctor," I told him as large black and green butterflies floated in and out of the shafts of sunlight.

"Good, *Bac-si.*" He grinned. "I like American doctor."

To the west I heard the *wap, wap, wap* of an approaching helicopter.

"Bac-si." Kien pointed. Twenty meters away, I spotted Duke Snider and his radio operator moving at the head of the 1st Platoon.

"Where the hell have you been?" I joked.

"You'd think they'd learn," Duke laughed and wiped the sweat from his face. "They musta tripped a dozen booby traps."

"Anything since we changed direction?"

"Can't say for sure," he said. "Canopy muffles the blast. Hard to figure distances."

Wap, wap, wap. The chopper passed low over the bamboo, and thousands of wilted leaves floated to the ground.

"Let me get up to the LZ," Duke said as the chopper touched down. "They're gonna pick up the wounded and drop off ammo, food, and demo."

Duke and his radio operator continued up the line while the rest of his platoon remained in position to our rear. Less than a minute later, the chopper lifted off.

"They bring ammunition?" Kien asked as the pulsating beat of the Huey faded to the west.

"Yeah," I said.

A few minutes later, we continued south and, a hundred meters ahead, passed Duke and his radio operator, who were waiting along the edge of a small oblong clearing.

"They get the wounded out?" I asked as we passed.

"Yup," Duke said. "Bob's got your resupply."

As our green-and-black column slipped in and out of the shadows, I looked at my map and figured that we were about a kilometer south of the enemy base camp. Since I hadn't heard any explosions for more than an hour I figured that we had successfully broken contact.

Whack-whack-whack. Whump-whump-whump. An exchange of fire, not more than two hundred meters ahead. Kien had the HT-1 radio pressed to his ear and monitored transmissions as we walked together.

"Recon kill two VC." He smiled.

"Uniforms?"

He held his finger to his lips and continued to listen.

"Black, *Bac-si*."

"Good." If they'd been wearing khaki, I'd have worried that they were trackers from the enemy base camp who had somehow anticipated our route of march and used high-speed trails to move ahead of us.

For what seemed like hours, we continued through bamboo and thorn-covered vines. At the base of a hill, we came to a large clearing and our movement slowed to a crawl. The open area measured a good two hundred by five hundred meters and was covered with eight-foot-high pale green elephant grass. A blazing late-day sun tortured the clearing, and around its perimeter the tall gray trunks of trees shimmered in waves of rising heat.

Fifty meters into the elephant grass, my boots began sinking ankle deep in black mud. With a seventy-pound rucksack on my back, I struggled to pull each step from the creamy suction, and my pores opened like faucets.

Running along the eastern edge of the clearing, we crossed a knee-deep stream and minutes later reentered dark triple-canopy jungle and began moving uphill through thick undergrowth. At the crest of the hill, we stopped in an area of fifty-foot palm trees to set up our mission support site. The trees were topped with large palm fronds and clumps of green coconuts, and their trunks were wrapped tight with vines. Growing from the vines were parasitic ferns and clumps of white flowers. Between the palms were large dark green ferns and two-story saplings.

As soon as we had our hammocks up and our listening post in position, we distributed the supplies that had been brought in on the chopper. Under an indigo sky, the Bodes took turns cleaning their weapons, and with the last light of day quickly fading, the squad leaders conducted a weapons-and-equipment inspection.

By the time I got to sit in my hammock, the first stars of the night appeared in the sky. I made a mental note of where everything was and leaned back with a cup of hot tea and a can of beans and franks—one of my favorites.

"Bac-si?"

"Yeah."

A ghostlike figure squatted next to my hammock.

"Is Kim Lai, *Bac-si.*"

"Kim, how are ya?"

"Bac-si, do you know about Sergeant England?" he asked. Kim was one of the best soldiers I had ever known. He had served as England's platoon sergeant on Blackjack-31—a monthlong operation south of Duc Phong Special Forces Camp, and on the Black Box Mission—the recovery of a top secret System 13A black box from a downed U-2 spy plane.

"Last I heard he was at the 24th Evac in Bien Hoa," I said as I sipped my tea.

"He come back Trang Sup?"

"No, he's gonna need major surgery," I said. "I think Bob told me he was goin' to a hospital in Japan."

"Bac-si." He grabbed my hand and held it tight. "You and England are special people of God. He not let VC kill you."

I was very moved and didn't know what to say.

"Thank you, my friend."

"Bac-si, I must ask you."

"Ask me what?"

"Bac-si, before Sergeant England wounded, Captain Gritz say many American come when we find VC. Why they not come?"

Kim's question left me without words.

"Why American not come, *Bac-si*?"

"I don't know, my friend."

8

1350 HOURS, 15 MAY 1967

An unforgiving sun beat down on us as our ten-man tail-gunner section slipped through the steaming tangle. The moisture-laden air was so humid it seemed at times almost suffocating to breathe. With a seventy-pound rucksack on my back, rivulets of sweat coursed down my face, and I could taste its salt on my lips.

We were two hundred meters behind the rest of the company and were following their trail to the southeast. Thach was the last man in our section and was walking backward as he watched for the enemy to our rear. I was a couple of paces in front of him, and ahead of me, Ly walked with the PRC-25 radio handset pressed to his ear. To Ly's front, the rest of the squad was spread out over twenty meters.

As tail gunners, our mission was to provide rear security for the main force. When the main force was moving along a course of known direction and distance, we would remain two hundred to four hundred meters behind them and periodically stop for fifteen to thirty minutes to set up a stay-behind ambush for trackers. If our direction and distance was unsure, we would stay with the main body.

Whoomph! A muffled explosion sounded to our rear. I turned and took a compass azimuth on the blast.

"Three hundred ten degrees," I whispered to Thach as we moved past two-story banana plants with large drooping leaves. "Maybe one of the booby traps we left in the MSS."

"I think so, *Bac-si,*" he responded as he used his scarf to wipe sweat from his leathery face. On earlier missions, we had learned that whenever the enemy discovered one of our mission support sites they would dig up the trash sumps and conduct a detailed search of the area.

We continued through thick secondary growth for 150 meters and then stopped where a decaying tree lay across the trail we were following. The rotting trunk measured at least two feet in diameter, and I could predict with reasonable certainty where the lead tracker's foot would strike the ground when he stepped over it.

"Good spot for a toe popper," I whispered to Thach. "Let's set up here."

While I waited with my M-16 at the ready, Thach positioned the squad with most of our firepower facing down our back trail. He also placed one-man security units ten meters to our left, right, and rear. With all-around security in place, I lowered my rucksack to the ground.

"I'll take care of the toe popper," I told Thach as Ly placed the PRC-25 on the ground next to my rucksack. "You set up claymores with trip wires and eight-hour time pencils to the left and right of the trail."

"Two claymore?" he asked.

"Yeah, at least ten meters up the trail," I whispered. "When their point hits the toe popper, they're gonna start skirtin' the trail."

"Okay, *Bac-si.*" He turned to move up the trail.

"One other thing," I added. "Don't arm 'em until we're on the other side."

I removed a toe popper mine from my pocket—it reminded me of a small hockey puck—and knelt on the ground next to the fallen tree. With Ly squatting beside me with his M-16 at the ready, I reached into my rucksack and pulled out a two-foot section of white detonating cord and a roll of green tape. Glancing to my rear, I saw Thach setting up the first claymore on the right side of the trail. I tore off a foot-long section of tape and handed it to Ly.

Whoomph! An explosion far to the west. It sounded like a 175-millimeter artillery round. I wrapped the detonating cord around the mine a few times and held it in place while Ly covered the cord with tape. Looking up again, I made sure that each of the men was alert and watching for the enemy. Using my knife, I dug a small hole in the soft moist earth and placed the plastic mine in it. The hole was too wide so I used my fingers to pack some dirt back in around it. When the mine was snug, I pulled its safety clip and covered the device with a thin layer of dirt and leaves. If a tracker stepped on it, the added detonating cord would insure that he lost more than just a few toes.

"Ain't no one-legged trackers," I whispered to Ly. "He'll have to find a new job."

Ly smiled and nodded his agreement, but I don't think he understood what was said. With the mine in place, I reached for the radio handset.

"Fox Control, this is Fox Three. Over," I said softly as a mosquito buzzed in my ear.

"Fox Control, this is Fox Three. Over," I repeated.

"Three, this is Control," Captain Gritz responded.

"Control, this is Three. We're at left 0.5, down 0.6. Will remain this position for three-zero minutes, over."

"Roger, Three. Control, out."

Glancing to my rear again, I saw that Thach had moved to the other side of the trail.

"We eat?" Ly asked.

"Yeah," I said as I looked at my watch. "I'm starvin'."

I pulled the rubber band from the top of a half-eaten bag of rice that I had mixed with instant soup, and sat with my back against my rucksack. The red volcanic soil was crawling with small black ants.

"Got a cold Pepsi?" I joked.

"No Pepsi, *Bac-si.*" He smiled and shook his head.

"Two claymore," Thach whispered as he returned and squatted next to his rucksack.

"Take a break," I said.

"I shit." Ly moved to a spot a few meters away and used his heel to dig a small hole.

Thach was a man of contrasting personalities. During off-duty hours, he was very relaxed and had a fatherly relationship with younger men; but when we were on an operation, he was very intense and accepted nothing less than instant, willing obedience. He removed a C-ration can and a small brown bottle of *nuoc-mam* from his rucksack and sat next to me.

"I like ham and egg." His smile revealed a set of gold capped teeth.

"Didn't you tell me you fought with the 5th Parachute Battalion at Dien Bien Phu?" I asked as he sprinkled a few drops of the fermented fish sauce on his ham and eggs.

"Yes, *Bac-si*." His scar-covered face filled with pride. "The 5th Parachute."

"When I was in Saigon, I met a guy who fought with the 5th at Eliane."

"Bac-si." He grabbed my arm. "All soldier fight Eliane, they die now," he said with great sadness.

"Most of his cheekbone was gone." I pointed to my face. "Said he fought with the 2d Company. His name was Le."

Thach's bloodshot eyes welled with tears.

"I know Le, *Bac-si*." He wiped his eyes. "I think he die."

"He lost his legs up in II Corps, but he's still armed, mobile, and dangerous." I smiled. "He and his wife own a restaurant in Cholon."

"Bac-si, when we go Trang Sup, we go see Le?"

"Sure," I said as Ly returned and sat with his back against his rucksack.

"My family live Cholon," Thach added with excitement. "We see them, too."

"As soon as we get back, we'll catch a hop down to Tan Son Nhut."

When we finished eating, we pulled in security, moved to the far side of the claymores, and waited while Thach placed blasting caps and time-delay devices in both mines. Soon after we moved out, I felt a bubble on my gum.

"Shit," I mumbled as I ran a finger over the inflamed area. A year earlier one of my front teeth had been shot out, and it was abscessed again. As soon as I had time, I'd have to drain it.

We proceeded southeast through thick secondary growth, and thirty minutes later stopped in a bamboo thicket. Thach and I moved forward and found Kien squatting at the edge of a meter-wide, hard-packed trail. Thach sent two-man security units fifty meters up and down the trail, and when they were in position, we moved to the other side. While I stood guard over him, he used his hat to sweep away our bootprints, straighten blades of grass on both sides of the trail, and sprinkled handfuls of leaves where our boots had sunk into the soft earth. Convinced that our back trail wouldn't be spotted by someone moving down the trail, we called in security and continued southeast.

Whack-whack-whack. Whump-whump-whump. An exchange of M-16 and AK-47 fire to the southeast. Ly handed me the radio handset, and as we pushed through a tangle of vines, Stik Rader informed Captain Gritz that his recon team had made contact with four Viet Cong wearing mixed black-and-green uniforms. The enemy appeared surprised and immediately broke contact, fleeing to the west.

"Local guerrillas," I whispered to Thach as we moved.

In Phuoc Long Province, local guerrillas were generally organized in three-to-twelve-man cells. They were responsible for the maintenance of base camps, agriculture, and the transportation of supplies. They also served as guides and couriers for Main Force Viet Cong and North Vietnamese Army units and performed limited intelligence missions.

As we continued to the southeast, the afternoon sun began its descent into Cambodia, and bright white beams of sunlight angled through the foliage. At an estimated 250 meters from our mission support site, we hit a shallow, spring-fed stream measuring a meter across and a foot deep. Both banks were crowded with large ferns, and in the branches above the stream, a few blue birds with bright red markings chirped as they fluttered from branch to branch.

"Take ten," I told Thach.

Once we had security in place, we took turns filling our canteens and washing up. When it was my turn, I brushed my teeth and lay in the shallow stream washing my hair with a bar of surgical soap. The smell of the soap and the taste of Colgate Dental Creme left me feeling like a new man.

When we finished, I led the squad uphill through dense undergrowth and stopped when I spotted one of our red-white-and-blue battle scarves hanging from a branch over the back trail.

"Wetsu," I called softly.

"Wetsu," a well-camouflaged Cambodian responded from behind a nearby tree.

"Hey, Jimmy," a voice with a New England accent called. When I turned, I saw Ray Fratus chomping on an unlit cigar.

"Good to see ya." I shook his hand. "What's goin' on?"

"High-speed trails everywhere," he told me. "We're gonna set up here for the night."

"We left a few toe poppers and claymores," I said. "How far to the MSS?"

"Top of the hill." He pointed. "About a hundred meters."

We preferred to set up our mission support sites on the high ground because there they were the most defendable. The enemy, on the other hand, generally set up his base camps in low areas that were on or close to a water supply.

With Thach leading, we moved uphill past enormous cypress trees whose mottled gray trunks measured eight to ten feet in diameter. The areas between the great trees were packed with thorn-covered vines and stalks of tan, brown, and green bamboo. Near the crest of the hill, I spotted three men from the 3d Platoon clearing fields of fire. There was no one on guard, and they didn't see us. Thach approached one of the men, and when he looked up, I saw that it was Set, a rifleman from the 2d Squad.

"Ah-brat!" Thach growled and kicked him in the stomach.

"Where's *Trung si* Cole?" I asked one of the other men.

He pointed to his right, and twenty meters down the line, I found Rinh heating a cup of water.

"Where's Bob?" I asked while looking for a spot to string my hammock.

"He went to see Captain Johnson," he said as Ly and I lowered our rucksacks to the ground a few feet from him.

Karoumph! A muffled explosion far to the south.

"Chon was wounded in the arm," Rinh said as he added a tea bag to his cup.

"What?" I said with surprise. "When?"

"Yesterday, when we attacked the base camp."

"How serious?" I asked as I stretched my hammock between two saplings.

"Shrapnel. He will need stitches," he said as Thach walked up and said something to him that I didn't understand.

"You set 'em straight?" I asked Thach.

"Yes, *Bac-si*," he responded. "Next time they die."

Thach was serious. He knew from experience that discipline was one of the keys to survival.

"Good man." I turned back to Rinh. "Why the hell didn't Chon say somethin'?"

"He thought you would send him back to Trang Sup," he smiled.

"You load 'im up on penicillin and streptomycin?"

"Yes, 1.2 million units of procaine penicillin G and a half gram of streptomycin."

"Good, get him over here. We'll sew 'im up before it gets dark," I said as I positioned my rucksack under my hammock. "What did Thach say?"

"He told me that three men need medical attention." Rinh smiled.

"That damned Thach is one of the best NCOs I've ever known." I chuckled as I removed my air force White Dot signal mirror and a twenty-five-gauge needle from my rucksack. While sitting in my hammock, I held the mirror in front of my open mouth and examined what was left of my tooth. It had been shot off at the gum level, and the tissue was raised and red.

Seconds later, Rinh returned with Chon and sat him on the ground a few feet in front of my hammock. While Rinh looked through our M-5 medical kit, I punctured my abscessed gum with the needle. When I pushed on the raised area with my finger, a stream of pus shot to the ground.

"*Kraqnac nas.*" Chon shook his head in disgust.

"Much better." I smiled. "Go ahead and get 'im ready."

Rinh removed an Ace bandage and gauze from Chon's arm and, halfway between his wrist and elbow, exposed a deep three-inch gash on the inside of his arm. I was relieved that there was no damage to his major blood vessels. I was also pleased that there was no discoloration of the tissue on either side of the wound. If there was any evidence of dead or dying tissue, it would have to be debrided before we closed the wound.

"Gimme some soap," I told Rinh as I rolled up my sleeves and knelt on the ground next to Chon.

Rinh reached into our M-5 kit and pulled out a plastic squirt bottle filled with a fifty-fifty mix of pHisoHex and hydrogen peroxide. After shaking it up, he squirted some of the creamy white mixture into the palm of my hand. I rubbed my hands together and worked my way up to my elbows.

"A little water," I said. He slowly poured water from a canteen and rinsed the soap from my hands and arms.

Whoomph! A muffled explosion to the northwest. It may have been one of our toe poppers. Rinh removed a sterile suture set from the M-5 kit and placed it on the ground next to Chon. It was wrapped with a green surgical towel, and after removing the tape, he peeled it open.

The suture set contained two straight and two curved five-inch forceps, a straight razor, a surgical knife, gut and black-silk suture thread, a general surgical scissors, an assortment of curved surgical needles, four eighteen-inch green surgical towels, an emesis basin, and a pair of tweezers. Everything we'd need to close the wound.

While Rinh hung a bottle of normal saline from a stalk of bamboo, I opened a pair of paper-wrapped, sterile surgical gloves and dropped them on the sterile surgical set. Rinh dropped some sterile pieces of gauze into the emesis basin and squirted pHisoHex and hydrogen peroxide on top of them. Looking closely at Chon's wound, I saw that there was some oozing.

"Flush 'er out," I said. Rinh extended the rubber tubing from the bottle of normal saline and used the clear, sterile salt water to flush pieces of foreign matter and blood clots from the wound.

"Okay, let's clean it up," I said as Bob returned.

Whoomph! A louder explosion cracked to the northwest. It may have been one of the claymores that we set up beside our back trail.

"He gonna need a medevac?" Bob asked while leaning over Chon to look at his wound.

"Don't think so," I said as I slipped into the surgical gloves.

Rinh picked up the plastic squirt bottle and filled the length of the wound with the soapy mixture. The hydrogen peroxide immediately began bubbling when it came in contact with the raw flesh.

"Sigma captured a nurse," Bob told me as I used a few soapy pieces of gauze to gently scrub the length of the wound. The news caught me by surprise. I wondered if it was the girl in the base camp.

"Around here?" I asked.

"No, outta the area," he said as Rinh flushed the soap from the wound. "I'm gonna check the perimeter."

I spread a sterile eighteen-inch towel on the ground and placed Chon's arm on it.

"Syringe," I said to Rinh.

He opened packages containing a 2cc plastic syringe and a twenty-five-gauge needle and dropped them both on the sterile towel.

"Anesthetic," I said as I attached the needle to the syringe.

Rinh removed a bottle of lidocaine hydrochloride from the kit and held it up while I pushed the needle through its rubber cap. When I pulled back on the plunger the syringe filled with the clear, painkilling liquid.

"Here we go." I smiled as I pushed the needle into the raw flesh at the end of Chon's wound and injected a small amount of the anesthetic. He didn't show any sign of pain. Working my way down both sides of the wound I injected the painkiller every quarter inch. With the wound anesthetized, I picked up a curved forceps, clamped it to a three-eighths-inch curved surgical needle, and threaded the needle with a piece of black-silk thread.

With the tweezers in my left hand, I gripped the skin halfway down the gash and pushed the needle through the skin and into the underlying tissue. When it came out, I pushed it into the raw flesh on the other side of the wound and out through the skin. Using the forceps, I then tied a tight surgical knot and cut away the excess thread.

"You hangin' in there?" I asked Chon.

"Okay, *Bac-si*." He smiled.

With the first stitch in place, I was pleased to see that both sides of the wound lined up perfectly. I repeated the procedure every quarter inch and finally closed the wound with thirteen stitches.

"Lookin' good." I smiled before covering the stitches with a few pieces of sterile gauze. "Gotta keep it clean and dry or it'll get infected."

"I will clean it once a day with hydrogen peroxide and keep him on penicillin and streptomycin," Rinh said as I held the gauze in place and he wrapped Chon's arm with a three-inch Ace bandage.

"They change the HT-1 batteries?" Bob asked Luc as they returned from the perimeter.

"Yes, *Trung si*."

"Don't throw 'em away. They can still use 'em in their

flashlights," Bob said as he sat on a fallen tree next to where Rinh and I were immobilizing Chon's arm with a sling.

Whack-whack-whack. Whump-whump-whump. An exchange of M-16 and AK-47 fire to the south. Bob picked up the radio handset and monitored radio transmissions.

"Duke made contact with four VC," he told us. "Porked one."

"Rucksacks?" I asked as I moved to my hammock and Rinh repacked our M-5 kit.

"Thank you, *Bac-si*." Chon smiled and shook my hand before heading back to the perimeter.

"No rucksacks," Bob said as he pulled his map from his pocket. "The guy they killed had a new khaki uniform and a Chicom Series-1956 AK."

"Main Force," I said as I leaned back in my hammock.

The fact that they weren't carrying rucksacks was a good indication that they were operating out of a nearby base camp.

"Ninth Division," Bob speculated as he looked at his map. "Gritz says that if we get hit during the night, we'll RV at the top of hill 105. Seven hundred meters southeast."

I marked the location on my map, applied a fresh coat of mosquito repellent, and sat back in my hammock with tins of bread and peanut butter. The once bright colors of the jungle were reduced to dull shades of gray, and something was screeching outside the perimeter.

"Monkeys," Rinh whispered as he sat on the tree next to Bob and removed a rubber band from the top of a bag of rice.

"This is the life," I said softly while enjoying my bread and peanut butter.

"Today 15 May." Luc sat on the ground in front of my hammock. "Bad day."

"Why's that?" Bob asked.

"Karl Marx birthday," Luc said as he sipped his tea. "Today, VC want many victory."

"Fuck him and Ho Chi Minh," Bob responded.

"Ho Chi Minh birthday 19 May," Luc said. "Very bad day."

"You ever think you're gettin' too old for this shit?" Bob chuckled.

"Yes, *Trung si,*" Luc said. "I soldier when I fourteen. Now I wounded seven time."

"Why the hell don't you find a job in Saigon?" Bob asked. "You could probably work security at the SF compound on *Avenue de Pasteur* or at Camp Goodman."

"I cannot, *Trung si.*"

"Why the hell not?"

"Freedom," he responded with emotion. "I want freedom for Khmer Krom people."

"You are free," Bob said.

"Not free, *Trung si*. VC and Saigon government want kill us."

"The world knows what the Chinese and the French did to the Vietnamese but not what the Vietnamese did to the Khmer people," Rinh said.

"I remember you tellin' me the Mekong Delta used to be part of Cambodia," Bob said.

"Yes," Rinh said. "During the seventeenth century the Vietnamese invaded the Kingdom of Kampuchea. When they reached the city of Prey Nakor, they forced the Khmer people to leave and changed the name to Saigon. Since then, we have been an oppressed minority."

"Vietnam not like Khmer," Ly added.

"Be careful not to spill your master's tea," Rinh said.

"Say again," Bob said.

"An old story," Rinh whispered. "Back in the 1800s, the Vietnamese used Khmer laborers to dig a canal in the Mekong Delta. When the canal was finished, they buried the Khmer up to their necks. Then they put their wood stoves on the heads of the laborers and started fires to heat their tea. When the Khmer cried out from pain, the Vietnamese told them to be careful not to spill their master's tea."

Ly said something in Cambodian that I didn't understand.

"He said that when the French came to Vietnam during the

1800s, we hoped they would free us from Vietnamese oppression," Rinh told us.

"Yeah," Bob responded with sarcasm. "Good luck."

"I never could figure out why we supported French reintervention at the end of World War II," I whispered. "It destroyed our credibility."

"Politics," Rinh said. "Your government caved in to French pressure."

"Big mistake," Bob said. "By supporting the French, we alienated the Nationalists and drove most of 'em into the hands of the Communists."

"No shit," I agreed. "The Nationalists were the most powerful force in Vietnam; the key to the future. Then we supported Ngo Dinh Diem for president. A mandarin Catholic in a country that's ninety percent Buddhist."

"Fucking politicians know how to screw things up," Bob whispered. "After we alienated the nationalists and Buddhists, who was left to fight the Communists?"

"You're right," I said. "Diem, Minh, Khanh, Huong, and Ky all made the same mistakes. Rather than isolate the VC and build a coalition government, they drove people to the other side and isolated themselves."

"So where do we go from here?" Bob asked.

"Other than the hard-core Marxist-Leninists, I think most people would support a president who offered a real democratic alternative to communism," I said. "Ideally, an elderly Buddhist; a democratic nationalist."

"The first thing I'd do is give the ethnic groups a piece of the pie," Bob said.

"What pie?" Luc asked. Everyone laughed.

"Khmer autonomy in the Delta and Montagnard autonomy in the highlands," Bob said.

Rinh explained what Bob had said.

"Saigon not agree," Luc responded.

"Sometimes you gotta give up a little or lose everything," Bob said.

As I lay listening to their whispers, the jungle came alive

with the sounds of the night, and I drifted off to sleep. Sometime later, an earth-shaking explosion woke me. I checked
my Seiko and saw that it was 2310 hours (11:10 P.M.). The
cool night air was filled with fireflies and the chirping of
crickets. I reached down to the foot of my hammock and
pulled my parachute nylon up to my neck.

"Sky Spot," Bob whispered from a few feet away. "Six to
seven hundred meters out."

"Yeah," I agreed. "The air force won't drop 'em any closer
than six hundred meters to friendly forces."

The TBQ-10 radar-controlled Sky Spot was a technical in-
novation that allowed us to call in air strikes at night. Once
Captain Gritz selected a target, Tom Horn would radio its encoded eight-digit coordinates to the Special Forces air liaison
officer at Company A in Bien Hoa. The air liaison officer then
relayed the information to the III Corps Direct Air Support
Center at Tan Son Nhut Air Base in Saigon. The coordinates
were then fed into a computer that controlled the aircraft's
course and bomb-release point. The system was capable of
accurately delivering bombs on targets within twenty to
thirty minutes and could also be used to make emergency resupply drops.

I rolled on my side and, in the warmth of my nylon cocoon,
quickly fell back to sleep. At 2400 hours (midnight), Bob
woke me for my two-hour watch. I slipped into my wet
boots and sat in my hammock, listening to the sounds of the
jungle.

A few meters behind me, Tom Horn was tapping out
Morse code. I felt my way in the direction of the tapping and
found him and Captain Johnson sitting shoulder to shoulder
with a poncho over their heads. Horn had his Morse code key
clamped to his right thigh, a Dianna one-time pad in his left
hand, and a red-tipped pen flashlight in his mouth. Captain
Johnson sat with a map spread on his outstretched legs, a
grease pencil in one hand and a pen flashlight in the other.

"Directing artillery fire," Johnson grinned. "Base camps, way
stations, likely avenues of approach, critical terrain features."

Horn continued to transmit.

"That's it, sir," he said to Johnson. "Thirteen targets."

They switched off their flashlights and pulled the poncho from their heads.

"We're in the belly of the beast," Gritz muttered from a nearby hammock.

"Yes, sir," I said. "The VC call this area the Forbidden Zone."

"Ninth Division headquarters may be in the area," Horn told me.

"That come from Sigma?" I asked.

"No," Johnson said. "The guy Snider killed was assigned to a headquarters security unit."

"Jimmy, how are the Bodes holding up?" Gritz asked.

"Not bad, sir," I said. "A few minor problems. One of 'em didn't tell me he'd been wounded because he didn't wanna go back to Trang Sup."

"A good example of why we picked the Bodes over the other ethnic groups," Gritz said.

"There's something special about 'em," Horn said.

"To know 'em is to love 'em," Johnson added.

"Sir, we gonna continue to the southeast?" I asked.

"South for a day and then west toward Phuoc Vinh on the seventeenth," Gritz said. "The next two or three days will be critical. Clyde's gonna make every effort to finish us."

"Better get back to the platoon," I said.

"Take care, Jimmy," Gritz responded.

I felt my way back to my hammock and, for the remainder of my watch, sat listening to exploding 175-millimeter artillery rounds and thinking about how we would survive the next few days.

During Operation Blackjack-31—our monthlong Mobile Guerrilla Force operation in War Zone D in January and February 1967—we entered an area previously unpenetrated by conventional military forces, fought fifty-one engagements, called in tactical air strikes against twenty-seven targets, and raided fifteen company- and battalion-size base camps. That

operation clearly demonstrated that a guerrilla force commanded by Americans could conduct unconventional operations in Viet Cong–controlled areas and secret zones; that we
could "outguerrilla the guerrilla."

Following the success of Blackjack-31, it was my hope that
the Mobile Guerrilla Force concept would be expanded to include similar units in every province in South Vietnam. The
primary objective of the Mobile Guerrilla Force units would
be to engage and destroy local Viet Cong forces—as opposed
to engaging Main Force units in decisive battles—and by so
doing substantially weaken the Viet Cong and its political
wing, the National Liberation Front, at its very foundation.

During the first phase of Blackjack-33, we were used conventionally to engage Main Force units, and on 3 May 1967,
some of the best soldiers in the world paid with their lives.
During the second phase of the operation, we returned to unconventional tactics, but were still being used to pursue Main
Force units. Even though the first six days of the operation had
gone well, I remained convinced that we were being misused.

I felt that finding Main Force units was a mission tailor-made
for Project Sigma's reconnaissance teams—two Americans and
four indigenous personnel who conducted reconnaissance
patrols throughout a targeted area—and roadrunner teams—
four indigenous personnel who dressed as Viet Cong and
conducted long-distance reconnaissance over enemy trails
and roads. Sigma's reconnaissance and roadrunner teams
were ideally suited for the mission because a team could be
covertly inserted by a single helicopter, their location was not
easily compromised, and it was generally easy for them to
break contact, and if necessary, arrange a timely helicopter
extraction. Once Sigma had a fix on a Main Force Viet Cong
or North Vietnamese Army unit, that company, battalion,
regiment, or division could be fought and finished by conventional American forces such as the 1st Infantry Division.

My two-hour watch passed quickly, and at 0200 hours
(2:00 A.M.), I woke Rinh to take over. Once again wrapped in
my nylon cocoon, I quickly fell back to sleep.

9

In the higher elevations the leaves disappeared into a thick morning mist as our two columns threaded southeast through wet vines and clumps of lime green bamboo. High in the trees, long-armed monkeys cried *hoot, hoot, hoot* and appeared to float through the mist as they bounded the distances between the trees.

Bob was on the point of the column on the right and was followed by myself, Ly, Luc, the machine-gun section, and the rest of the 3d Herd. To our rear were the *bo-chi-huy* and Bill Ferguson's 2d Platoon. Duke Snider's 1st Platoon was twenty meters to our left and was followed by Glen Bevans's 4th Platoon and Ray Fratus's Recon Platoon.

Three hundred meters southeast of our mission support site, we entered dark triple-canopy jungle and headed south over relatively flat terrain. In the lower levels of the canopy, small yellow birds sang morning arias as they fluttered from branch to branch. While pushing through a tangle of dripping vines, Bob suddenly stopped and dropped to one knee. I moved forward and found him crouched at the edge of a meter-wide trail.

"Hasn't been used for a while," he whispered.

Above the trail's foot-long grass, hundreds of spider webs like white silk fishing nets were stretched from one side to the other. Thousands of insects were stuck to the webs, and many were mummified in gray cocoons. We continued on our southerly azimuth, and a hundred meters past the trail, Bob again stopped in a tangle of vines and ferns.

"Smoke," he whispered.

As we stood in silence, we heard what sounded like someone chopping wood.

"A hundred meters," Bob estimated.

I extended my hand, and Ly handed me the radio handset.

"Fox Control, this is Fox Three. Over," I whispered.

"Three, this is Control. Over," Captain Gritz responded.

"Control, got smoke and someone chopping wood a hundred meters south. Over."

"Roger Three. I'm coming forward."

As Bob and I waited, Duke Snider and Dave Rose joined us.

"Someone's cookin'," Dave whispered.

"Hope we ain't late for breakfast." Duke grinned.

Captain Gritz had his radio handset pressed to his ear when he and Tom Horn joined us.

"That's a Roger, Memphis," Gritz said to the forward air controller. "Control, out."

"Could be a base camp, sir," Bob said.

"FAC'll be up in five minutes," Gritz told us as he looked at his map. "Let's hit 'em before we're spotted."

"Yes, sir," Bob responded.

"Okay, 1st and 3d got the assault," Gritz said. "Once you move through the objective, set up security on the south side."

"*Bo-chi-huy* got the search?" Duke asked.

"Yeah," Gritz responded.

"Let's do it," I said.

"If we get into deep shit, we'll RV at 148 562," Gritz said, "eleven hundred meters southeast."

"At the top of the hill," Dave commented as we used our grease pencils to mark the location on our maps.

As soon as Gritz and the other Americans left, Luc used his HT-1 radio to issue instructions to the squad leaders. Within seconds, the 3d Herd was silently deploying on line to our right. I moved twenty meters down the line and, standing behind the men, watched for Bob's signal to move forward.

A few minutes passed before he raised his hand over his head and, by lowering it forward, gave the signal to advance. As we pushed through wet foliage, the morning dew sparkled like diamonds; the first rays of sunlight were just angling to the jungle floor.

"Keep 'em on line," I whispered to Binh as we moved.

Thirty meters ahead, we entered an area where calf-high pungi stakes with fire-hardened tips had to be carefully sidestepped.

"Dich!" A high-pitched Vietnamese voice broke the silence and a surge of adrenaline electrified my system.

Ta-tow-tow-tow. Whack-whack-whack. Our line erupted, and the Bodes surged forward yelling *"Chey-yo!"*

Whump-whump-whump. The enemy returned fire, and a few green tracers cut through the foliage. We advanced at a fast walk and soon came to an area where the lower levels of the canopy had been cut and cleared. Only the great trees remained, and they supported an umbrella of leaves that kept the camp in near darkness. A few glowing white shafts of sunlight angled to the jungle floor and left me with the feeling that I had entered a church.

With the roar of automatic fire and *"Chey-yo"* echoing through the base camp, we moved past a line of empty spider holes. Ahead of our advancing line, red tracers streaked through the camp at waist level, chickens and ducks scurried for cover, and exploding M-79 rounds flashed as they hit their targets.

I slipped between two thatch-roofed structures with open sides and fired quick bursts at the backs of two shirtless enemy soldiers as they ran for their lives. One of them was knocked to the ground but immediately got back on his feet and quickly disappeared. When we reached the spot where he had fallen, Binh reached down to remove a watch from a severed arm. Further into the camp, I passed a well and a below-ground-level kitchen whose thatch roof was covered with clear plastic.

Twenty-five meters past the kitchen, we reentered thick jungle and stopped a few meters into the foliage to set up a defensive line. The firing on our side of the camp had stopped, but on our left flank, there were still sporadic shots and explosions. The fact that the enemy had made no serious effort to defend the camp may have been an indication that it didn't contain anything important.

I ran back into the camp and found the *bo-chi-huy* set up next to the kitchen. Captain Gritz was on the radio and Caption Johnson and Tom Horn had slit open fifty-pound bags of rice and were dumping them down the well.

Dien and I jumped down into the kitchen—its dirt floor was four feet below ground level—and found a bamboo table crowded with baseball-size sticky rice balls, half of which were wrapped in leaves. On the other side of the table were two large brown bottles of *nuoc mam*, pieces of breadfruit, and a basket of vegetables. At the far end of the kitchen, two blackened vats boiled on fireplaces that had been dug into the kitchen's red-clay wall. On the other side of the vats, two smoke-filled underground chimneys continued to the east. Even though both fires were going strong, they weren't producing any visible smoke. The underground chimneys appeared to be absorbing the smoke before it could be released into the air. An ingenious system.

I tossed a piece of burning wood onto the roof, and Dien kicked over the boiling vats. Glancing twenty meters to my left, I saw Bob kneeling in one of the camp's open-sided hootches. I ran to where he had removed a trapdoor and was about to enter an underground bunker. A half dozen bamboo mats were spread on the floor around him, and a few sets of black pajamas hung from a section of bamboo that extended the length of the hootch.

"Anything in there?" I asked.

"Looks like a few satchel charges," he said. "Let's check 'em out."

I dropped my rucksack to the floor of the hootch and followed him into a dark, moldy bunker. It measured about ten feet across, with a log ceiling only four feet above its dirt floor. In the near darkness of the far corner, four shoe-box-shaped devices were encased in clear plastic. Around each satchel, a few tightly wrapped bamboo strips held the plastic in place, and protruding from the top of one of them was an olive drab fuse. A fine trip wire was attached to the fuse and wrapped a dozen times around the satchel. If the wire was tripped, it would pull the retaining pin from the striker and detonate the satchel. Without touching the device, Bob used his flashlight to take a closer look.

"Russian MUV pull-fuse," he told me. "I'm gonna rig it."

"Be careful," I said. "If they used potassium chlorate, it could be unstable."

While lying on the floor, Bob lifted the end of the device just enough to shine a ray of light under it.

"Not booby-trapped," he said as he handed me the flashlight.

While I held the light, he screwed an M-5 pressure-release firing device into the well of an M-26 high-explosive hand grenade and then used his knife to dig a grenade-size hole in the floor.

"Trung si," Hien called into the bunker. "We go."

"One minute," I told him.

Bob placed the grenade in the hole and saw that the plate on the M-5 device was flush with the dirt floor. To keep the grenade stable, he packed some dirt back in around it and then pulled the satchel over most of the release plate. He then carefully pulled the safety pin from the M-5 device and slid the satchel over the remainder of the exposed release plate. If the satchel was moved, a swing lever within the M-5 device would be released. When it struck the percussion cap, the grenade would explode and kill everyone in the bunker.

"Let's go," he said as he used his hat to spread some loose dirt from around the satchel.

I followed Bob out of the bunker and choked on the smoke-filled air. A few feet above our heads, the building's thatch roof was engulfed in flames. We quickly replaced the trap-door, grabbed our rucksacks, and ran from the burning building.

The Bodes from the *bo-chi-huy* were busy throwing kitchen utensils, uniforms, tools, and a few dead chickens into the well while Captain Johnson stood waiting with a grenade in his hand. On the north side of the camp, Glen Bevans and Stik Rader appeared to be burying toe poppers.

"Fire in the hole!" Johnson yelled as Bob and I ran by.

Whoomph! A fountainlike column of water exploded from the well. By the time we got back to the platoon, Luc had the men lined up and ready to move. Minutes later, we continued south with Bob on point and, one hundred meters from the base camp, stopped at the edge of another grass-covered east-west trail.

"Booby trap," Bob whispered as he pointed to his right.

A meter down the trail, a piece of clear monofilament fishing line glowed where a beam of sunlight penetrated to the jungle floor. It was stretched tight through the foot-long grass and would have been invisible if it weren't in the direct sunlight.

"What's it connected to?" I asked.

"Don't move," Bob cautioned as he leaned in the direction of the fishing line.

I reached back, and Ly handed me the radio handset.

"Fox Control, this is Fox Three. Over," I whispered.

"Three, this is Control. Over," Gritz responded.

"Control, we're checkin' a booby trap on an overgrown east-west trail. Over."

"Roger, Three. Control, out."

"Jim." Bob pointed to a well-camouflaged green sapling that was close enough to touch. It had been stripped of its branches and bent—at waist level—in the direction of the trail. Near the path's edge, it was bent around the trunk of a tree. I carefully pushed aside a few large featherlike ferns and, near the end of the sapling, spotted six pungi stakes lashed to it. If the fishing line was tripped, that would release the sapling and its pungi stakes would strike the average American in his midsection.

"Gonna trip this sucker," Bob whispered. He picked up a three-foot section of moldy bamboo and, while standing at a safe distance, tossed it on the fishing line.

Wuushhh! The sapling was released, and the razor-sharp pungi stakes whipped across the trail with tremendous force.

We crossed the trail, and while pushing through hanging vines and large heart-shaped leaves, I thought about the booby trap. The Viet Cong were geniuses when it came to the employment of nonelectric booby traps. Although the devices were generally well camouflaged, most could be detected if you took your time and thought about what you were doing.

I made it a practice to ask myself continually what I would do if I were them. Over time, I had learned that in enemy-controlled areas and secret zones, they generally employed the things when they had something to protect. You were most likely to find them along trails and roads, on likely avenues of approach to their base camps, around their base camps, and sometimes *in* their base camps. Whenever you found a booby trap in an enemy-controlled area, you could generally conclude that Mister Charles was in the neighborhood.

We proceeded downhill through thick undergrowth and, an hour later, crossed a hard-packed east-west trail that had a single strand of black communications wire running along it. The wire was a good sign that battalion-size or larger enemy units were operating in the area. Two hundred meters south of the trail, we came to the bank of a spring-fed, ankle-deep stream.

Whack-whack-whack. Whump-whump-whump. An exchange of M-16 and AK-47 fire to our rear.

"Bac-si." Luc handed me the radio handset.

"Control, this is Five. Over." It was Ray Fratus.

"Five, this is Control. Over," Captain Gritz responded.

SFC Robert "Bob" Cole.

S.Sgt. Dale England and his Cambodian radio operator.

Luc, platoon sergeant, 3d Platoon.

Capt. James "Bo" Gritz and his Cambodian radio operator.

The Mobile Guerrilla Force compound adjacent to Trang Sup Special Forces Camp. In the background is Nui Ba Den, Black Virgin Mountain.

S.Sgt. Tom Horn.

Col. Francis "Blackjack" Kelly.

S.Sgt. Jim Donahue.

Kien Rinh, senior
Cambodian medic.

Viet Cong troops on the move in War Zone D.

M.Sgt. Donald "Ranger" Melvin.

Thang Kieng, rifleman, 3d Platoon.

Capt. Tom Johnson.

Kim Lai (right) and members of his 2d Platoon.

Viet Cong mortar crew.

S.Sgt. Dave Rose (left) and three Cambodians.

A-1E aircraft dropping napalm containers attached to T-7A reserve parachutes.

S.Sgt. Larry "Stik" Rader.

Viet Cong meeting in bunker.

S.Sgt. Ernest "Duke" Snider.

S.Sgt. Ray Fratus.

Viet Cong soldier washing his shirt in a stream. Note the AK-47 rifle leaning against the tree.

SFC Bill Ferguson.

Viet Cong awards
ceremony.

SFC Glen Bevans
(left) and S.Sgt.
Jim Battle
(saluting) at awards
ceremony, Phuoc
Vinh. The awards
are being presented
by Maj. Gen. John
Hay, Commanding
General, 1st
Infantry Division.

Left to right: Jim Donahue, Steve Yedinak, Son Thai Hien,
and Phil Downey at Kim Lai's grave.

"Control, made contact with an undetermined number of Victor Charlies moving west on the trail. They broke contact to the east. Negative casualties. Over."

"What were they wearing? Over."

"Pith helmets and khaki uniforms. Point man had an AK; the second guy an RPG. Over."

"Recon made contact on the trail," I whispered to Bob.

"Roger, Five," Gritz responded to Fratus. "Booby-trap our back trail and set up an ambush one to two hundred meters south of the POC. Control, out."

We moved uphill past three-story chestnut trees and clumps of green bamboo, and at the crest, we set up our mission support site. Once we had the Bodes in position, Bob, Luc, Ly, and I strung our hammocks. A few meters away, Rinh sat removing the Ace bandage from Chon's arm.

"How's it goin'?" I asked as I squatted next to them.

"Good, *Bac-si*." Chon smiled.

Rinh removed the squares of sterile gauze from the wound, and I was pleased to see that there were no signs of infection.

"Keep him on penicillin and streptomycin," I said as Rinh dabbed the stitches with gauze soaked with hydrogen peroxide. "We'll take 'em out when we get back to Trang Sup."

"Jim." I turned. Bob was kneeling with his map spread out in front of him.

"Yeah," I said as I squatted next to him.

"You wanna take Thach's squad out?"

"Sure."

"Gritz wants us to keep two squads and the machine-gun section on the perimeter," he said. "You can take Luc and the radio with ya."

"Where am I goin'?" I asked.

"Seven hundred meters southeast," he said as he used his pen to point to a stream on his map.

"Okay." I marked the location on my map. "I'll go directly to it, skirt it east for maybe two hundred meters, then shoot an azimuth back to the MSS."

"Sounds good," he said. "Give yourself time to get back before dark."

"*Trung si*." I looked up, and Luc was standing with Thach's squad lined up behind him.

"They ready to roll?" I smiled.

"Yes, *Bac-si,*" Luc responded.

"Okay, check their weapons and equipment," I said. "We'll head out in ten minutes."

As a reconnaissance patrol, our mission was to collect information. But we also had to be prepared to engage and destroy the enemy. While Luc and Thach conducted their inspection, I ran a couple of patches through the bore of my M-16 and wiped it down with my silicone cloth. When they completed the inspection, I gathered the squad in a small circle and informed them of our mission, route of march, and what action we would take if we made contact with the enemy. Our tactics were simple and aggressive: if we made contact we would shoot first and move fast. Back at Trang Sup, we had spent many hours practicing immediate action drills, and before departing, I quickly reviewed how each member of the patrol would react if we made point, flank, or rear contact. When I was convinced that every man knew his job, we headed downhill to the southeast with Thach on point. I was a few paces behind him, and to my rear were Ly, Luc, and the rest of the squad.

Halfway down the hill, Thach suddenly froze in midstep with his fist clenched above his head. As we waited in silence, my heart raced in my chest. Seconds later, two small female deer walked into an open area to our right front. At the base of the hill, we came to a shallow, meter-wide stream. Stalks of lime green bamboo grew to both banks, and red dragonflies the size of canaries skimmed its surface at amazing speeds.

When we finished filling our canteens, we continued southeast past clumps of green and tan bamboo. Fifty meters past the stream, Thach stopped at the edge of a meter-wide east-west trail with calf-high grass growing along its surface.

While Thach sent two-man patrols fifty meters up and down the trail, I checked the ends of the branches that grew to both edges of the footpath. I didn't find any evidence that any of them had been cut or broken in recent days.

When the patrols returned, the one that had gone to the left reported an enemy booby-trap warning thirty meters down the trail. We skirted the trail to the east and, lying on the trail, found a moldy piece of bamboo broken at a right angle. Since there was no bamboo growing in the immediate area, it was likely that someone had placed it there.

So that they wouldn't kill their own men, the Viet Cong often left warnings that an area was booby-trapped: three evenly spaced stones or sticks, a broken stick or piece of bamboo with the break pointing at, or in the direction of, a booby trap, a clump of grass tied together, or a horizontal stick tied to two vertical sticks in the shape of a goal post.

We continued to skirt the trail to the east, and forty meters past the warning, Thach stopped in a clump of green bamboo and pointed to his right.

"Booby trap," he whispered.

From the center of the narrow trail, a ten-foot section of brown bamboo extended to an overhead branch. Anyone moving down the path would have to push it aside.

"That it?" I questioned.

He nodded. "VC."

Once we had security in place, Thach and I approached the trail and found the section of bamboo covered with mold and spider webs.

"Been here a while," I whispered.

Hidden in the leaves where the bamboo rested against an overhead branch were what appeared to be a few gray sections of serrated cast iron. Since most booby traps were found in, on, or near the ground, most people wouldn't look for an overhead device. A potentially fatal mistake.

"Nice work," I whispered. "Probably a pull device."

Most Viet Cong booby traps consisted of either a pull or

pressure-release mechanism attached to an explosive device. From what I could see, I had to conclude that the cast-iron explosive device was connected to the bamboo with a wire. If the bamboo was moved, it would detonate the explosive and, because of its elevated position, kill or wound everyone on the trail below. Since only a fool would try to defuse it, I decided to rig it so that it would detonate when we were well out of the area.

"Gimme a blasting cap and get the demo bag," I told Thach as I pulled a time pencil from my pocket.

He removed a small wooden box from his pocket, opened it, and handed me a blasting cap.

"I get bag," he told me.

When he returned with the demolition bag, I removed crimping pliers, a roll of green tape, and an eighteen-inch section of white detonating cord. While he stood guard, I crimped the time pencil to the blasting cap and then taped the blasting cap to the end of the detonating cord. At chest level, I wrapped the detonating cord around the bamboo a few times and held it in place while he wrapped it tight with green tape. With everything set, I crushed the time pencil's glass vial between my fingers and pulled its safety tab. In eight hours, the exploding detonating cord would cut the bamboo and detonate the overhead device.

We continued to the southeast and, thirty minutes later, hit our objective—a two-meter-wide stream that sparkled as it flowed over moss-covered rocks. Stalks of green bamboo grew along its far bank, and above the bamboo, featherlike palm fronds were silhouetted against a clear blue sky. Running along our side of the stream was a well-used, meter-wide, grass-free trail. The path's red-clay surface was as smooth as glass, and the grass at both edges lay pressed to the ground. When grass is stepped on, it generally returns to an upright position in less than a day. The fact that the grass remained pressed to the ground was a good indication that the enemy had recently used the trail. With my head extended over the trail, I saw that straight sections continued for fifty feet in both directions before they disappeared into the green.

"Set up on that rise," I whispered to Thach as I pointed to an area overlooking the trail.

We backed off fifteen meters and set up a small defensive perimeter with most of our firepower covering the trail. From there, we had a good view of the one-hundred-foot section of straight trail.

"Beaucoup VC use trail," Luc whispered as I examined my map and realized that I didn't have the coordinates of the day's reference point.

"Fox Control, this is Fox Three. Over," I whispered into the radio handset.

"Three, this is Control. Over," Captain Gritz responded with his familiar Oklahoma twang.

"Control, we've reached our objective. Got a well-used, high-speed, east-west trail running along the north bank. Over."

"Roger, Three. Set up an overnight ambush and return to base at first light. I'll relay your coordinates to FDC. Over."

"Roger, Control. Can you give me the coordinates of the RP? Over."

"Wait one."

While waiting for Captain Gritz to get back to me, I watched the trail and worried that the enemy might come marching down it before we had the ambush in place.

"Three, this is Control. Are you prepared to copy? Over."

"Ready to copy. Over."

"Today's RP is at Juliet, Mike, Sierra, Sierra. I say again, Juliet, Mike, Sierra, Sierra. Over."

"Roger, Control. That's Juliet, Mike, Sierra, Sierra. Wait one. Over."

We had developed a system for encoding and decoding numbers so that the information couldn't be used by the enemy if they intercepted our radio transmissions. To encode a number we converted it to a letter in the captain's name.

JAMES   GRITZ
1 2 3 4 5   6 7 8 9 0

The number 1 would be encoded as a *J*, the number 2 an *A*, the number 3 an *M*, etc. Accordingly, Juliet, Mike, Sierra, Sierra or JMSS would be decoded as 1355. In other words, the day's reference point was where the 13 and 55 grid lines intersected on my map.

Using my grease pencil, I marked the reference point on the map and saw that we were sixteen hundred meters right and twelve hundred meters down from the reference point.

"Control, this is Three. Over."

"Three, this is Control. Over," Gritz responded.

"Control, we're at right 1.6, down 1.2. Over."

"Roger, Three. Control, out."

"Overnight ambush," I told Luc and Thach. "We'll set up here."

"Okay, *Bac-si*." They nodded.

Since the enemy's route of march would be confined to the trail, I decided that our ambush's killing zone would be the one-hundred-foot section of straight trail. Total surprise would be required, and once the ambush was sprung, we would have to instantly fill the killing zone with the maximum volume of fire. If it was to be successful, it had to be short and violent—not more than a few seconds.

"Two-man OPs fifty meters to the left and right," I whispered to Thach. "They're there to watch, listen, and report, not to shoot."

"Okay, *Bac-si*."

"And tell 'em to find a position where they can bug out if they see something comin' down the trail."

"Okay," Thach nodded.

"If we get split up, we'll RV back at the MSS," I added.

Thach briefed his men, and as soon as they were in position, he sent a two-man patrol to check the far side of the creek.

"How many claymores d'ya have?" I asked Thach.

"Four."

"I want 'em covering the trail," I told him and Luc. "Two to the right, two to the left."

They nodded, and while Ly and I waited, they positioned the mines and ran their detonating wires back to our position. With the claymores in position, their deadly spherical steel balls would sweep the length of the one-hundred-foot section of trail. From our position, we would also be able to cover the killing zone with automatic-rifle fire, and anyone caught in the ambush would find himself in a deadly cross fire. I felt confident that, with total surprise, we could ambush and destroy a much larger enemy force.

While we waited for the patrol to return from the other side of the stream, we cleared a five-meter-wide circular area of ferns, leaves, downed branches, and twigs. After the foliage was removed, I squished three leeches and a large brown scorpion with the heel of my boot.

"We take bath?" Ly asked.

"No baths and no brushing your teeth." I worried that the enemy might detect the the smell of soap and toothpaste.

Within our cleared circle, I assigned Luc, myself, Ly, and Thach to positions facing the trail. Luc and I would be responsible for the two claymores facing to our left, and Ly and Thach for the two to our right. When the patrol returned, the men reported that they had gone a hundred meters without seeing any sign of the enemy. I positioned them on the far side of the circle, where they would be responsible for covering our rear. When the outposts were pulled in, they would occupy the left and right sides of the circle. With all-around security, each man would be a spoke in a wheel. Our feet would touch at its hub, and during the night, we would be able to communicate with minimum movement.

A few minutes before last light, Luc and Thach left to retrieve the outposts. I would have preferred to leave them in position overnight, but without radios, they would have no way of warning us of an approaching enemy force. During the day they could position themselves so that they could bug out and warn us, but at night they wouldn't see the enemy until it was too late. When Luc and Thach arrived with the four Bodes, one of them was carrying a headless four-foot snake whose dark brown patches were edged with white. It was a Russell's viper—one of the deadliest snakes in the world.

"Don't wanna give Charlie a chance to return fire," I told Luc, Thach, and Ly. "The instant I blow my claymore, I wanna hear the other three. At the same time, I want ya to fire a magazine—on automatic—on your part of the trail."

"Okay, *Bac-si*." They nodded.

"One-hundred-percent security?" Luc asked.

"Yeah, no one sleeps."

Simplicity was one of the keys to a successful ambush. That was especially true when commanding troops who had a limited knowledge of the English language. Each man had to know the plan and what his role would be in executing it.

"Bac-si." Luc handed me a small leather bag containing ground-up charcoal. Our weapons and uniforms blended with our surroundings, but on a starlit night, exposed skin might be visible from the trail. While Luc and Thach briefed each of the men, I applied charcoal to my face, neck, and hands. When I finished, I passed the bag to Ly.

I settled into a prone position between Luc and Ly and, reaching forward a few feet, picked up a foot-long section of rotting wood that I would use as a bench rest. I laid my M-16 on the wood and, with the butt under my chin, adjusted the wood until my sights were lined up on the trail. Once it was dark I would use the wood to cover my section of the trail with grazing fire—the most deadly form of fire. I wanted to insure that the trajectory of my bullets would pass through the enemy formation at a level never higher than the chest or lower than the hip.

With my rifle in position, I moved the selector switch to automatic and pushed the safety bail on my claymore's M-57 firing device to the armed position. When I depressed the handle on the device, it would generate a three-volt electrical pulse that would travel through the one-hundred-foot firing wire and detonate the electric blasting cap in the claymore.

"Claymores armed, weapons on automatic," I whispered.

While digging out a couple of half-buried rocks from under my chest, I noticed the hissing sound coming from our PRC-25 radio and worried that it might be heard from the trail. After making a communications check with Tom Horn, I switched the radio's function switch to SQUELCH, and the hissing stopped.

Through a few holes in the canopy, I saw that the night sky was white with stars. Most of the jungle was as black as midnight, but where the starlight penetrated the canopy, a few small sections of jungle appeared in shades of gray. As I lay in the darkness, I thought about our situation and worried that an enemy force might be spread out over more than the one-hundred-foot section of trail in front of us. If we ambushed a large, well-trained force, those not caught in the killing zone would likely move quickly to assault our position.

"Check the men every thirty minutes," I whispered to Thach.

Whoomph, whoomph, whoomph. Muffled explosions far to the west. Probably an artillery barrage.

As we lay on the soft moist earth, our body heat was attracting leeches. Every few minutes, I picked one of the slippery bloodsuckers from my skin, squished it between my fingers, and tossed it outside our circle. I thought about applying a fresh coat of mosquito repellent but again worried that the enemy would smell it.

"Bac-si," Luc whispered in my ear. "I think many snake live here."

"Hey, that's why I'm in the middle." I chuckled and nudged him with my elbow.

Sometime around midnight, one of the men to my right starting coughing.

"Give 'im some codeine," I whispered to Thach.

I heard him open a bottle and hand the Bode a half-grain tablet. We used codeine to control moderate levels of pain, but it also served as an excellent cough suppressant. Within minutes, his coughing stopped.

Whoomph! A loud explosion to our rear. I checked my watch.

"Time pencil on the trail," I whispered to Luc. "It's been eight hours."

By 0200 (2:00 A.M.), I was cold, damp, and shivering. With my finger on the trigger and the firing device cupped in my left hand, I strained to make out signs of movement on the trail but couldn't see much. The areas to my front and right were as black as a windowless bunker. Only a small area at the extreme left end of the killing zone was illuminated by starlight. It measured about five meters across, and within it everything appeared gray.

Someone coughed down the trail to our right, and a surge of adrenaline raced through my system.

"VC!" Thach whispered.

I felt him and Luc checking the men and then everything was still. With my rifle resting on the piece of wood and the stock under my chin, I adjusted my grip on the claymore's firing device.

"*Di cham lai*," a voice called. They weren't more than fifty meters down the trail. My only option would be to spring the ambush when I saw the first man enter the gray area at the left end of the killing zone.

Looking back to my right front, I caught a glimpse of what appeared to be the glowing red tip of a cigarette. I couldn't tell if he was the first man in the column. Seconds later, I heard the scraping of metal on metal on the trail in front of us and detected a moldy smell in the air. The Viet Cong often smelled of mold.

My eyes were focused on the gray area, and my nostrils filled with the smell of a Vietnamese cigarette. I took up the slack in my trigger and a shadow appeared in the gray area.

Whoomph, whoomph, whoomph, whoomph! Whack-whack-whack. I had squeezed my firing device and trigger, and for three or four seconds a series of flashes lit the jungle as though someone were using flashbulbs.

"Yaaahhh!" For a split second I saw the upper half of a man being blown down the trail like a feather that had been dropped in front of a fan.

"Ban tra lai!" Someone barked orders.

Whump-whump-whump. Automatic fire erupted fifty to one hundred meters down the trail to our right. I thought we might have hit the lead element of a large enemy force.

"We go, *Bac-si,*" Luc whispered as the air filled with the scents of spent gunpowder and scorched foliage.

"Let's go!" I snapped as I sprang to my feet.

With Ly gripping one of the straps on the back of my harness I moved a few steps to the north.

"Got everyone?" I whispered as the firing and screaming continued.

"Okay," someone responded.

With everyone in tow, I began moving away from the trail in two-inch steps. After moving about thirty meters, I stopped to make a whispered radio contact with Captain Gritz.

"Fox Control, this is Fox Three. Over."

"Three, this is Control. Over."

"Control, we ambushed an undetermined number of VC on the trail. We broke contact and are movin' north. Negative casualties. Over."

"Roger, Three. Do you want supporting fire? Over."

"Control, gimme a spotter round on the trail one hundred meters west of the POC. Over."

"Roger, Three. Control, out."

In total darkness, we continued to feel our way north through sweating leaves and vines.

Karoumph! An artillery round flashed to our rear.

"Control, Three. Round on target. Fire for effect. Over."

"Roger, Three. I'll walk 'em down the trail to the east. Control, out."

I continued to the north because I didn't want to leave a

back trail that would lead enemy trackers northwest to the
mission support site.

Karoumph, karoumph, karoumph. An artillery barrage
flashed to our rear and a few pieces of shrapnel cut through
the overhead foliage.

Thirty minutes before first light, the jungle came alive with
the grunts and groans of animals and the chirping of birds.
With the dawn of the new day, we found ourselves in a
bamboo thicket two hundred meters north of the point of contact. A pearl mist filled the space beneath the canopy, and
everything appeared dull green and brown. In the soft earth to
our rear, we were leaving a trail that couldn't be missed.

With monkeys screeching high in the mist, we stopped and
waited while Thach buried a toe popper in the center of our
back trail. Twenty meters past the mine, we again stopped and
waited while Luc and Thach buried additional mines to the
left and the right of our back trail. If an enemy point man
stepped on the first mine, the remainder of the force would
likely move to either side of our trail and begin moving parallel to it.

Thirty meters farther north, we hit the west side of a meter-
wide north-south trail. While we waited in silence, Thach
sent two-man security teams to skirt the trail fifty meters to
the north and south. Once they were in position, we intention-
ally left a trail of our distinct jungle-boot prints heading south
on the path. When we reached the security team, we removed
our boots, reversed direction, and in our bare feet moved
north on the trail until we found the other security team.

High in the branches, the morning mist glowed a dull rose
as we spread out on the trail—a few paces between each
man—and slipped back into the jungle. Still in our bare feet,
we moved a few meters before stopping to slip back into our
boots. Once Thach had everyone back in line, I shot an azimuth that would take us back to the mission support site and
led the squad downhill through thick undergrowth.

At the base of the hill, we hit the same shallow, meter-wide stream that we had crossed the day before. We were only two hundred and fifty meters from the mission support site, so I decided to stop and wash up. Once security was in place, we took turns using Ly's bar of soap to wash the charcoal from our skin. Then I contacted the *bo-chi-huy* to inform them that we would be entering the perimeter from the east.

Just inside the perimeter, I found Bob, Rinh, and Son kneeling on a poncho where they were working on our M-60 machine gun. In two small holes next to the poncho, glowing pieces of C-4 heated a canteen cup of tea and a can of beans and franks.

"Smells good," I said as I leaned my rifle against a tree.

"It's yours." Bob reached out and handed me the steaming cup.

"Thanks." I turned and saw Captain Gritz approaching.

"Mornin', sir," I said as Bob rose to his feet.

"Morning, Jimmy, Bob." The captain smiled. "Everyone make it back?"

"Yes, sir." I sipped the tea.

"Anything more on the contact?" Gritz asked.

"No, sir. Couldn't see much," I said. "Like being at the bottom of a well at midnight. All I know is that they were spread out over more than a hundred feet. Their point could'a been fifty to a hundred meters ahead of the main body. Then again, on a dark night, they might'a been back to chest."

"Yeah," Bob agreed. "Sometimes ya can't see shit."

"I'll tell ya one thing," I said. "Anyone caught in the killing zone went down hard."

"Okay." Gritz checked his watch. "We move in thirty minutes."

"West, sir?" Bob asked.

"Yeah, on two-seven-zero." Gritz headed back to the *bo-chi-huy*.

"Don't touch that three-eighty-six." Bob pointed to an olive drab PRC-25 radio battery lying on the ground where it wouldn't be missed by the enemy. "Got a grenade under it and another one in sump."

"Right." I picked up the can of beans and franks and sat in my hammock.

"Be glad to get outta here," Bob said as he stuffed his hammock into his rucksack. "Got more trails than New York has streets."

"Mmmm, beans are *good*." I smacked my lips. "Any updated intel from Sigma or the FOB?"

"Sigma roadrunners spotted thirty VC," Bob said as Son and Rinh finished reassembling the M-60. "One of their recon teams made contact with a squad."

"Bac-si." I turned and saw Ly standing without his fatigue jacket. At least a dozen leeches were attached to his chest and arms. The inch-long creatures were bloated with blood and looked like balloons that were ready to burst.

"Can I light a cigarette?" Rinh asked.

"Yeah, go ahead," Bob said.

As Rinh used the tip of the lit cigarette to remove Ly's leeches, I stripped and found over twenty of them attached to my body.

"I'm next," I told Rinh when he finished with Ly.

While I stood naked, sipping my tea, Rinh touched each of the slimy blood-filled suckers with the tip of the hot cigarette. When a leech released its grip, he lifted it from my skin and tossed it over his shoulder. He then dabbed iodine on the raised red spot where it had been attached.

"Thanks, my friend," I said before pulling the quick releases on my hammock.

By the time I had my rucksack packed, our point elements were already moving west in two parallel columns. The column on the left was led by Ray Fratus's Recon Platoon and was followed by Glen Bevans's 4th Platoon and Bill Ferguson's 2d Platoon. Duke Snider's 1st Platoon led the column on the right and was followed by the *bo-chi-huy* and the 3d Herd. Bob was at the head of the platoon, and I brought up the rear with Luc and Kien.

A fading red mist drifted high in the leaves; we headed downhill through triple-canopy jungle. At the base of the hill, we crossed a stagnant, moss-covered, waist-deep stream and entered a mosquito-infested swamp. With our boots sinking into soft, black mud, we moved past dying clumps of black and brown bamboo and rotting tree stumps.

After struggling though the muck for close to two hours, we hit solid ground and continued west past clumps of bright green bamboo.

Thirty minutes later, the column stopped in an area of mango trees with spreading leaves and flat tops. While Luc stood with the HT-1 radio pressed to his ear, I buried a toe popper mine in the center of our back trail.

"North-south trail," Luc told me. "Patrol check."

"Break time!" I said.

As soon as we had security in place and a claymore covering our back trail, I dropped my rucksack to the ground and sat with my back against it. It was a beautiful morning. Brilliant white shafts of sunlight angled through the foliage, and where they came in contact with the wet jungle floor, trails of steam worked their way skyward. A few small yellow birds chirped as they fluttered from branch to branch, and large black-and-green butterflies drifted in the still, hot air. I was tired and could easily have drifted off to sleep.

"Jim."

I turned and saw Bob approaching. "Base camp two hundred meters south," he whispered as he pulled his map from his pocket.

Adrenaline surged into my system, and I suddenly felt full of energy.

"Occupied?" I asked as I rose to my feet.

"Yeah, Charlie's home."

"How many, *Trung si*?" Luc asked.

"Captain Johnson says it's company-size," Bob responded.

"What's the plan?" I asked.

"Got a high-speed trail up ahead," he said as he looked closely at his map. "Camp's on the east side of the trail." He pointed with the tip of his pen. "We're gonna move south along the east side."

"Recon and the 1st got the assault?" I asked.

"Yeah, 2d and 4th got flank security," he responded. "*Bo-chi-huy*'s got the search."

"We got the rear?" I asked.

"Yeah. If we get split up, we'll RV at 118 550."

"At the top of the hill?" I asked as I used my grease pencil to mark the location on my map.

"Right."

"And the RP?" I asked.

"Fifty-four, ten."

"Fifty-four, ten," I repeated as I marked where the two grid lines crossed.

Bob returned to the head of the platoon, and within a few minutes, we were moving south through thick secondary growth.

Whoomph. Whack-whack-whack. An explosion followed by M-16 fire. The pace picked up to a fast walk, and AK-47s joined the firing as I slipped past hundreds of pungi stakes. Twenty meters past the pungi stakes, I spotted Bob deploying the platoon on line.

"Take the right flank," he told me when I reached him.

While moving down the line, I passed a smelly slit trench latrine that was buzzing with blue-green flies. From the latrine, a narrow path led across a small bamboo bridge and into the camp. At the end of the line, I found Binh standing with his M-16 at the ready.

Ta-tow-tow-tow. Whump-whump-whump. The firing continued.

"VC!" I yelled when I spotted two figures in black running away from the camp. By the time I had my weapon pointing in their direction, they were thirty meters away.

Whack-whack-whack. I fired a quick burst but missed. With my M-16 resting against the side of a sapling, I lined up my front sight blade on the second man.

Whack-whack-whack. I fired, and he jerked as if he had been hit by an invisible force, then disappeared beneath the foliage.

Binh and I ran to where he fell and found him lying on his back among large ferns. He was a young man—somewhere around eighteen—with straight black hair and a confused expression on his face. Much of his throat had been shot away, and when he exhaled, a bloody spray blew from the gaping hole. The second round had hit him in his armpit, and the third had taken off the tip of his nose.

"Watch for the other one," I told Binh as I knelt at the wounded soldier's side.

He grabbed my arm and tried to say something, but only a sickening sucking sound gurgled from what was his throat. When his fingers touched the bloody orifice a terrified expression appeared on his face.

Whack-whack-whack. Binh fired a burst from behind a large fallen tree.

"VC." He smiled and ran his finger across his throat with a slashing movement.

The sucking sound stopped, and when I looked back at the soldier, I saw a man screaming in silence. His airway had closed, and he was suffocating. With his mouth agape and his eyes bulging, he clawed desperately at the sides of his wound.

I pulled a bandage scissors from my pocket and, just above his clavicles, found the end of his torn trachea. I pushed aside some bloody tissue and worked the closed end of the scissors into it. With the scissors an inch into his airway, I attempted to spread its sides by opening the scissors. With his body shaking violently, he again grabbed my arm.

Whoomph! An earth-shaking explosion from within the camp.

When I looked back at the soldier's face, I saw the faraway look of death.

"Let's go," I yelled to Binh as I pulled the soldier's bloody hand from my arm. I wiped the scissors on my trousers, and by the time we got back to the 3d Herd, most of the firing had stopped. With the platoon in position covering our rear, I moved to the edge of the camp, where I found Duke Snider kneeling in a trench with Dave Rose standing guard over him.

The camp was filled with thick gray smoke, and a short distance beyond them, bamboo popped and cracked as orange-and-yellow flames leaped from the thatch roofs of a few hootches.

"Everyone okay?" I asked.

"Yeah, "Dave said. "They broke contact as soon as they saw us."

"Complete surprise," Duke said as he used his knife to dig a hole. "Didn't have a chance to get in the trenches."

Lying on the ground next to Dave were a few old cast-iron MK-11 fragmentation hand grenades with what appeared to be nails sticking out of their wells.

"What d'ya got?" I pointed.

"Charlie removed the fuse assemblies and dropped in non-electric blasting caps," Dave explained as he picked up one of the grenades and showed it to me. "Then they held the tip of a nail against the blasting cap and filled the well with wax to hold everything in place."

"Gotta give 'em credit." I shook my head.

"We'll put 'em to good use," Duke said as he buried a grenade in the floor of the trench.

"Mind if I take one?" I asked.

"Go ahead," Dave said.

With the grenade in my hand I ran to the path that led to the latrine. A few meters down the path I stopped where three ten-foot sections of bamboo had been lashed together to serve as a bridge over a thorn-filled ditch. I examined the bridge and found that, while the two outside poles were pressed against the ground, the center one was an inch above it. When I stepped on the center pole, it squeaked to the ground, and when I removed my foot, it returned to its original position. I saw Thang standing a few meters away and signaled him to join me.

"Gonna booby-trap this," I told him as I dropped my rucksack to the ground.

"Okay, *Bac-si*."

We picked up the end of the bridge and moved it a foot to

the side. He stood guard over me as I used my knife to dig a grenade-size hole where the center pole would strike the ground when someone stepped on it. I then slipped the grenade into the hole and saw that the top of the nail extended a quarter of an inch above ground level.

"Perfect," I told Thang as I pushed dirt in around it and packed it tight with my fingers.

"Jim," Bob called.

I turned and saw him approaching.

"They're movin' out," he told me.

"Okay."

Thang and I picked up the end of the bridge and carefully repositioned it with the center pole less than a half inch above the nail.

"Stay here until the last man moves west," I told him as I wiped my hands on my trousers. "Make sure no one steps on it."

"Okay, *Bac-si*."

I moved back into the base camp and found that I couldn't see more than twenty meters through the thick gray smoke. Near the center of the camp, the ghostlike figures of the *bo-chi-huy* were moving west through the smoke. With the welcome drone of the FAC's aircraft approaching from the west, I pulled my map from my pocket and recorded the base camp as being at coordinates 120 535. Seconds later, Bob and Ly entered the camp at the head of the 3d Herd.

"Jim," he said. "Ly's gonna stay with you and Luc. If I need a radio, I'll use the *bo-chi-huy*'s."

"Right," I gave him a thumbs-up.

Bob fell in behind the *bo-chi-huy*, and Luc, Kien, Ly, and I returned to our tail-gunner positions. Twenty meters to my left, Jim Battle and Hien—2d Platoon's machine gunner—were at the end of the other column.

On the far side of the base camp, we entered a bright area of two- and three-story chestnut trees. Luc was the lead man in the tail-gunner section and was followed by Ly, myself, and

Kien. Kien was the last man in the column and walked backward with a silencer-equipped Sten at the ready. The column was moving at a slow pace, so we took the opportunity to bury three toe poppers. We then moved quickly to close the gap with the rest of the platoon.

"Bac-si." Ly reached back to hand me the radio handset.

"Fox Three, this is Fox Control. Over," Captain Gritz radioed.

"Control, this is Three. Over," I responded as I walked.

"Three, are you clear of the base camp? Over."

"Roger, Control, we're fifty to seventy-five meters out. Over."

"Memphis, this is Fox Control. Over," Gritz radioed the FAC.

"Control, this is Memphis. Over," Captain Gammons responded.

"Memphis, we're clear of the base camp. Can you hit it with a load of CBU? Over."

"That's a can-do, Control. I'm in contact with a flight of Thuds. They'll be on station in zero-two minutes. Over."

"Memphis, we're movin' west on two-seven-zero. Over."

"Roger, Control. Got a lot of smoke down there. I'll bring 'em in north to south. Memphis, out."

The pace picked up, and we entered a relatively open area that was crisscrossed by a maze of recently used trails.

"Here we go," I said to Luc as an F-105 screeched in low from the north.

Whumph-whumph-whumph. Like drops of rain, hundreds of evenly spaced bomblets blanketed the base camp to our rear. Anyone caught above ground level would be cut to pieces by shrapnel. We were moving at a blistering pace, and with little overhead cover, my pores were running like faucets. As another jet made its final approach, I wiped the sweat from my eyes.

Kawhoosh! Napalm splashed through the foliage. As it poured down into the trenches and bunkers, there would be no escaping its liquid hell. Seconds later, another Thud knifed toward the base camp at close to four hundred miles an hour.

Karoumph, karoumph, karoumph. Seven-hundred-and-fifty-pound bombs exploded to our rear, the earth shook, and shock waves rippled through the foliage.

"Fox Three, this is Fox Control. Over," Gritz radioed.

"Control, this is Three. Over," I responded.

"Three, we're moving northwest on three-two-zero. Give Memphis another smoke as soon as you begin moving on the new azimuth, over."

"Roger, Control. Three, out."

Minutes later the men ahead of me changed direction and began moving to the northwest. I dropped a smoke canister to the ground, and within seconds, a plume of red smoke was working its way skyward.

"Control, this is Memphis," Captain Gammons radioed. "Got your red smoke. Over."

"Roger, Memphis. We're moving northwest. Can you give us twenty Mike-Mike between the red smoke and the base camp? Over."

"Roger, Control. They'll be approaching the target from the west. Memphis, out."

The pitch on the FAC's engine changed as he rolled in to mark the target.

Whooosh . . . pop! A white phosphorous round exploded to our rear, and through the trees, an umbrella of molten white streamers appeared against the blue sky. In his radio communications with the F-105s, Captain Gammons would use the white smoke as a reference point.

The whine of a Pratt & Whitney J-75 engine rose to a scream as another Thud approached from the west.

Burrrrr. The jet streaked through the still, hot air with its twenty-millimeter cannons tearing apart the foliage and any trackers who may have been on our back trail.

"Memphis, this is Fox Three. Over," I radioed.

"Three, this is Memphis. Over," Captain Gammons responded.

"Memphis, you're lookin' good. Over."

"Roger, Three. We aim to please. Memphis, out."

With the hot sun beating down on us, we continued northwest for 150 meters and then returned to our westerly azimuth. Soon after the F-105s completed their last run, the sound of their engines faded to the south. Fifteen minutes later, we crossed an intermittent stream, and our movement slowed to a crawl as we moved uphill through thick undergrowth.

"Fox Control, this is Fox One. Over," Duke Snider radioed Captain Gritz.

"One, this is Control. Over," Gritz responded.

"Control, this is One. We're at the top of the hill. Got a deuce-and-a-half parked at the side of a well-used, north-south road. Over."

"Control, this is Five," Ray Fratus broke in. "We're in a platoon-size base camp thirty meters south of One. Over."

"Roger, Five. Any sign of Clyde? Over."

"Control, this is Five," Fratus responded. "They left uneaten food. Probably bugged out when they heard the shooting. Over."

"Roger, Five. Wait one. Fox Four, Three, and Two, are you there? Over," Gritz called.

"Roger, Control. This is Four," Glen Bevans responded.

"This is Two," Jim Battle radioed.

"Three here," I said into the handset.

"Okay, let's set up a hasty perimeter and conduct a quick search," Gritz ordered. "Control, out."

As soon as we had the 3d Herd tied in with the 1st and 2d platoons, Bob, Ly, and I moved forward until we found Captain Johnson, Duke Snider, and Dave Rose standing in the sun at the center of a one-lane, red-laterite road. Both sides were lined with tall trees and thick underbrush. Ten meters past the road, Captain Gritz and Tom Horn were talking to Stik Rader, Glen Bevans, and Bill Ferguson. A few meters to our right, a large military truck was parked at the side of the road and covered with leafy branches.

"How many claymores d'ya have?" Captain Johnson asked Duke.

"Six, sir."

"Where you gonna put 'em?"

"Forty meters south," Dave responded.

"Okay," Johnson said. "Bob, you and Jim booby-trap the truck."

"Yes, sir," we responded.

"Connect this to the starter," Duke told Bob as he handed him an M-26 fragmentation hand grenade with two wires dangling from its fuse well. "I took out the fuse and put in an electric blasting cap."

"One wire to the starter and the other to the ground?" Bob asked.

"Yup."

"It'll get the driver's attention." Dave smirked.

"Got the demo bag?" I asked Ly.

"Yes, *Bac-si*."

"Okay, let's get it done," the captain said. "We move in ten."

Bob, Ly, and I moved to the empty, ten-wheeled, olive drab truck. Twenty meters past the truck, Duke's M-60 machine gun was set up at the side of the road. We dropped our rucksacks to the road's hard surface, and with Ly standing guard, Bob opened the hood. I stepped up onto the running board and crawled into the cab.

"Russian," I told Bob when I saw the cyrillic lettering on the dashboard.

"Three-ton ZIL-151," he responded. "It's in good shape."

I mumbled, "108 531," as I sat on the seat. I used a grease pencil to mark its location on my map. "Need any help?" I asked.

"Na, why don't ya leave a toe popper at the rear," he responded. "Once this blows, they'll have to tow it."

I jumped from the running board and tapped the sides of its external gas tank as I moved to the rear of the truck.

"Plenty of gas," I said as I pulled a branch from the truck. The leaves were soft, and the cut was still light colored. "Fresh branches."

High above the road, the FAC's O-1E soared like an eagle

with outstretched wings, drifting in a lazy circle. I removed a toe popper mine from my pocket and knelt on the road where I figured someone would stand when attaching a tow rope to the vehicle.

"Gimme some det cord and green tape," I told Ly.

Using the blade of my knife, I pushed aside some of the red laterite and dug a small hole in the clay.

"Bac-si." Ly handed me a foot and a half of white detonating cord, and I wrapped it around the mine a few times. While I held the cord in place, he covered it with green tape.

"Need the tape," Bob said as he straddled the engine.

While Ly helped Bob, I buried the toe popper and carefully arranged the laterite over it so that the mine would not be detected.

"All set," Bob said as he and Ly lowered the hood and then jumped to the ground.

As we moved back to where we first hit the road, we checked for jungle-boot prints but didn't find any on the road's hard surface. However, at the crossing point, we found bootprints in the soft soil on both sides of the road.

Minutes later, Bob returned to his position at the head of the platoon and again followed the *bo-chi-huy* west. Once the last member of the 3d Herd was across the road, Luc, Ly, Kien, and I used branches to sweep both sides free of our bootprints.

The four of us returned to our tail-gunner positions, and twenty meters west of the road, I again stopped to bury three toe poppers. A fifty-meter gap had developed between us and the rest of the platoon, and as small brown monkeys watched our every move, we quickly closed it. With the 2d Platoon only fifteen meters to our right, we entered an area of monstrous cypress trees whose mottled gray trunks were wrapped with thick, snakelike vines. In the higher elevations, the foliage was bright and green, but in the darkness of the lower levels, everything was dead or dying.

Whoomph! An explosion—not more than one hundred meters to our rear. It was too loud to be a toe popper. A few meters to my rear, Kien walked backward with his Sten at the ready.

"Bac-si," Ly handed me the radio handset.

Whump-whump-whump. Whoomph, whoomph, whoomph. Automatic fire and more explosions to our rear.

"Claymores on the road," I whispered to Luc.

Our movement slowed to a crawl, and minutes later, we came to a slow-moving stream with a ten-foot-high bank. On the far side of the stream, the Bodes were using a thick green vine to scale the bank. I watched for movement to our rear but didn't see anything.

"Fox Control, this is Memphis. Over," Captain Gammons radioed.

"Memphis, this is Control. Over," Captain Gritz responded as I waited my turn to cross the stream.

"Control, we've got somewhere between a squad and a platoon of dead Victor Charlie on the road. Also got movement south of the POC. Over."

"Roger, Memphis. Can you put a strike on 'em? Over."

"Control, we're talkin' a good two-zero minutes. Over."

"Memphis, we need it now. Suggest you request artillery support from Phuoc Vinh. Over."

"Roger. I'll put 'em in at the POC; then walk 'em south on the road. Memphis, out."

When the enemy triggered the claymore on the road, they must have thought that they had walked into an ambush. Apparently, they assaulted what they thought were the ambush positions and, in the process, triggered additional claymores.

"Fox Control, this is Fox Five. Over," Fratus radioed Gritz.

"Five, this is Control. Over," Gritz responded.

"Control, I'm standin' next to what's gotta be the world's biggest rice cache. No sign of Charlie. Over."

"Roger, Five. I'm comin' forward. Out."

Like an Olympic skier, I slid down the muddy bank and splashed into the slow-moving, waist-deep stream. After filling my empty canteens, I dug the toes of my boots into the soft bank and used the thick green vine to pull myself to the top.

Karoumph, karoumph, karoumph. Artillery rounds exploded to our rear.

While Ly, Kien, and I watched for movement to our rear, Luc leaned over the side of the bank and taped an M-26 high-explosive hand grenade to the base of a sapling. He then attached one end of a wire to the grenade's safety pin and the other to the vine. Before straightening the bent-over ends of the safety pin, he covered the wire with mud, and the grenade with a few leaves. If enemy trackers used the same vine to climb the bank, the wire would pull the pin from the grenade and kill or wound everyone between the banks.

With artillery rounds exploding to the east, we again moved quickly to close the gap with the rest of the platoon. Fifty meters past the stream, we found Bob deploying the platoon on line.

"A good twenty tons of rice," he told me as he stood next to a small open-sided hootch.

"Twenty *tons*?" I questioned.

"Yeah." He smiled. "Check it out."

Thirty meters ahead, I saw Captain Gritz and a few others standing next to a large open-sided structure with an overhanging thatch roof that was covered with clear plastic. As I walked toward them, I saw that it was packed—floor to ceiling—with fifty-pound bags of rice.

"Roger, Memphis," Gritz said to the FAC. "Twenty tons."

Captain Johnson and Tom Horn reached up to pull a burlap bag from the top of the pile, and when it hit the ground, it split open.

"I'll be damned," Johnson said as he used a knife to cut a section of burlap from the bag. "The Continental Grain Company." He shook his head with disgust and held it up for everyone to see.

"That's the Continental Grain Company of New York, not Hanoi," Horn said.

"I don't believe this shit," Duke Snider said as he and Dave Rose walked around from the rear of the structure.

I looked at my map and estimated our coordinates as 108 531.

"That's a Roger," Gritz said to the FAC as I marked the location on my map. "No time to dump it in the stream. We'll mark it with smoke. Over."

"Enough to feed the whole 9th Division," Dave said.

"Roger, Memphis." Gritz laughed. "Tell the pilots they're invited to dinner. We'll cook it with napalm and serve it hot. Control, out."

"Sir, you wanna ground panel on the roof?" Duke asked.

"Yeah, a panel and smoke with a fifteen-minute delay," Gritz said.

"Got a ladder round back, sir," Dave told Gritz.

As I headed back to the platoon, artillery rounds continued to explode to the east. Just inside our perimeter, I found Bob and Ly kneeling next to a fire pit.

"Rice is from New York," I told him as he finished using his knife to dig a hole in the ashes.

"You shittin' me?" Ly handed him a strip of green tape.

"No, the Continental Grain Company," I said as he wrapped the tape around an M-26 high-explosive hand grenade.

"Someone needs their ass kicked."

Bob pulled the pin and placed the grenade in the hole with the safety lever facing up. As artillery rounds continued to explode to our rear, he covered it with ashes and small pieces of half-burned wood. If someone started another fire, the tape would burn, and the safety lever would fly from the grenade. It would kill or wound everyone within ten meters.

"That should do it," I said as Bob stood up and wiped his hands on his trousers.

With a flight of jets approaching from the south, the company continued to the west and Luc, Ly, myself, and Kien returned to our tail-gunner positions. When we were twenty-five meters west of the cache, Captain Gritz radioed the FAC that we were clear of the target. The FAC again rolled and dived towards the rice cache.

Whoosh . . . pop! His marker round exploded to our rear

and streaks of phosphorous arced against the sky to form a giant white mushroom. A minute later, the whine of a Supersabre's engine rose to a scream as it streaked in low from the north.

"Fox Control, this is Memphis," the FAC radioed to Gritz. "Nape on the way. Over."

"Napalm!" I yelled to the Bodes as I dived into a depression.

Kawhooosh. Seventy-five meters to our rear a boiling orange-yellow and black mass spilled through the canopy. A second later an invisible wall of heat hit our positions and brought with it the pungent petroleum smell of burning gas. Calling in napalm always scared the hell out of me because if it hit too close to your position, its insatiable fireball could suck the air from your lungs and suffocate you. With a billowing black cloud to our rear, we hurried to close the gap with the rest of the platoon. Minutes later, we crossed a well-used, north-south trail as another jet roared over the cache.

Karoumph! A bomb exploded to our rear, shock waves rippled through the foliage, and more thick black smoke erupted into the pale blue sky.

"Fox Control, this is Memphis," the FAC called as thousands of leaves floated to earth. "Dead center. Over."

"Roger, Memphis," Gritz responded. "Suggest you put your remaining ordnance in on the road. Over."

"Control, we've got movement in the area of the cache. Looks like they're trying to carry away whatever they can scoop up. Goin' down to check it out. Memphis, out."

The pitch of the O-1E's engine again changed as he rolled in for a closer look.

"VC!" Kien hissed. He fired a burst from his silenced Sten.

I turned and caught a glimpse of khaki fifty meters to our rear.

Ta-tow-tow-tow. Whack-whack-whack. Jim Battle's tailgunner section opened up. I switched my selector switch to automatic, and as I moved to get a clear shot, I saw four more khaki-clad Viet Cong with green pith helmets and tubular sacks of rice over their shoulders. I fired three quick bursts, hit one in the face, and within seconds, the roar of M-16s and AKs resounded through the jungle.

"Memphis, this is Fox Two," Jim Battle radioed the FAC from a position twenty meters away.

"Two, this is Memphis. Over."

"Memphis this is Two. Got an enemy force of unknown size thirty meters east of my position. Request immediate air support. Over."

"Roger, Two. Gimme a smoke. We're stacked up and ready to deliver. Over."

A plume of yellow smoke twisted skyward from Battle's position.

"Memphis this is Two. They're thirty meters east of the yellow smoke. I say again, thirty meters east of the yellow smoke. Suggest you again bring in on a north-south line. Over."

"Roger, Two. Smoke in sight. CBU comin' your way. Memphis, out."

"Get down," I yelled as an F-100 streaked in just above the treetops. We again dove for cover, and seconds later, a load of cluster bomb units exploded like a string of firecrackers across our rear.

"Let's go," I yelled as I emptied a magazine into the area where I had last seen the enemy. We jumped to our feet and ran to close the gap with the rest of the platoon. With Jim Battle directing air strikes to our rear, we continued at a fast pace over relatively flat terrain.

Four hundred meters west of the point of contact, we entered triple-canopy jungle. A few minutes later, Recon and the 1st Platoon walked into a platoon-size base camp. By the time I reached the camp, its three thatch-roof hootches were engulfed in flames, and I choked on the smoke that was trapped beneath the canopy. We quickly moved through the base camp and didn't stop until we hit a fast-moving stream seventy-five meters farther west. Both banks were packed with large, oval, green-and-white leaves, and five feet below, the water foamed as it cascaded over smooth black rocks. As I stood waiting my turn to cross, I wiped the pungent taste of burnt petroleum from my lips.

On the far bank, we continued through thick undergrowth and, six hundred meters farther west, entered the Ba Ta swamp. Clouds of mosquitoes drifted among leafless trees, and the ground was littered with decaying trunks that were crawling with insects. With the roar of the jets fading to the south, the only sounds that remained were those of our boots being pulled from the creamy black mud and the croaking of frogs.

After struggling through the muck for close to thirty minutes, the column suddenly stopped shortly after we hit dry ground and reentered triple-canopy jungle. I checked my map and figured that we were close to the southern edge of the village of Cam So. Twenty meters ahead, I saw the men lowering their rucksacks to the ground, and Bob and Thach and a few Bodes moving down the line.

"Take ten," Bob told us. "Jim, we're gonna check out a deserted village. Wanna come?"

"Sure." I dropped my rucksack to the ground.

"*Bac-si,* I go?" Kien asked.

"Okay." I smiled. Kien was the world's greatest scrounger and never missed an opportunity to pick up something of value.

As soon as Luc had security in place, Kien and I followed Bob, Thach, and the rest of the Bodes to an overgrown north-south trail. We skirted the trail to the north and, a few minutes later, stopped at the edge of an oval clearing. The area measured a good three hundred meters across and was covered with foot-long, straw-colored grass. A short distance into the clearing, a few partially collapsed thatch and bamboo hootches were shaded by fifty-foot palm trees. Also growing around the structures were large banana plants with drooping leaves shaped like elephant ears. On the far side of the village, a checkerboard pattern of overgrown rice-paddy dikes extended to a wood line that shimmered in the late-day heat.

Except for a woodpecker tapping out what sounded like Morse code, everything was silent.

We set up a small defensive perimeter just inside the wood line and sent Thang and Kien to check out the village. While waiting for them to return, I spotted a six-foot-long slit-trench latrine a few meters from where I was standing. There were no flies hovering around it, and when I probed its feces with the end of a branch, I found them hard and dry. Both indications that the village had been deserted for a long time.

"No VC," Thang told Bob as he returned and handed him a dirt-covered round which measured a good six inches in length. When Bob wiped it on his trousers, he exposed a purple tip and a narrow black band just below the end of the round.

"Chicom 14.5 millimeter," Bob told us as he examined the round. "Heavy machine gun."

"Booby trap, *Trung si*," Thang said as he held up a hollowed-out four-inch section of bamboo. At its base, the bamboo was attached to a block of wood. A nail had been hammered through the wood and served as the device's firing pin.

"An ass kicker," Bob said.

"I show you, *Trung si*." Thang smiled as he extended his hand.

Bob gave him the round, and he slipped it into the hollowed-out section of bamboo and moved it up and down a few times.

"Soldier walk on bullet, soldier die," Thach said.

"Where'd you get it?" Bob asked Thang.

"Come," he said.

"Trung si." We turned and saw Kien returning with a two-foot section of board under his arm and a large galvanized metal can in his hand. "No go, *Trung si*." He shook his head and handed Bob the piece of wood.

On the board the word *CAM* was printed in large black letters.

"In Vietnam, *cam* is booby trap," Thach said.

"Good man," Bob told Kien.

"The whole clearing's probably booby-trapped," I said.

"Yeah," Bob agreed. "Best LZ in the area. Let's get the hell outta here."

As Bob and Thach turned to leave, Kien handed me the galvanized container. On its side, a purple strip matched the tip of the bullet, and printed in black were a number of Arabic numbers and Chinese characters.

"Ammunition container," I told him as I tossed it into the latrine.

We skirted the trail back to the platoon and, a few minutes later, continued west through thick undergrowth. An hour later, we waded across the Suoi Lach Be—a slow-moving, waist-deep stream—and on its far bank, we quickly moved through another smoke-filled platoon-size base camp. Near the center of the camp, thick gray smoke poured from the moldy thatch roofs of two open-sided structures.

On the west side of the base camp, we buried three toe poppers, and one hundred meters farther west, we found SFC Glen Bevans and one of his squads set up in an ambush.

"Jimmy, any sign of trackers?" he asked.

"No, looks like the air strikes and mines slowed 'em down."

"Four hundred meters to the MSS," he said.

"Okay, see ya in the mornin'." We continued uphill past massive cypress trees with moss-covered trunks. In between the great trees, a cluster of gnarled brown vines twisted off in every direction. Near the crest of the hill, we found Captain Johnson standing at the base of a tree whose trunk measured twelve feet in diameter.

"Ninety to one-eighty," he whispered and pointed. "Tie 'em in tight."

"Yes, sir," I said.

We pushed through vines that hung like limp tentacles and worked our way around a few fallen trees that appeared to have been uprooted by a tropical storm. In the higher elevations, small black monkeys with skin-color faces and white beards scurried from branch to branch, and through a few holes in the canopy, a steel gray sky was streaked with red. When we reached our sector of the perimeter, I found Bob and Rinh stringing their hammocks.

"Home sweet home." I smiled as I lowered my rucksack to the ground.

"I'm gonna set up the LP," Bob whispered. "Would ya heat me some water?"

"Sure," I said as I used my knife to clear an area of vines.

"Everyone holdin' up?" I asked Rinh.

"A soldier in the headquarters section has malaria," he said.

"You put 'im on chloroquine?" I asked as I finished stringing my hammock and Luc arrived.

"Yes, one gram at 1300 (1:00 P.M.)."

"Good," I said. "Give 'im a half gram tonight and then a half gram a day for two days."

"Dien has two soldiers carrying his gear," Rinh added.

"Any vomiting?"

"No."

"Good. Keep an eye on his temperature and hook 'im up to an IV if there's any sign of dehydration. If we have to bring in a Dustoff, we'll send him out."

"Very good, Donahue."

"Make sure they clean their weapons before it gets dark," I told Luc as he squatted next to his rucksack. We had a problem with high-carbon-content ammunition, and if the M-16s weren't cleaned after every firing, a carbon buildup could cause malfunctions.

"They do, *Bac-si*," he said softly. "Squad leader check all weapons."

"Don't give 'em any slack," I said. "They tend to relax after we've been out for a few days."

"All soldier know many VC this area," he assured me before heading back to the perimeter.

While kneeling next to my rucksack, I added dried minnows and water to two dehydrated rice meals.

Karoumph, karoumph, karoumph. Artillery rounds exploded to the east. With the last light of day quickly fading, I filled my canteen cup with water, dropped a tea bag into it, and placed it over a piece of glowing C-4. While kneeling in the shadows, I quickly fieldstripped my M-16 and cleaned it with Hoppe's #9. The cleaning solvent dissolved the carbon and had a refreshing smell.

"LP's fifty meters out at 125 degrees," Bob whispered as he returned and leaned his M-16 against a tree.

"Here ya go." I handed him an indigenous meal. "Gimme your canteen cup."

"Thanks." He handed me his cup, and I filled it half full of steaming tea.

"Can't figure it," he said as he sat in his hammock.

"What's that?" I wiped down the outside of the M-16 with my silicone cloth.

"Why would Charlie have base camps and twenty tons of rice this close to Phuoc Vinh?" he whispered as he sipped his tea. "We're only eleven klicks out."

"Gotta be massing for an attack on Phuoc Vinh or Dong Xoai," I said as I picked up my hot cup and sat in my hammock.

"Could be," he responded as artillery rounds exploded to the south. "But how could they be this close to Phuoc Vinh and no one know about it?"

"You'd think they'd be patrollin' the area," I said.

"Someone ain't doin' their job." He shook his head as Luc returned from the perimeter. "Their S-2 needs his ass kicked."

"All weapon clean," Luc told us. "Claymore out."

"Good man," Bob said as he used a C-ration spoon to eat his rice.

"There have always been many VC in Phuoc Long Province," Rinh said. "In 1965, they overran every camp in the province."

"When we get back to Trang Sup, dinner's on me." Bob changed the subject.

"We get to pick the restaurant?" I mused as I placed my cup on the ground and picked up my bag of rice.

"Any place you guys wanna go."

"You ever been to François's in Nha Trang?" I asked as I sprinkled some Tabasco sauce on my rice.

"The place down at the boat landing that's owned by the French Legionnaire?" Bob asked.

"Yeah," I said. "Not much to look at, but it's got the best lobster in Vietnam."

"Like your Cambodian friend in Tay Ninh," Bob joked.

"Hey, watch it," I cracked. "She'll kick your ass."

"I'll never forget the time I saw her chasin' you down the middle of the street with that butcher knife." He laughed. "Funniest thing I ever saw."

"Old Ha *was* fast." I laughed.

"Donahue is in love with Ngoi," Rinh said. "She is very beautiful."

"The girl in Bien Hoa?" Bob questioned.

"Yes," Rinh said. "I think Donahue will marry her and take her to America."

"I'm too young to get married." I laughed.

"Hey, what d'ya say we go to Saigon?" Bob suggested. "I'd like to pick up a few things for the family."

"Great," I said. "We'll catch a flight down and pick up a jeep at the PX."

"If we go to Saigon, the Le Loi Restaurant has excellent Vietnamese food," Rinh told us. "It's near the central market."

"Rinh, do you remember the time we went to the My Canh floating restaurant?" I asked.

"Yes, the boat docked on the Saigon River at the foot of Tu Do Street," he said. "Across from the Majestic Hotel."

"Best seafood in Saigon and great coconut ice cream," I said as I lay back in my hammock. "Get a table at the railing and watch the sampans and ships as you're eating. At night, ya can sit for hours; talkin', sippin' coffee, and watchin' the lights of Gia Dinh."

"After dinner, we'll go to that air-conditioned bar on the roof of the Caravelle Hotel," Bob said.

"Whenever I go to Saigon I like to drink French coffee at a sidewalk cafe," Rinh said.

"We'll take Thach," I said. "He wants to visit an old friend in Cholon."

"Danh should be out of the hospital," Rinh said. "I think we should take him."

"Anything you guys want is okay with me," Bob said. "We'll stay for a couple days and hit all of the good restaurants."

"Tomorrow we go west to Phuoc Vinh?" Luc asked in the darkness.

"No, Gritz has a skin feelin' that 9th Division headquarters might be somewhere along the Suoi Loch Be," Bob said. "We're gonna follow it south to where it hits the Rach Rat."

"Ya know, this is a lot like a mouse huntin' a big cat," I mused.

"Gotta be one fast mouse," Bob chuckled.

"Ain't no slow mouses in this game." I laughed. "Only the quick and the dead."

"Hey, let's get some sleep," Bob said. "Tomorrow's gonna be a long day."

10

Our columns snaked south through emerald forest and pearl mist. The air smelled of mold and cinnamon bark, and in the branches above our heads, a few yellow-eyed brown monkeys sat eating leaves while others scurried from branch to branch.

Kien was on the point of the column on the right and was followed by myself, Bob, Ly, Luc, and the rest of the 3d Herd. To our rear were the *bo-chi-huy* and Bill Ferguson's 2d Platoon. Duke Snider's 1st Platoon was fifteen meters to our left, and to their rear were Glen Bevans's 4th Platoon and Ray Fratus's Recon Platoon.

Slipping silently through dripping leaves and waist-high ferns, Kien's black eyes flashed back and forth, searching for signs of the enemy: a shadow, a footprint, a glimpse of khaki. At the same time, he strained for a sound that didn't fit: a hushed voice, the snap of a twig, a rifle bolt. Like a finely tuned machine, his rifle followed his eyes to his left, front, and right.

Every few minutes, Kien stopped to listen as he looked up into the trees or squatted close to the ground where, beneath the lowest level of vegetation, he could sometimes see for thirty to fifty meters. With his finger on the trigger of a silenced Sten, he was prepared to instantly respond to contact with the enemy. On point, the difference between life and death was often measured in split seconds, and nothing could be overlooked.

Hanging from a fine gold chain around Kien's neck was a small Buddha that had been carved from a boar's tusk. Most Buddhists wore jade or ivory Buddhas, but our Khmer Serei believed that if their Buddhas were carved from a boar's tusk, they could not be killed by the enemy unless they violated one of the Buddha's commandments against lying, drinking, stealing, adultery, or cursing.

Wrapped inside a colorful scarf around his neck, he also carried a *Yon*—a white handkerchief with intricate Buddhist symbols and sacred text. The *Yon* was written in Pali—the ancient language of the Buddha—and the Cambodians believed that it, too, provided protection to those who carried it into battle.

With my map in my left hand and my compass in my right, I checked Kien's direction and saw that he was moving on an azimuth of two hundred degrees.

"Psst!" I hissed. He looked to the rear, and I adjusted his course to 180 degrees by pointing 20 degrees to his left.

At the base of the hill, we hit the east side of a shallow north-south stream whose fast-moving water sparkled as it flowed around moss-covered rocks. Along its muddy banks, a few gray birds with white chests and long beaks paced back and forth, stabbing at insects. We skirted the stream to the south, and fifteen minutes later, we reached the point where it flowed into the Suoi Lach Be, the same slow-moving, waist-deep stream we had crossed the day before.

Both banks of the Suoi Lach Be were crowded with thirty-foot, flat-topped mango trees and large heart-shaped leaves growing from green stems. In the branches above the stream, a few black birds with bright yellow stripes sat chirping.

A short distance past the stream, we entered an area of ferns and new-growth bamboo. The smooth, twelve-foot stalks were bright green and free of leaves. Growing from the ground around them were thousands of three- to four-inch asparaguslike bamboo shoots that in time would grow into thirty- to fifty-foot stalks. When peeled and cooked, the sprouts provided a tasty meal; so, too, did the small leaves at the top of fully grown stalks. The potatolike tubers, which grew at the base of the large heart-shaped leaves, and parts of the ferns could also be eaten. If you knew what you were looking for, edible plants were abundant in the jungle. When I was an adviser to a Montagnard light infantry company at Duc Phong Special Forces Camp, they taught me to watch the monkeys. If you ate what they ate, you wouldn't get sick, and if you wanted to add meat to your meals, you could also eat the monkeys.

With a blanket of mist drifting a few feet above the ground, we continued south through dripping vines and large ferns.

Karoumph! Something exploded far to the west, and Kien suddenly dropped to one knee.

"VC!" He pointed. The ground beneath the branches was covered with medium-green ferns, and running through them was a meter-wide, east-west line of dark green ferns. The plants appeared a darker shade of green where something, or someone, had knocked the dew from them.

"What d'ya got?" Bob whispered from behind me.

"Somethin' moved through here." I pointed. "Let me check it out."

Kien and I advanced a few meters and, beneath the dark green ferns, found the outlines of sandals in the soft earth. You could tell which direction they were moving in because the heel end of the sandals made a deeper imprint than the toe end. While Kien stood guard, I moved back to where Bob was waiting.

"Five to eight men headed west," I whispered.

"Smoke." Bob's nostrils flared as the faint smell of someone cooking meat drifted through our ranks.

"Probably on the stream," I said as I looked at my map.

"Fox Control, this is Fox Three. Over," Bob radioed Captain Gritz.

"Venison," Duke said softly as he joined us. "Gotta be a base camp."

There was something wrong with Duke. He looked pale and exhausted.

"Your eyes look like a couple of pee holes in the snow," I said.

"Been up all night," he whispered. "Got the green-apple two-step."

"Diarrhea can kick your butt," I said. "Dave get your temperature?"

"Yeah, a hundred and one."

"Takin' anything?"

"Dave thinks it might be dengue fever. He loaded me up on tetracycline, paregoric, Kaopectate, and APC's."

"Fox Control, this is Fox Three. Over." Bob again tried to contact Captain Gritz.

"Without a lab test, there's no way of knowing for sure," I said. "If it is dengue, there's no specific treatment. All ya do is treat the symptoms."

"Everything aches," he said. "My head, my joints, my back. Even my eyeballs."

"Complete bed rest is the treatment of choice." I smiled.

"Yeah," he responded sarcastically.

"What d'ya say we carry ya in a hammock?"

"Yeah," he mused. "Like King Tut."

"If your headache gets any worse, take some codeine," I said as I pinched the skin on the back of his hand and saw that it had lost some of its elasticity. "You're dehydrated."

"I'm fine," he insisted.

"Give your gear to the Bodes and drink a lot of water," I said. "If the dehydration gets any worse, we'll hook ya up to an IV."

"Hey," he said. "I'll drink the water, but ain't no one carryin' my gear."

"Another bullhead." I shook my head.

"Control, this is Three," Bob said softly into the handset. "Got smoke and fresh footprints—maybe a squad—movin' west. Could be a base camp on the stream. Over."

"A hundred meters to the stream," I told Bob as Duke

moved to the far side of a nearby tree, dropped his trousers, and sprayed the ground with explosive diarrhea.

"Roger, Control. Three, out," Bob whispered before giving the handset back to Ly. "Captain says to follow the trail."

Ly heard what was being said and slipped his Buddha into his mouth. When the Bodes sensed imminent danger, they put them in their mouths because they believed it brought them closer to him.

"Got a skin feelin' on this one," I said.

"Here ya go," Duke said as he returned and handed me a white phosphorous and two CS gas grenades that had been taped together. The fuse had been removed from the white phosphorous grenade, and taped into the grenade's well was a piece of time fuse. Attached to the other end of the time fuse was an M-1 pull-type firing device.

"What's the delay on the fuse?" I asked as I handed them to Kien.

"Ten seconds," Duke said. "When the CS mixes with hot white phosphorous ya get one nasty gas. It'll stop 'em in their tracks."

"Let's do it," Bob said as he bounced to adjust the weight of his rucksack on his back.

With Duke's platoon twenty meters to our left and brilliant shafts of sunlight angling through the canopy, we skirted the trail west through wet ferns and leaf-covered vines.

If there was a base camp on the stream, we would deploy on line, achieve fire superiority, and assault. If it was defended by a smaller force, we would quickly overpower them and destroy the camp. If it was occupied by a larger force, surprise would be the key to our survival; we would have to hit them with the full force of our firepower before they had a chance to get into their defensive positions. If we were able to overrun the camp, we would secure it only long enough to conduct a search and destroy everything of military value.

Minutes later, the crow of a rooster broke the silence, and Kien again dropped to one knee. I advanced to where he was kneeling among waist-high ferns and, ten meters ahead, saw the slow-moving waters of Suoi Lach Be. On the stream's far side, a six-foot-high red-clay bank had been worn smooth. In the foliage above the stream, numerous small yellow birds chirped as they fluttered from branch to branch.

"Trinh!" A voice on the far side of the stream broke the silence, and adrenaline surged through me.

With my heart pounding in my ears, I turned to Bob with my fist over my head—the signal to freeze. I moved the selector switch from safe to automatic, and Kien and I lay on our sides beneath the plants. I wanted to dump my heavy rucksack, but knew that if I did, I might never get back to it. Through featherlike ferns, I saw a head bobbing toward the stream. I turned and gave Bob a thumbs-down—enemy in sight. When the top half of the enemy soldier came into view, I saw that he wasn't wearing a shirt and that he had a blue towel draped over his shoulder.

With my finger on the trigger I kept my front sight blade centered on his chest as he moved down a set of stairs that had been dug into the bank. He was wearing khaki trousers with a brass belt buckle, appeared to be in his late teens, was well fed, and had short, straight black hair. His khaki trousers, muscular build, and recent haircut were all good indications that he was Main Force Viet Cong.

When he reached the edge of the stream, he yawned, squatted, and placed his toothbrush on a flat rock. He was only fifteen meters away, and I worried that he would spot my light-colored skin in the foliage.

As he lathered up a bar of soap and washed his face, Kien turned to me. I pointed to the Viet Cong and ran my finger across my throat in a slashing movement.

"Kill him," I mouthed with my lips.

Kien nodded and turned back to the enemy soldier. It had to be a fatal shot. I had no idea how many troops might be in the base camp, and if he wasn't killed instantly, he would surely alert them.

Go for the head, I said to myself as Kien lined up his sights. Go for the head.

The enemy soldier looked up and sniffed the air. He sensed something. After more than a week in the jungle, we had to smell pretty bad.

Chunk! Kien coughed as the bolt on his silencer-equipped Sten slammed shut and a nine-millimeter round hit the soldier in the center of his chest. With a shocked expression on his face and his mouth agape, he was knocked flat on his back. I hoped that Kien's cough had disguised the metal-on-metal *Chunk* of his bolt. Kien and I jumped to our feet and moved to the edge of the stream.

"Ooohhh," the soldier moaned as he tried to sit up.

Chunk! Kien again fired and coughed. The soldier's head jerked to the rear as the round splattered his eye and a stream of blood, brain, and bone fragments exploded from the top of his head. As Kien and I waded across the meter-deep stream, the enemy soldier lay quivering on the bank. By the time we reached him, he was still.

"He die," Kien whispered as he chomped on his unlit cigar and kicked the side of the soldier's head.

We quickly moved to the six-foot-high bank and carefully peered over the top.

"Holy shit," I said to myself. Much of the lower levels of the canopy had been cleared, and a thin layer of mist and smoke drifted just above the ground. Forty meters into the camp, three khaki-uniformed soldiers sat smoking on a log with their backs to us. A few meters to their left was a machine-gun bunker made of logs and covered with dirt and grass. Twenty meters past the enemy soldiers was an open-sided hootch with a corrugated tin roof covered with leafy branches. Beyond the hootch were clumps of drooping banana plants and what appeared to be fruit trees. On the far side of the trees were a number of smaller thatch and bamboo hootches, and beyond them were parts of what appeared to be at least two large structures. With my head extended just above the bank, I could hear the singsong chatter of voices, laughter, and coughing. They appeared to have no idea that we were in the area.

"VC here long time," Kien whispered as his eyes flashed back and forth under the brim of his hat.

"No shit." I found myself wondering how patrols from Phuoc Vinh could have missed it. With state-of-the-art Red Haze infrared detection devices, side-looking airborne radar, and aerial photographs, you would also think that analysts at the MACV intelligence center in Saigon would have pinpointed its location. I turned and saw Bob, Ly, and Luc slipping across the stream.

"Ssshhh." I slid to the base of the bank and used my hand to signal them to stay low. Thirty meters to the south, Duke's platoon was pouring across the stream.

"Big time base camp," I whispered to Bob as he squatted next to me. "If we get pinned down in there, they're gonna kick our ass."

"Get 'em on line and keep 'em low," Bob said to Luc as the birds continued to chirp in the branches above our heads. "Let me take a look."

Bob joined Kien high on the bank, and as each of the Bodes slipped across the stream, Luc directed them upstream.

"Bac-si." Ly handed me the radio handset.

"Fox Three, this is Fox Control. Over."

"Control, this is Three," I whispered. "Got an occupied base camp on the west bank of the stream. From what I can see, it extends west for over a hundred meters, over."

"Control, this is One," Duke broke in. "I'm on line south of Three. This boy continues south for a good two hundred meters. VC everywhere. Gonna spot us pretty quick. Over."

I looked downstream but couldn't see any of Duke's troops.

"Roger, One, Roger, Three. Hit 'em before you're spotted," Gritz ordered. "Recon, Two, Four, and the *bo-chi-huy* will be prepared to reinforce. Control, out."

"One, this is Three," I called to Duke. "Are you ready to move? Over."

"On your command. Over."

"Wait one."

Bob slid back down the bank.

"Captain says to hit 'em before they see us," I whispered. "Duke's ready to move on your command."

"Okay, you and Kien got the search," Bob said.

"Keep 'em movin'," I cautioned Luc. "Don't let 'em get pinned down."

"Okay, *Bac-si*."

I had learned from experience that during the initial stages of a raid on a base camp, the enemy commander would cautiously assess the strength of the attacking force. It was during this short-lived assessment period that a small, well-trained, raiding party could wreak havoc on a large base camp. If the enemy commander concluded that he was being hit by a superior force, his rear-guard elements would fight a delaying action. At the same time, his headquarters personnel and main force would break down into small units and withdraw to preplanned rendezvous points outside the base camp. If he concluded that he was being hit by an inferior force, he would immediately counterattack and attempt to destroy it. During a raid, our survival depended on our ability to think fast and react aggressively. The jungle was littered with the bleached bones of procrastinators.

I rejoined Kien high on the bank, and Bob, Luc, and Ly moved upstream to a position near the center of our line. The three enemy soldiers were still sitting on the log talking. I looked back at Bob and saw him standing with his hand over his head and his radio handset pressed to his ear. Seconds later, he lowered it forward.

"Here we go," I said to myself as I swallowed and climbed to the top of the bank. With my finger on the trigger and my weapon pointed at the three enemy soldiers, I suddenly felt very exposed. I could only hope that some enemy soldier wasn't in a concealed position with the front sight blade of his automatic weapon centered on my chest. To my right, the platoon was on line and advancing into the camp at a slow walk.

Whack-whack-whack. Someone from Duke's platoon opened up with a burst of automatic fire, and the Viet Cong sitting on the log sprang to their feet. Our entire line erupted, and I fired a sweeping burst at the three soldiers. Two of them were knocked off their feet; the third was hit in the chest by an exploding M-79 round.

"*Chey-yo*," the Bodes yelled as we swept forward with red tracers skimming the knee-high mist.

At the side of the log and earthen bunker, Kien and I stepped over a headless enemy soldier who lay in a pool of blood with his lungs protruding from the top of his torso. At the rear of the bunker, I tried to squeeze through its narrow entrance, but my bulging rucksack stopped me. Kien and I dropped our rucksacks to the ground and inside the dark, musty bunker found a Soviet 7.62mm light machine gun RP-46 silhouetted against the bright light of the aperture. It was set up on a bipod, with its flash suppressor extending out into the light, and was loaded with a 250-round metallic belt of ammunition.

"Get the gun," I told Kien.

"*Russi*," he said as he grabbed its carrying handle, telling me it was Russian.

Lined up on a ledge to the right of the aperture were four old American MK-2 fragmentation hand grenades. The cast-iron devices were covered with so much mold that you could barely see the yellow bands that identified them as TNT-filled grenades. On the floor against the rear wall was a wooden ammunition box and an open galvanized metal can of ammunition. Chinese characters and the Arabic numbers 7.62 were stenciled on both the box and the can. Dug into the floor in the darkness of the far corner was what appeared to be the entrance to a tunnel.

I quickly dropped the ammunition and three of the four grenades into the tunnel and heard them hit the ground a few feet below. Once outside the bunker I pulled the pin on the fourth grenade, reached back in through the entrance, and tossed it into the hole.

"One thousand, two thousand, three thousand," I counted as Kien and I ran for cover behind a nearby tree.

Whoomph! The grenade exploded and black smoke poured from the bunker.

Kien and I shouldered our rucksacks and ran to catch up with our advancing line. A short distance past the bunker, we came to the open-sided hootch with the corrugated tin roof. Inside, we found a long bamboo table with benches along both sides. I quickly grabbed a couple of papers that lay on the table and stuffed them into my pocket.

Whack-whack-whack. Poing . . . whumph. The firing continued as we again ran to close the gap with the platoon. We caught up as the men were moving past a line of spider holes. Lying next to one of the holes were two dead, khaki-clad Viet Cong.

A short distance past the spider holes, we found digging tools and baskets lying next to a new four-foot-deep, open trench. As the enemy dug the trench, they formed an underground tunnel by covering it with segments of green bamboo, a layer of thatch, and a few inches of dirt. They were using the baskets to carry away the extra dirt and had done an excellent job of camouflaging the completed section.

I leaned down into the open trench and, looking back into the completed section, saw that it led back to the machine-gun bunker.

Viet Cong base camps were generally characterized by defense in depth, and the tunnel was likely intended to be used to reinforce or resupply the machine-gun bunker. If necessary, the troops manning the bunker could also use it to withdraw to another line of resistance. I fired a burst into the dark tunnel and Kien tossed in a CS gas grenade.

A deafening cacophony of automatic fire and explosions filled the space beneath the canopy. Kien and I again ran forward and quickly came to a bamboo structure whose roof and sides were covered with American ponchos that had been sewn together.

We fired bursts into the structure, and when I pushed aside one of the ponchos, I found a smoke-filled room with a large earthen oven and racks of drying meat, the venison that we had smelled earlier. We ran from the smokehouse and saw that thirty meters ahead, our line of Bodes had hit the ground and was exchanging fire with the enemy. With green enemy tracers cutting through the foliage and thumping into the tree trunks, we continued forward and hit the ground next to Lieu, a rifleman in the first squad. Fifty meters farther into the base camp, a khaki-uniformed soldier ran from behind a tree, and a split second later disappeared beneath the blanket of knee-high mist. It didn't appear that he had been hit.

"VC *endout*." Lieu pointed. The Viet Cong were in a trench.

"Pon man?" I asked how many there were.

"Muoi pourk." A squad.

I couldn't see much of anything below the mist, but based on the level of firing, I figured that the trench extended across our entire front. Beyond the trench, M-79 rounds were exploding into the sides and roofs of eight to ten of the largest thatch and bamboo structures I had ever seen. They appeared to be living quarters.

Fifteen meters to our right and a few meters behind the line of Bodes, I spotted what appeared to be the side of another bunker. Running in a low crouch, Kien and I found it to be a mortar pit with an attached log and earthen ammunition bunker. In the center of the pit, the caustic gray smoke of a thermite grenade poured from the four-foot tube of a Soviet 82mm mortar. The grenade's intense heat would quickly burn through the tube and its base plate.

I jumped into the pit and lifted the torn burlap that hung over the entrance to the attached bunker. At the rear of the dark bunker, Thach was crouched with his arm wedged between a pile of ammunition boxes and the wall.

"I booby-trap!" He grinned.

"Good man," I yelled before crawling from the pit.

Twenty meters farther down the line, I saw Luc. Again running in a low crouch, Kien and I found him squatting in a pile of straw inside a fenced-in pen. Lying next to him with a bullet hole between its eyes was what had to be the world's biggest pig.

"Bunker," Luc yelled over the shooting and pointed to a square hole in the ground about eighteen inches across. "VC hide door under grass."

Kneeling in the straw next to him, I looked down into the dark moldy bunker and saw Binh lying on top of a pile of galvanized ammunition containers. He was positioning a claymore mine between the ammunition and the wall. Stacked against the wall to his right were twenty to thirty one-pound blocks of Soviet TNT. Most were wrapped in wax paper and labeled with cyrillic script and the Arabic number 400.

"*Bac-si*, do you know this?" Luc asked as he handed me a five-kilo sheet metal container that had a red horse stenciled on it and was labeled in both English and Chinese. In English it read: RED HORSE BRAND, MADE IN THE PEOPLE'S REPUBLIC OF CHINA, and DANGER—HANDLE WITH CARE.

"Red phosphorus," I told him. "They mix it with potassium chlorate or potassium nitrate to make explosive fillers for mines and booby traps. Don't mess with it."

"Jim." I turned and saw Bob approaching with the radio handset pressed to his ear. "They're movin' on our right flank," he panted and wiped the sweat from his eyes. "Maybe a company."

The news scared the hell out of me.

"Get down," I yelled to him as Luc reached down and pulled Binh from the bunker. "They're in a trench up ahead."

"Let's get outta here before they close the back door," Bob ordered.

"Okay," I said as Binh handed Luc the claymore's firing device and one hundred feet of S-rolled firing wire.

Luc raised his HT-1 radio to his lips and calmly issued instructions to the squad leaders.

Clap-clap-clap. A burst of rounds passed over my head. The clapping sound was an indication that they had only missed by inches.

Bob raised his whistle to his mouth and blew three long blasts.

"Break contact!" I yelled.

"Jim, I'll catch ya back on the stream," Bob said before heading back down the line to our right.

"Gimme those CS and Willy Pete grenades," I yelled to Kien as the platoon began leapfrogging to the rear. As one squad laid down a base of fire and the other two moved a short distance to the rear, Luc walked backward, unraveling the firing wire. As soon as everyone was clear of the bunker, I pulled the ring on the M-1 firing device, sprung to my feet, and ran to the rear. Fifty feet from the bunker, I found Luc and Thach standing behind a large tree with claymore firing devices cupped in their hands.

"All clear," I yelled as I joined them behind the tree.

They swung the safeties to the armed position and squeezed the handles on the firing devices.

Whoomph! Whoomph! Two earth-rending explosions pounded my eardrums. Looking around the side of the tree, I saw logs from the ammunition bunker's roof falling through thick black smoke in what appeared to be slow motion.

"Go!" I yelled.

We ran to the rear, and when we caught up with the platoon, I looked back and saw a noxious gray-white cloud of CS gas and white phosphorous smoke filling the space beneath the canopy. The squads continued to leapfrog to the rear, and when we reached the bank of the Suoi Lach Be, I found Son lying high on the bank with his M-60 pointed back into the camp. To our rear, the world's biggest pig was floating slowly downstream.

"Chloey sang kream!" Binh yelled that he had a prisoner as he and Sarine dragged a screaming khaki-uniformed soldier toward me.

"Aaahhh!" The wounded soldier yelled as they pulled him over the bank and he slammed to the ground below. He appeared to be in his late teens, was well built, and had a brush cut. His right leg and hip had been blown away, and with his dirt-covered intestines dragging behind him, he left a trail of blood and undigested food to where they left him lying. By the time I reached him, he lay choking on vomit.

"What the fuck am I supposed to do with this guy?" I yelled to Binh.

The young soldier looked up at me through terror-filled eyes, gagged as he tried to say something, and then lay still in the hot sun at the edge of the stream.

"He's dead," I said.

Ta-tow-tow. Son fired a machine-gun burst back into the camp.

When I looked up, I saw Bob peering over the top of the bank with a claymore mine firing device in each hand.

"Recon, Two, Four, and the *bo-chi-huy* are movin' east," he yelled to Luc as he looked to his rear. "Get 'em across."

"We got everyone?" I asked Rinh as we waded into the water.

"Yes, Donahue," he said. "Two minor shrapnel wounds. Nothing serious."

Whoomph! Whoomph! Bob detonated the claymores before he and Ly slid down the bank and splashed across the stream.

"I'll leave the machine gun and radio with you," he told me.

"Okay," I said.

Bob assumed his position at the head of the platoon and moved quickly to close the gap with the rest of the company.

"How many claymores you got?" I asked Thach as I reached into my pocket and counted four toe poppers.

"Two, *Bac-si,*" he responded as AK-47 fire continued to our rear.

As the platoon moved east, our five-man tail-gunner section fell in behind the last man. Thach was the first man in our section, followed by Son with the machine gun, Ly with the radio, myself, and Kien.

While pushing through wet, leaf-covered vines, I saw Duke Snider twenty meters to our right. He was walking

backward and was the last man in the other column. I gave
him a thumbs-up. With his radio pressed to his ear, he and his
radio operator moved to close the gap between us.

"Roger, Control," he said to Captain Gritz. "Everyone's
clear and movin' east. One, out."

"Biggest base camp I ever saw," I said as we walked together.

"Looked like Fort Bragg." He shook his head.

"How far in ya get?" I asked.

"Hundred meters."

"Same here," I said. "Hit a trench line."

"Same on the left." He used his scarf to wipe his face. "Got
out just in time."

"Trackers gonna be on us pretty quick," I said. "Got any
more of those Willy Pete–CS contraptions?"

"Ya liked that?" He grinned.

"I'll tell ya what. No one came through that gas."

"That was the last of the CS," he said as he handed me a
bulging claymore mine M-7 bandolier.

"What's this?"

"A Willy Pete taped to the front of the claymore," he said.
"It'll put a hurtin' on 'em."

"Thanks."

"Here we go again," he grimaced as he stopped and
dropped his drawers.

While Kien stood guard, I quickly buried a toe popper in
the center of the trail we were leaving.

"Damned green-apple two-step," Duke said.

"Whew!" I held my nose. "That'll kill 'em for sure."

When Duke finished, he returned to his platoon, and we
moved quickly to close the gap with the rest of the 3d Herd.
High above the canopy, I heard the welcome drone of the
FAC's O-1E approaching from the west. I crushed the vial on
the time pencil in one of my fragmentation hand grenades,
pulled the safety, and left it in the grass next to our back trail.
It probably wouldn't kill anyone, but when it exploded in
thirty minutes, it might convince enemy trackers that we were
someplace we weren't.

A hundred meters farther east, our route of march changed direction to the north. Ten meters to our right, Dave Rose popped a smoke canister, and a plume of yellow smoke was soon working its way up through the leafy stalks of green and tan bamboo. I crushed the vial in the time pencil on my last grenade and again left it in the grass at the side of our back trail.

"Bac-si." Ly handed me the radio handset as we moved.

"Control, this is Memphis," the FAC radioed Captain Gritz. "Got your yellow smoke. Over."

"Can ya give us a couple passes of twenty Mike-Mike between the yellow smoke and the base camp? Over," Gritz responded.

"Roger, Control. I'll have a flight of fast movers on station in zero-two minutes. Got a lot of smoke all along the stream. Over."

"Memphis, the center of the base camp is due west of the yellow smoke. Control, out."

We continued to the north, and a long minute later, I heard the welcome whine of jets approaching from the west. When they arrived overhead, the sound of the FAC's engine changed as he dived to fire a marker round.

Whooosh . . . pop! A white phosphorous round exploded to our rear, and molten white streamers blew up through the canopy and arced against the blue sky. Seconds later, a jet streaked in low from the west.

Burrrrr! Its twenty-millimeter cannons tore into our back trail and any trackers who might be on it. As we continued north past flat-top mango trees, another jet strafed the same area. Minutes later, we again hit the slow-moving waters of the Suoi Lach Be. Looking at my map, I figured that we had put about four hundred meters between us and the base camp.

We crossed the stream and headed west past clumps of black-and-brown bamboo. The dead and dying stalks were covered with mold and bowed to the ground.

Karoumph, karoumph, karoumph. Seven-hundred-fifty-pound bombs exploded in the enemy base camp. There was a muffled secondary explosion, and a second later, a jet screeched low over the canopy.

By 1000 hours (10:00 A.M.), the jungle had turned into a steam bath. We were moving through an area of towering trees and thick secondary growth, and the few patches of mist that remained drifted among the leaves in the upper reaches of the canopy.

Whack-whack-whack. Whump-whump-whump. An exchange of M-16 and AK-47 fire erupted at the end of the other column.

Ly handed me the radio handset as we continued to move.

"Fox Control, this is Fox One. Over," Duke radioed.

"One, this is Control. Over," Captain Gritz responded.

"Control, had three khaki-uniformed Victor Charlie sniffin' our back trail. They broke contact to the east. Negative casualties. Over."

"Trackers," I whispered to Kien as we walked backward with our weapons at the ready.

"Roger, One; wait one," Gritz said. "Memphis, this is Fox Control. Over."

"Control, this is Memphis," the FAC responded.

"Memphis, Clyde's on our tail. Can you divert a couple fast movers? Over."

"Roger, Control. I've got nape and HE," the FAC responded. "Where d'ya want it? Over."

"Memphis, this is One," Duke broke in. Can you give me napalm seventy-five meters east of the red smoke? Over."

"Can do, One. Got your smoke."

Whooosh . . . pop! The FAC's marker rocket exploded to the rear, and our pace suddenly picked up. Less than a minute later, an F-4 Phantom's engines screamed as it streaked in low. For a second, I saw the F-4 and its silver napalm containers tumbling lazily end over end.

Kawhoosh! An orange-yellow-and-black fireball erupted to our rear, and an agonizing human scream reverberated beneath the canopy.

"Memphis, this is One. You do good work. Over."

"Roger, One. Got one more nape," the FAC replied as the pungent smell of burning gas permeated the air. "Where d'ya want it? Over."

"Memphis, they gotta be backpedalin'. Lay it in fifty meters east of the first strike, over."

"Roger, One. Fifty meters east."

Seconds later another Phantom streaked in just above the canopy and left its load of liquid hell spilling down through the trees.

With Kien walking backward a couple of paces behind me, I looked at my map as we continued west under the spreading leaves of the great trees.

Karoumph, karoumph, karoumph. More bombs exploded to the southeast.

"The base camp," I said to Luc as another Phantom roared overhead.

There weren't any prominent terrain features that I could use to give me an exact fix on our location. However, based on our pace, route of march, and azimuth to the exploding bombs, I figured that we were about five hundred meters west of the Suoi Lach Be.

As we pressed on over relatively flat terrain, I thought about the trackers and hoped that they weren't the three-man point element of a large enemy force. Viet Cong Main Force units were generally organized in groups of three: three men to a cell, three cells to a squad, three squads to a platoon, three platoons to a company, three companies to a battalion, three battalions to a regiment, and three regiments to a division.

By late morning, the heat was stifling, and for over an hour, we threaded our way west through a steaming tangle of thick undergrowth and thorn-covered vines. Suddenly, our pace slowed and then stopped. While bending forward to relieve the strain on my shoulders, I saw Duke and his radio operator standing less than ten meters away.

"Feelin' any better?" I asked as I closed the gap between us.

"Yeah, diarrhea stopped," he said as he wiped the sweat from his eyes.

"Worst thing I ever smelled," I joked. "Attractin' every VC in the area."

"That ain't no lie," he mused. "Hey, looks like we're takin' a break. I'll catch ya later."

Twenty meters ahead, the Bodes were lowering their rucksacks to the ground, and Bob and Luc were moving down the line in my direction. I checked my Seiko and saw that it was 1140 hours (11:40 A.M.).

"Jim, captain wants to see ya," Bob whispered.

"What's goin' on?"

"Fresh tracks up ahead," he said. "We're gonna stop while they check it out."

"Okay," I said as I lowered my rucksack to the ground.

"Tie 'em in tight with the first and second platoons," Bob told Luc. "Four-man claymore ambush on our back trail."

"Okay, *Trung-si*."

Near the center of our cigar-shaped hasty perimeter, I found the captain kneeling in a depression with his map spread out in front of him. Tom Horn and two Bodes were busy clearing a path for his PRC-74 radio antenna, and Captain Johnson was looking skyward, with his radio handset pressed to his ear. High above the canopy, the FAC was approaching from the south.

"Jimmy," Gritz smiled. "Got the colors in your ruck?"

"Yes, sir. American and Khmer Serei flags," I said. "We gonna make it into Phuoc Vinh today?"

"Yeah, late in the day." He nodded.

"Now!" Johnson said into the handset as the FAC passed directly overhead.

"We're about ten klicks out," Gritz told me. "Break 'em out after we cross the Rach Rat. From there, it'll be a straight shot into Dodge."

"Yes, sir." I smiled.

"Roger, Memphis," Captain Johnson said to the FAC.

"Get the coordinates?" Gritz asked Johnson.

"Yeah, 060 506."

Gritz marked the position on his map, and I headed back to

the perimeter, where I found Rinh and Sarine sitting next to my rucksack.

"Bac-si." Sarine smiled as Rinh poured some calamine lotion into the palm of his hand.

"How ya doin', my friend?"

"Poison ivy," Rinh told me.

Ten meters to our right, Bob was positioning our M-60 machine gun, and five meters to our left, two members of Duke's platoon were setting up a claymore mine in front of their position. Ten meters to their left, Duke and Dave were talking to Chote, the first platoon interpreter.

I still had the claymore mine with the white phosphorous grenade taped across its front, so I carried it to a position ten meters outside the perimeter and pushed its legs into the ground on the far side of a decaying stump. If I had to detonate the mine, the stump would shield us from its backblast.

Security in place, I sat with my back against my rucksack and swallowed a couple of salt tablets with a long drink of water. In the branches above our heads, a few small yellow birds chirped as they fluttered from branch to branch, and high above the canopy, large cotton-white clouds drifted in a pale blue sky.

As I sat watching the Bodes, I sensed the excitement that always existed on the last day of an operation. We would probably spend the night at Phuoc Vinh and fly back to Trang Sup in the morning. I was looking forward to getting back to Trang Sup and down to Bien Hoa to see Ngoi again. Whenever I got into town for more than a few hours, I took her out to a movie and dinner. The last movie we saw was a Turkish-made cowboy movie with Vietnamese subtitles.

"Looks like we're gonna make it into Phuoc Vinh today," I told Rinh.

"Yes. I am very happy." He smiled.

Sarine said something I didn't understand.

"What's that?" I asked.

"He says that his wife is waiting at Trang Sup," Rinh told me. "She took a bus from Soc Trang."

"You should take her into Tay Ninh to visit the Cao Dai Temple," I told Sarine. "Let me know if you need a ride."

As Rinh translated my words, I reached into my pocket and pulled out the documents I had picked up in the base camp. They were soaked with sweat but could still be read.

"Thank you, *Bac-si,*" Sarine responded.

"What's this?" I handed Rinh a four-page document.

"We're tied in tight," Bob whispered as he and Luc lowered their rucksacks to the ground to my right.

"Everyone's excited about goin' back to Trang Sup," I said.

"Yeah, I told Luc to stay on the squad leaders," Bob said. "We ain't outta here yet."

"Anxious to see your family?" I asked Luc as he used a pliers to remove the bullet from a 7.62-mm AK-47 brass shell casing.

"Yes, *Bac-si.*" He grinned. "My son now have son. Now I ahhh . . ."

"Grandfather," Rinh said.

"Yes, grandfather." Luc smiled.

"An old fart." Bob chuckled as Luc poured the powder from the brass casing and replaced it with a piece of white detonating cord.

"This is propaganda," Rinh said softly as he examined the document, and Luc used the pliers to push the bullet back into the end of the shell casing. "It says that in December 1961"—he paused—"the Vietnamese Marxist-Leninists met and decided to form the"—he again paused—"ahhh, the Vietnamese People's Revolutionary Party. Then it lists the objectives of the party."

"I leave on trail," Luc told us as he slipped the booby-trapped AK-47 round into his pocket. If the round was picked up and used by the enemy, it would explode and kill or wound whoever fired it.

"And this?" I unfolded another wet document and handed it to Rinh.

"Ambush in position?" Bob asked Luc.

"Yes, *Trung si.* Seventy-five meter east."

"This is more propaganda," Rinh told me as he examined the document.

"What's it say?" I asked.

"Mmmm." He strained to read the faded print. "That the South Vietnamese workers realize that to defend their interests"—he hesitated—"they must have a party that is allied with the peasants . . ."

"VC!" Luc pointed.

The sight scared me. Fifty meters to our left front, a large number of heavily armed, khaki-clad Viet Cong in green pith helmets skirted our perimeter as they moved from north to south. They were bunched up—five to six abreast—and appeared to be in a hurry.

Whack-whack-whack. Whoomph, whoomph. Duke's platoon opened up with the ripple of M-16s and exploding claymore mines.

I moved my selector switch to automatic and, from a kneeling position, fired a full magazine into the enemy formation. Falling forward into a prone position, I quickly changed magazines and chambered a round.

Twenty meters away, the Viet Cong yelled "Yaaaaa" as they ran toward us with their mouths wide open and weapons flashing.

Whoomph! Bob fired the claymore with the attached white phosphorous grenade and burned a gaping hole in the enemy formation. I fired a second sweeping burst into the enemy ranks and, glancing to my right, saw Luc jerk violently as a round exited his lower back in what appeared to be slow motion.

Clap-clap-clap. A burst of rounds just missed my head.

I ducked, changed magazines, chambered a round, and when I looked up, four Viet Cong were running toward us through swirling white smoke. I fired a burst and hit the first one high in the chest. The top half of his body was knocked to the rear and he landed flat on his back. Bob fired and the second soldier's head exploded into a fine red mist.

Whoomph! Sarine fired a canister round from his M-79

and, at close range, caught the third Viet Cong in the mid-section. Pieces of intestines, blood, and undigested food exploded from his back, and he slammed to the ground a few feet in front of us.

"Aaahhh!" He looked up, and Ly fired a round into his open mouth.

I glanced to my left and saw Sarine firing another canister round from a kneeling position. A split second later, a piece of skull and hair exploded from the side of his head, and he slumped to the ground.

To our front, the space beneath the canopy was filled with white smoke. Standing motionless in the smoke was a man with no face. The top half of his khaki uniform was black and smoldering, and all that remained of his face was a mass of bleeding flesh and bone.

Ta-tow-tow-tow. Son cut him down with a burst from his M-60.

"Control, this is Three," Bob radioed Captain Gritz, as he lay on the ground with his M-16 at the ready and the firing and explosions continued.

Rinh and I crawled to Luc and found him lying on his side with his hands over his abdominal area. His bloodshot eyes were glassy, and his ashen skin was wet with sweat.

"I okay, *Bac-si,*" he said and pointed to Sarine.

"Control, this is Three," Bob said into the handset. "Got a large enemy force at six o'clock. We're takin' casualties. Can you get us TAC air? Over."

Rinh and I crawled to Sarine and found him lying on his back. The ground beneath his head was wet with cerebrospinal fluid and blood, and his light brown skin had turned a pale sallow color. He appeared to be close to death.

"*Bac-si,* I die," he said softly as I cradled his head in my hands and examined his wound.

I was overcome with emotion and couldn't say anything. It didn't look good. A three-inch section of skull had been blown from the side of his head. Part of his brain was exposed and a stream of blood was pulsating from a severed blood vessel. I took in a deep breath.

"Mit neung ot ei te," I said assuring him he would be okay.

Rinh handed me a hemostat clamp, and I clamped it to the end of the bleeding vessel. While I held the clamp, Rinh tied off the vessel using a piece of black surgical thread.

"Get a dressing," I told Rinh as blood continued to pour down the side of his neck.

"Chheu reu te?" I asked Sarine if he was in pain.

"Te, ot chheu te." He said that he wasn't.

"No air for ten minutes," Bob yelled as he tossed a smoke grenade in front of our position. "FAC's in contact with FDC at Phuoc Vinh. Gonna get us artillery."

Rinh removed a battle dressing from its paper wrapper, and while I held it in place over the wound, he tied it to Sarine's head. Blood quickly saturated the dressing and continued to run over my hands and down the side of Sarine's neck.

"Need more pressure," I told Rinh. "Get an Ace."

"Roger, Memphis. Troops in the open. Fifty meters east of the purple smoke," Bob said to the FAC.

Whoomph! A trail of gray smoke led to where a rocket-propelled grenade exploded against a nearby tree.

"RPG," I yelled to Bob as we were showered with pieces of bark and wood. "Smoke's attractin' fire."

"Negative VT. I say again, negative VT," Bob said to the FAC. "We're between the guns and the target. Gimme a Willy Pete fifty meters east of the purple smoke. Will adjust HE. Over."

A variable time artillery round produced an air burst and was the most effective type of round against troops in the open. However, when you were between the guns and a target, there was a danger that a short round would explode over your head rather than the enemy's.

"Get it tight," I told Rinh as I held Sarine's head, and he rolled an Ace bandage over the battle dressing and around his head.

With a tight Ace bandage in place, the bleeding finally

stopped. Glancing down the line I saw Duke and Dave carrying a wounded Bode toward the *bo-chi-huy*.

"Let's get to Luc," I said as I carefully lowered Sarine's head to the ground.

Luc was still lying on his side with his hands over his wound.

"Bac-si." He grimaced. "Not good."

"Don't worry, partner," I said. "We're gonna get ya outta here."

Karoumph! A white phosphorous artillery round exploded to the east, and white streamers arced high above the canopy.

"Memphis, this is Three," Bob radioed the FAC. "You're on target. Fire for effect."

"Let's get ya outta that harness," I said as I carefully unbuckled Luc's BAR belt.

Rinh pulled the harness from Luc's shoulders, and I unbuttoned his fatigue jacket. His belly was as hard as a bowling ball, and two inches to the left of his belly button was a small, dark red bullet hole that was ringed in black and oozed bright red blood.

Karoumph, karoumph, karoumph. The ground shook as an artillery barrage exploded to the east and shock waves rippled through the foliage.

"No serious bleeding." I smiled as hundreds of leaves floated through the white smoke.

"Do you want to start an IV?" Rinh asked.

"Yeah, get his blood pressure," I said as I lifted Luc's jacket. On the left side of his lower back, I found an exit wound that was the size of a dime. Although there was no observable bleeding, I worried that he might be bleeding to death internally.

"Roger, Memphis," Bob said to the FAC. "They were movin' north to south. Walk it north in fifty-meter increments. Over."

While Rinh wrapped a blood-pressure cuff around Luc's arm, I placed four-inch squares of sterile gauze over the entrance and exit wounds, and covered them with surgical tape.

"His systolic blood pressure is eighty-four," Rinh said with concern.

That worried me too. The fact that his systolic blood pressure had fallen below ninety was a good indication that he had serious internal bleeding. When a fast-moving bullet tore through soft tissue, it often destroyed large amounts of the surrounding tissue. Even if no major blood vessels were damaged, shock could result if a large volume of blood leaked into the surrounding tissues from damaged smaller vessels. If we didn't quickly stabilize his blood pressure, he could go into irreversible shock and die.

"Okay," I said as more artillery rounds exploded. "Get some epinephrine ready. I'll start the IV."

I taped a bottle of normal saline to a sapling and extended its plastic tubing while Rinh prepared the epinephrine injection. Using my thumb to hold a vein in place on the back of his hand, I worked the needle into the vessel. I then taped the needle in place and opened the regulator on the IV tubing.

"Looking good," I said as the clear salt water flowed through the tube and into his vein.

"Should I give him morphine?" Rinh asked as he injected 0.2 milligrams of epinephrine into the IV tubing.

"Yeah, doesn't appear to be any respiratory involvement," I said as artillery rounds exploded to the northeast.

The epinephrine would constrict his blood vessels and increase his blood pressure, and the morphine would ease the pain and, I hoped, slow his descent into irreversible shock.

"Jim." Bob grabbed my arm. "Gritz wants to see ya."

"Okay," I said. "Rinh, hook Sarine up to an IV and hit 'im with some Demerol."

"Okay, Donahue."

Running in a low crouch, I found Captain Gritz standing in the depression with his radio handset pressed to his ear. To his rear, Captain Johnson and Tom Horn were kneeling over a wounded Bode who had a battle dressing covering his abdominal area and an IV running into his arm.

"Roger, One," Gritz said into the handset. "Jimmy, we

gotta break contact. How d'ya wanna handle the dead and wounded?"

"Got a count, sir?" I asked.

"Two dead." He paused. "Maybe a dozen with serious wounds."

"Too many to cache," I said as firing erupted along the southern side of our perimeter. "Let's get 'em in hammocks and up to the *bo-chi-huy*."

Carrying the dead and wounded would slow us down, but sometimes there were no easy solutions. If we had only one or two casualties, we could hide them in the underbrush, move quickly to break contact, and then return to recover them later in the day. However, if we tried to hide more than a few men, the enemy would likely find and kill them.

"Jim, take a look at this," Captain Johnson said as he gently lifted the dressing over the Bode's abdominal wound. "Mitch was our first sergeant on Blackjack-32."

"Roger, Memphis," Gritz said to the FAC. "Gimme a distance and direction to an LZ."

Mitch's wound was similar to Luc's. There was a small, round bullet hole an inch below his belly button.

"Got an exit wound?" I asked.

"No," Johnson said. "It's still in there."

"We gave him morphine," Horn said.

"All ya can do is start an IV and try to control the pain," I said. "He's gonna need major surgery."

Captain Johnson called me aside.

"Mitch gonna make it?" he asked with concern.

"Sir, it depends on what the bullet hit," I said. "If he's alive in thirty minutes, we'll know it didn't hit anything important."

"He's probably survived a hundred battles," Captain Johnson shook his head. "Now it's come down to this."

"Roger, Memphis," Gritz said as a flight of jets arrived overhead. "Can you clear the way to the north? Over."

"Got an LZ?" Johnson asked Gritz as firing continued along the south side of the perimeter.

"Yeah, a sandbar on the Rach Rat," Gritz said. "Seven hundred meters on two-seven-zero. We'll move north for a hundred meters, then west to the LZ."

"Three columns?" Johnson asked.

"Yeah, Recon, Four, and One on the right; Two and Three on the left; the *bo-chi-huy* and the wounded in between."

I returned to the perimeter and found the air filled with the acrid scents of spent gunpowder and white phosphorous. Bob had assigned Thach as the acting platoon sergeant, and he and two other Bodes were out in front of the platoon picking up weapons and searching enemy bodies for anything of intelligence value. Many of the smaller trees around them had been split like matchsticks, and here and there, wispy, ghostlike tendrils of smoke drifted in the still, hot air.

Rinh had placed Luc and Sarine in hammocks attached to ten-foot sections of green bamboo and moved them to the relative safety of a nearby depression. A bright shaft of sunlight angled through a hole in the canopy and illuminated the area around their hammocks. The unexpected beauty of dust, smoke, and colorful butterflies dancing through the light stopped me in midstep.

"Jim!" Bob's voice brought me back to reality. "You and Rinh stay with the wounded."

"Okay," I said. "Ambush back?"

"Yeah, scared the piss outta 'em."

"See ya on the LZ," I said as I lifted my rucksack to my back, and another jet streaked in low from the east.

"Donahue," Rinh called as he approached with four men to carry the hammocks.

"Let's get 'em up to the *bo-chi-huy*," I said. "Tell the guys to keep the IVs above the hammocks."

Kawhoosh! Napalm spilled down through the trees on the north side of the perimeter.

Rinh issued instructions to the men, and with heavy rucksacks on their backs, they struggled to lift the bamboo poles to their shoulders.

"We'll get ya to an American doctor," I assured Luc as we moved toward the *bo-chi-huy*.

"Okay, *Bac-si*." He forced a smile.

Nearing the *bo-chi-huy*, we ran into Dave Rose and twelve men from the 1st Platoon carrying six more hammocks.

"Two dead, four wounded. All gunshot wounds," he told me as we walked together.

I looked into one of his hammocks and saw a Bode with a tourniquet, a blood-soaked battle dressing, and an improvised bamboo splint attached to his lower leg.

"Nasty compound fracture." Dave shook his head. "He could lose it."

By the time we reached the *bo-chi-huy*, the columns to our left and right were moving north, and another jet was screeching in low from the east. I reached into Sarine's hammock to check his IV and found him unconscious but still breathing.

Kawhoosh! More napalm spilled through the trees to the north.

I was relieved that we were moving north rather than continuing directly west to the landing zone. Predictability was an invitation to sudden death.

"Here we go, partner," I said to Luc as an F-105 knifed in from the east with its twenty-millimeter cannons spitting out six thousand rounds a minute.

As we followed the *bo-chi-huy* north, I thought about our contact with the enemy. My guess was that they were working with the three trackers that Duke's platoon ran into earlier in the morning. While the trackers followed our back trail and maintained a fix on our location, the main force likely remained one to two hundred meters behind them. When we stopped, the enemy commander probably viewed it as an opportunity to move ahead of us to set up an ambush. While moving on our flank, he must have thought that he was farther west than he actually was, and when he turned south to set up his ambush, he ran into us. His troops paid the price for his miscalculation.

Thinking about what might have been sent a shiver up the length of my spine. If they had succeeded in moving ahead of us, and had had time to set up a large horseshoe-shaped ambush, it might have meant the end of the Mobile Guerrilla Force. Vietnam was like that. It was the small things that made the difference between life and death.

A short distance outside the perimeter, we entered an area where the napalm had done its work. The steaming ground beneath my feet was covered with a layer of fine black ash, and foliage hung in blackened shreds from the charred trunks of trees. A blanket of slow-moving, blue-gray smoke drifted across the silent battlescape, and the nauseating scent of burnt flesh filled my nostrils.

One hundred meters north of our perimeter, we changed direction and headed west toward the landing zone. With the added weight of their rucksacks on their backs, the two Bodes who were carrying Luc were drenched with sweat, stumbling, and were close to passing out.

"Let's take 'im," I told Rinh.

Without losing a step, we transferred Luc to our shoulders and soon entered an area of fifty-foot stalks of tan bamboo. With little overhead cover to protect us, a blistering sun beat down on us.

"Bac-si," Luc said softly from his hammock.

"Yeah."

"If I die, take me my son?"

"Hey, you're goin' to the 24th Evac in Bien Hoa," I said as I tried to conceal my emotions. "One of the best hospitals in the world."

"Bac-si." He looked up at me through sad bloodshot eyes. There was no bullshitting the old soldier. He knew that his survival was a crap shoot.

"You know I will," I assured him as I wiped tears and sweat from my eyes. "He at Trang Sup?"

"No, he work B-Team in Tay Ninh," he said. "Thach know his house."

The fact that Luc was still alive was a good indication that the bullet hadn't severed a major blood vessel. If we could get him to an American surgeon within five or six hours, he had a good chance of surviving. The surgeon would cut open his abdomen and conduct a detailed examination of the organs in his peritoneal cavity. Generally, a gunshot wound of this type caused multiple perforations of the intestines. If he wasn't properly cared for, his feces would contaminate the cavity, and he would die of a peritoneal infection. Sarine was in the same boat. We had to get him to a competent neurosurgeon, and we had to do it quickly.

As we struggled with the hammocks, jets continued to clear the way to the west and pound our back trail to the east. In between the air strikes, the FAC worked both flanks with artillery fire from Phuoc Vinh.

At 1410 hours (2:10 P.M.), we hit a shallow creek and, on its far side, reached the sandbar. It was twenty meters wide and was a good seventy-five meters long. Growing from its gravelly soil were scattered stalks of green bamboo and small saplings. By the time I reached the center of the sandbar, Captain Gritz had security in place, and Tom Horn and a dozen Bodes were busy clearing an area that would be large enough to accommodate a Huey.

"Get 'em off to the side." Gritz pointed as he stood with his nine-millimeter Swedish-K submachine gun under his arm and his radio handset pressed to his ear. "Choppers two minutes out."

Dave and I lined the hammocks up along the bank of the Rach Rat. The slow-moving stream measured about ten meters across and appeared to be well over our heads. I dropped my rucksack to the ground and swallowed two salt tablets with a long drink of water. I was light-headed, and I don't think I could have carried Luc much farther. Looking up, I saw the welcome sight of the FAC's O-1E drifting in the pale blue sky.

Wap, wap, wap. Choppers were approaching from the south.

"Roger, Memphis," Gritz said into his radio handset. "Give 'em a smoke," he told Tom Horn.

"Get 'em ready," Dave told the Bodes.

I knelt next to Sarine's hammock and pulled the nylon from his face. He was still unconscious but had a strong pulse.

"Here they come," Dave said.

"Good luck, my friend," I said as I squeezed Sarine's hand.

A twisting trail of purple smoke poured from the canister and filled the clearing. Gliding in over the leafy stalks of bamboo, the green hull of the first Huey appeared to shimmer as it descended through wave after wave of rising heat. Nearing the sandbar, its nose suddenly rose to slow its speed. With its main rotor slapping the humid air at over three hundred rpm, the pilot lowered the nose at the last possible second, kicked up a cloud of dust, and sat down in a clearing that wasn't much larger than the length of the chopper.

"Let's go!" Dave yelled.

Rinh and I shouldered the bamboo attached to Luc's hammock, covered our eyes with our arms to protect them against blowing grass and dust, and moved to the side of the chopper. With the rotor pulsating a few feet above our heads, Rinh handed his end of the bamboo to a crew member, and we slid Luc across the chopper's floor.

"The wounded go to the 24th Evac in Bien Hoa and the dead to Trang Sup Special Forces Camp in Tay Ninh Province," I told the American.

"The Viets go to Cong Hoa hospital in Saigon," he yelled as Dave Rose and the Bodes slid three more hammocks into the chopper next to Luc.

Luc and Sarine would die if they were evacuated to a Vietnamese hospital. "General Hay wants the wounded taken directly to the 24th," I said with authority.

"Yes, sir." He nodded.

"I'll be down to see ya in a few days," I said to Luc as a few additional Bodes climbed aboard and took up seats with their backs against the fire wall.

"Bac-si." Luc shook my hand.

We ran the short distance back to the edge of the stream, and when we turned back to the chopper, it appeared that the pilot was having difficulty hovering straight up until he cleared the bamboo. With hot black fumes pouring from its engine, the Huey finally tilted forward, transitioned to forward flight, and climbed above the bamboo.

Seconds later, another chopper touched down, and we soon had it loaded with the remainder of the wounded. One of the Bodes was sitting with his back to the pilot's station with a guilty-as-hell expression on his face.

"Wait a minute," I said to myself.

It was Hoi, the guy Rinh was treating for gonorrhea. I reached into the cabin and grabbed him by his harness.

"Mit trove robours canlang nar?" I asked him where he was wounded.

He didn't respond.

"Chheu nas," Thach bellowed as he grabbed Hoi's arm, and we yanked him from the chopper.

"Jimmy, what was that about?" Captain Gritz asked as Thach dragged Hoi into the bamboo.

"The bullheaded clap, sir," I yelled over the noise of the engine and rotors. "He ain't wounded."

"Depends on how you look at it." He shook his head and laughed.

With the last of the wounded on board, we ran back to the edge of the stream.

"We're gonna cross a hundred meters north," Bob told me as we shielded our eyes from the blowing dust, and the chopper lifted from the clearing. "Three, the *bo-chi-huy*, and Four on the right; Two and One on the left. Recon's gonna set up stay-behinds."

"Okay," I said as I lifted my rucksack to my back and bounced up and down to settle the load.

From the clearing, we moved north along the bank of the Rach Rat in two columns. Kien was on the point of the column on the right and was followed by myself, Bob, Ly, and

Thach. Jim Battle was on the point of the column on the left and was followed by Bill Ferguson and his radio operator, Kim, and Hien with the machine gun. Both banks of the stream were lined with clumps of green-tan-and-brown bamboo. Near the ground, the fifty-foot stalks were bundled together, but at the higher levels, the weight of their leaves bowed them out over the Rach Rat. In the shade of the bamboo, hungry red dragonflies cruised the water's surface in search of mosquitoes. Near the center of the stream, the sunlight penetrated the foliage, and in those areas, large yellow butterflies drifted in and out of the light.

A short distance north of the sandbar, we found Ray Fratus and Recon Team Bravo set up along the bank of the stream.

"Only crossing in the area," Fratus whispered. "Stik's on the other side."

I followed Kien into the waist-deep stream, and while moving across, I washed the dried blood from my hands, splashed some water on my face, and rinsed the dirt and sweat from my camouflaged bush hat. Standing on the far bank, I found Stik Rader and a Bode from Recon Team Delta.

"Hey, Jim," Stik smiled as he reached down to pull me up on the bank.

"Any sign of Charlie?" I asked.

"No, we got teams a hundred meters north, south, and west," he told me. "Once we get everyone across we're gonna booby-trap the hell outta the area."

"See ya in Phuoc Vinh," I said as I checked my compass and pointed Kien west on 270 degrees.

One hundred meters from the stream, we stopped in a bamboo thicket to wait for the rest of the company to complete the crossing. While Bob and Thach positioned two-man security teams to the north, south, and west, I dropped my rucksack to the ground.

"We need a piece of green bamboo for the flags," I whispered to Rinh as I pulled a clear plastic bag from the bottom of my rucksack. When I removed the folded American and

Khmer-Serai flags from the bag, I discovered that my rucksack and the flags had been hit by a bullet.

"Is this okay?" Rinh asked as he handed me an eight-foot section of bamboo.

"Claymores out," Bob said as he lowered his rucksack to the ground next to mine.

"Perfect," I told Rinh.

While I held the pole, Rinh cut pieces of 550 parachute line and used them to attach the flags.

"Lookin' good." Bob grinned as I waved the flags back and forth over my head.

"The holes add somethin'." I smiled.

"Who's gonna carry 'em?" Bob asked.

"Old Kien's been bustin' his butt," I whispered. "He deserves the honor."

"Watch this." Bob chuckled. "Rinh, tell Kien to take the flags and report to Captain Gritz. He's gonna carry 'em into Phuoc Vinh."

Kien overheard what was said and snapped to attention with a shit-eating grin on his face.

"I do, *Trung si.*" He saluted.

As Kien hurried to tuck his trousers in his boots and straighten his hat, Bob, Rinh, and I were doubled over with laughter.

"Here ya go, buddy." I handed him the flags and shook his hand.

Old Kien was something to behold. With the pole pressed to his shoulder he moved down the line with a peacock-proud, kick-my-ass-if-you-can strut.

"Trung si." Ly handed Bob the radio handset.

"Fox Control, this is Fox Three. Over," Bob said.

"Let's get on home, my friend," I said to Rinh as the expression on Bob's face turned serious.

"Roger, Control," Bob said. "Three, out."

"What's up?" I asked.

"We're movin' to an LZ," Bob said as he looked at his map.

"How far?"

"Four thousand meters."

"We're not walkin' in?" I asked as he marked the location on his map.

"No, a Sigma chopper was shot down," he said. "Gritz volunteered to secure the crash site."

"Any casualties?"

"Five wounded," he said. "Two SF, a pilot, an interpreter, and a roadrunner."

"The LZ hot?" I asked.

"Don't know."

Carrying Luc had exhausted me, but with the news of the downed chopper, adrenaline awakened my system, and I suddenly felt full of energy.

"Want me to take point?" I asked.

"Yeah; I'll navigate," Bob said.

With Bob a few paces behind me and the 2d Platoon thirty meters to our left, we continued west past clumps of tan bamboo. Thirty minutes later, we entered an area of two- and three-story trees with nothing but sun-bleached grass growing between them. With little overhead cover and a blazing sun beating down on me, sweat dripped from the tip of my nose and blurred my vision. After struggling through the oppressive heat and humidity for close to two hours, I slowed the pace when I heard what sounded like someone chopping wood to the southwest.

"Woodcutters," I turned and whispered to Bob.

"Yeah, I hear 'em," he said. "Gritz says to press on to the LZ. Don't stop for nothin'."

We resumed our brisk pace and soon saw smoke and heard more woodcutters to the north of our route of march. My guess was that they were making charcoal that would be sold in Phuoc Vinh. Close to an hour later, I felt a great sense of relief when we hit the eastern end of the landing zone. The clearing measured a good thousand meters long and two hundred meters across and was surrounded by tall cypress trees that appeared to shimmer in the heat. The area was covered with foot-long grass and was crisscrossed with overgrown rice-paddy dikes.

"Three hundred meters down the north side," Bob whispered and pointed. "Two and One got the south side."

"Right."

We continued just inside the wood line, and when we reached the three-hundred-meter point, I stopped, turned to Bob, and pointed to the ground.

"Two-man patrols fifty meters west and north," Bob whispered to Thach as I stood guard with my M-16 at the ready.

Once the patrols left and we had security in place, we dropped our rucksacks to the ground.

"Thach," I said. "Before we get on those choppers, make sure the weapons are on safe, the blasting caps are outta the claymores, and the pins on the grenades are taped down."

"Okay, *Bac-si,*" he nodded.

"Where we headed?" I asked Bob as he monitored radio transmissions and used a grease pencil to mark a location on his map.

"To 963 638," he pointed to another clearing on his map. "About fourteen klicks north-northwest."

"That's only three klicks from where Williams was killed," I said.

"Yeah, I know."

The Bodes overheard what was being said and immediately slipped their Buddhas back into their mouths.

"No VC," Thach told us when the patrols returned.

"Choppers one minute out," Bob said as he continued to monitor radio transmissions.

"What's the plan?" I asked.

"They'll lift out the Huey as soon as the LZ's secure," Bob said as we shouldered our rucksacks. "Third Herd's got the south side. Shouldn't be on the ground for more than fifteen minutes."

With the FAC circling overhead, I heard choppers approaching from the south. Someone from the *bo-chi-huy* tossed a canister into the clearing, and a coil of red smoke was soon drifting across the dry grass.

"Get 'em ready," Bob told Thach.

Thach radioed instructions to the squad leaders, and the platoon quickly moved out onto the landing zone in groups of eight to ten men. With a good twenty-five meters between each group, the platoon was spread out over an area the length of a football field.

Under a large, flat-bottomed white cloud, two lines of helicopters snaked in just above the trees. Seconds later, they lowered their noses and touched down simultaneously near each of our groups. As groups of men with heavy rucksacks on their backs moved through, blowing dust, the air filled with the smell of burnt aviation fuel. When we reached the side of the lead chopper on the right, we found the door gunner sitting nervously with his finger on the trigger of his M-60 machine gun.

"Let's go!" Bob yelled as he and I helped a few Bodes on board and then took up seats on the Huey's floor with our feet hanging out over the skid. Looking to our rear, I saw Thach and Rinh sitting in the other door.

Seconds later, the pilot pulled back on his collective, and the chopper shook as it kicked up more dust. Like a synchronized swim team, the two lines of choppers lifted to a few feet off the ground and transitioned to forward flight.

"Yahoo!" I yelled as we picked up speed. With a refreshing breeze blowing through the cabin, we were soon headed north-northwest beneath a dense, white cloud formation that billowed like a towering mountain into the blue sky. A thousand feet below, slow-moving shadows drifted across the broccoli-topped trees and wheat-colored clearings of War Zone D.

"The road to Dong Xoai." Bob pointed to a green-and-yellow civilian bus traveling north on the faded blacktop of Highway 1A. Its roof rack was crowded with cardboard boxes, suitcases, animals in bamboo crates, and three men in black who waved as we passed overhead.

The aircraft commander turned and yelled something to Bob that I couldn't understand.

"Movement south of the LZ," Bob hollered in my ear. "Could be hot." The news scared me. One or two automatic weapons in the wood line could cut us to pieces.

As soon as we reached altitude, the pilot slightly raised the nose of the chopper, and we began our descent back into the Forbidden Zone. I reached to place both feet on the skid, and with the prop wash tugging on my uniform and rucksack, I hung out the side of the chopper. Looking down and to our front, I saw that we were descending onto another sun-bleached clearing that measured more than a thousand meters long and three hundred meters across. The grassy area was surrounded by tall trees with dirty white trunks. A muddy east-west creek ran through its center.

"Helicopter," Thach yelled from the other door as he pointed down and to our left front.

I strained to look but couldn't see the downed Huey from our side of the chopper. Seconds later, the pilot lowered the nose of the chopper, and I moved my selector switch from safe to automatic. Just as we were about to set down in blowing grass, I jumped from the skid and fell to my knees in a foot of water.

"Shit," I mumbled as I struggled to my feet.

"Get 'em on line!" Bob yelled to Thach as the two lines of choppers lifted off simultaneously.

Looking across to the north side of the landing zone I saw our flags and a line of black-and-green uniforms moving toward the tall trees. I couldn't see the downed Sigma chopper but figured it had to be just inside the wood line. High above our heads, the everpresent O-1E drifted in a lazy circle, and just above the tree line, two helicopter gunships patrolled the perimeter like hungry dragonflies.

By the time Thach had the platoon on line and moving toward the southern side of the clearing, artillery rounds were exploding two to three hundred meters south of the wood line. We splashed through the water for a good fifty meters and stopped when we came to an east-west dike that had been built up a foot above the level of the water. The sides of the dike were overgrown with dry grass, and running along the top of it was a hard-packed clay trail that had been worn smooth by foot traffic.

"Set 'em up along the dike," Bob yelled to Thach.

"Okay, *Trung si.*"

While Thach and the squad leaders were positioning the men along our side of the dike, a Huey and a twin-engine CH-47A Chinook helicopter had arrived over the other side of the clearing.

"Fox Control, this is Fox Three. Over," Bob radioed Captain Gritz as the Huey landed near our flags and the Chinook continued to hover above the tree line.

"Control, this is Three," Bob said. "We're in knee-deep water about seventy-five meters from the wood line. We're settin' up along a north-south dike. Over."

"Keep 'em off the dike," I told Thach. "Could be booby-trapped."

"Okay, *Bac-si.*"

"Roger, Control. Three, out," Bob said as a few men ran from the Huey. They were carrying what looked like a large canvas bag and disappeared into the wood line.

"Lifting straps," I said to Bob as the Chinook continued to hover and lowered a cable into the trees.

"My last one." Bob handed Thach a toe popper and pointed to the dike.

"Okay, *Trung-si,*" Thach said as he removed his knife from its sheath and moved to the dike.

"Damn buffalo leeches." Bob pulled a five-inch leech from his trousers and tossed it to the other side of the dike. "Place is crawlin' with 'em."

"Many VC walk here," Thach said as he straddled the dike and used his knife to chip out a small hole in the sun-baked clay.

"There it is," I said as the Chinook lifted the Sigma

chopper into full view. The Huey's main rotors had been removed to keep it stable during the sling-load operation. There didn't appear to be any serious structural damage.

With the four-ton Huey dangling from the cable beneath the Chinook, the CH-47 slowly picked up speed and altitude as its Lycoming T-55 turbo engines screamed. Seconds later, the Huey on the ground lifted off, and someone on the far side of the clearing popped a yellow smoke.

More choppers were approaching from the south.

"Let's move it," I told Thach as he pulled the safety clip from the toe popper and placed the olive drab device in the hole.

"Get 'em ready," Bob said. "We're goin' home."

"Go ahead," I told Thach. "I'll finish it."

I pulled a canteen from my BAR belt, straddled the dike, and poured some water on the dry clay chips that covered the mine. As the gunships continued to work the perimeter, I added more water and gently rubbed the surface chips until they turned to mud. I then used my finger to smooth a thin coat of mud and blend it into the surrounding clay. Once it dried, the booby trap would be impossible to spot.

"Jim!" Bob yelled. "Let's go!"

"Okay," I said as I quickly used my hat to brush away loose chips and straighten the grass at the sides of the dike.

By the time I finished, the platoon was breaking down into eight- to ten-man groups. As Bob and I splashed toward the nearest group, two lines of Hueys glided in over the tree line from the west.

A chopper touched down in the water a short distance from each of our groups. When Bob and I reached the door to ours, we again took up seats with our feet dangling out over the skid. Seconds later, the pilot pulled up on the collective, and with our main rotors slapping and popping, the chopper shook as we lifted a few feet off the ground.

"Chey-yo!" the Bodes cheered as we transitioned to forward flight and picked up speed and altitude.

With a refreshing prop wash blowing through the cabin, Thach began chanting:

> Puc a puc a Ho Chi Minh.
> Puc a puc a Ho Chi Minh.

"He sings fuck Ho Chi Minh." Rinh grinned.
Soon, everyone was singing:

> Puc a puc a Ho Chi Minh.
> Puc a puc a Ho Chi Minh.

"We made it." Bob shook my hand.

A golden sun was silhouetted against a black-and-red sky, and a thousand feet below, the shadows lengthened as night descended on the Forbidden Zone.

I felt a tap on my shoulder, and when I turned, I saw that it was the door gunner reaching to hand me a set of earphones. I placed them over my ears and found that I was listening to Simon and Garfunkel's "Homeward Bound." I flashed him a thumbs-up, leaned back against my rucksack, and closed my eyes. Life was good. . . .

EPILOGUE

Following operation Blackjack-33, Maj. Gen. John H. Hay, commanding general, 1st Infantry Division, decorated the American members of the Mobile Guerrilla Force and commended them for their outstanding display of aggressiveness, devotion to duty, and personal bravery.

On 1 August 1967, the Mobile Guerrilla Force was redesignated Project Rapid Fire (Provisional Detachment B-36) and, under B-36, Detachments A-303 and A-304, became A-361 and A-362. B-36 was also augmented with twenty long-range reconnaissance patrol personnel from the American infantry divisions in the III Corps Tactical Zone of South Vietnam.

In September 1967, Detachment B-36 moved from Trang Sup to a site on the South China Sea at Long Hai. When Projects Omega and Sigma were transferred to MACV-SOG on 1 November 1967, Detachment B-36 assumed the added responsibility of developing tactical and strategic reconnaissance for II Field Force Vietnam. Project Rapid Fire was redesignated the 3d Mobile Strike Force on 23 May 1968, and grew to a force of three light-infantry battalions, a reconnaissance company, and a headquarters company.

In July 1969, the Khmer Serei leader, Dr. Son Ngoc Thanh, sent a representative to Phnom Penh, Cambodia, to secretly meet with Gen. Lon Nol, commander of Cambodia's military forces. Both Gen. Lon Nol and Dr. Son Ngoc Thanh were unhappy with Prince Norodom Sihanouk's policies toward the Communists and feared the presence of an estimated forty-five thousand North Vietnamese and Viet Cong troops in eastern and northeastern Cambodia. At the meeting, it was decided that Special Forces–trained Khmer Serei troops from Vietnam would assist the thirty-two thousand poorly trained troops of Gen. Lon Nol in the overthrow of Prince Sihanouk.

Khmer Serei leaders within the 3d Mobile Strike Force were informed of their role in the pending coup d'etat in January 1970, and sent Thach Rinh to Phnom Penh for a final planning meeting with Gen. Lon Nol. In May 1970, the Cambodians of the 3d Mobile Strike Force were flown by U.S. Air Force C-130 aircraft from Long Hai to Phnom Penh's Pochentong Airport. Shortly after their arrival, they engaged Main Force North Vietnamese Army troops, and over the months that followed were integrated into the Cambodian Army.

THE AMERICANS AND CAMBODIANS

Hal Slusher—Recon Section Leader, Recon Platoon

I linked up with Hal at the 1992 Special Forces Association convention in Fayetteville, North Carolina. That night he told me that following the battle on 3 May 1967, he was medevacked to the 1st Infantry Division medical clearing station at Phuoc Vinh and then to the 3d Field Hospital in Saigon. While recovering from his wounds, Hal heard that Loc Ninh Special Forces Camp had lost its medic. He volunteered to fill the position, and while on an operation in Tay Ninh Province, he developed hepatitis and was medevacked to the C-Team hospital in Bien Hoa.

Hal completed his tour in Vietnam in November 1967 and received orders to the 10th Special Forces Group (Airborne) in Bad Tolz, Germany. While assigned to the 10th Group, he participated in submarine training in Italy, mountain-climbing training in Oberammergau, desert training in Libya, ski training in Norway and at Berchtesgaden, HALO training in Germany and Spain, and counterterrorist training with the British Special Air Services and Royal Marines in Northern Ireland.

In November 1968, Hal volunteered to return to Vietnam and was assigned to Detachment A-375 at Katum Special Forces Camp. Hal was seriously wounded by AK-47 fire in a March 1969 battle with North Vietnamese Army forces and was medevacked to the medical clearing station at Cu Chi where a vascular surgeon saved his life. From Cu Chi, he was evacuated to hospitals in the Philippines and on Okinawa and then to Ireland Army Hospital at Fort Knox, Kentucky.

While hospitalized, Hal was informed that he was no longer fit for Special Forces duty and that he would be assigned as the first sergeant of a medical holding company pending a medical discharge from the army. Hal was unhappy with the army's plans to discharge him and made a telephone call to Mrs. Billie Alexander at the Pentagon. Billie handled Special Forces assignments, and Hal soon had orders to report to Special Forces Training Group (Airborne) at Fort Bragg where he served as an instructor in the surgical phase of medical training.

In June 1971, Hal was transferred to Fort Sam Houston, Texas, where he interviewed and tested candidates for Special Forces medical training. While at Fort Sam, he was selected to become a member of the first class of army medics trained as physician assistants and finished the program as the distinguished honor graduate.

Hal's first assignment as a physician assistant was with the 2d Battalion, 508th Infantry, 82d Airborne Division, where he served as the division's first physician assistant. From Fort Bragg, he received orders to the Internal Medicine Section of Ireland Army Hospital at Fort Knox, Kentucky.

Hal retired as a chief warrant officer in 1978, and currently works in the outpatient clinic of the Emergency/Urgent Care Section of the Veterans' Administration Hospital in Fort Myers, Florida. He is the immediate past president of the Veterans' Caucus of the American Academy of Physician Assistants and the executive director of the Society of Army Physician Assistants. For the past nine years, he has served in the House of Delegates of the American Academy of Physician Assistants.

Hal and his wife live in Fort Myers and have two grown children. In his spare time, he enjoys traveling, fishing, and time with his grandchildren.

Hal earned a number of military awards and decorations but only wore his Combat Medical Badge, Master Parachutist Badge, and three Purple Hearts.

Kien Rinh—Chief Cambodian Medic

Rinh remained with the Mobile Guerrilla Force, Project Rapid Fire, and the 3d Mobile Strike Force until 1970. With the American-sponsored overthrow of Cambodia's Prince Norodom Sihanouk in the spring of 1970, he was airlifted to Phnom Penh, Cambodia. Once the government of Lon Nol was in power, Rinh was selected to attend the Khmer National Military Academy in Phnom Penh. He graduated in 1973, was assigned to the 101st Evacuation Hospital in Phnom Penh, and quickly rose to the rank of captain.

By 1975, the Khmer Rouge had taken over in Cambodia and were systematically tracking down and murdering everyone who had served with the Americans or the Lon Nol government. Rinh avoided capture and, in April, headed back to Vietnam on foot. Twenty-nine days later, he arrived at his former village in Vinh Binh Province. By then the Communists had also taken over in Vietnam, but with the help of friends, Rinh managed to conceal his past from the Communist authorities.

Rinh's luck ran out in July 1982, when an informer told the police that he had worked with Special Forces. Rinh once again avoided capture and headed back to Cambodia, where he hid and lived as a woodcutter near Kampong Speu. Vietnamese security forces were soon on his trail, but he evaded them and headed northwest to the city of Battambang.

When he arrived there, security forces from the Cambodian National Front arrested and jailed him. After four days of intense interrogation, Rinh convinced his captors that he had never worked with the Americans or the government of Lon Nol. He also convinced them that he was on his way to a job in Paris and that if they didn't execute him, he would send them money from France. They believed his story, and a few days later, Rinh made it to the Thai border and the Site #2 refugee camp. While at Site #2, he applied for permission to emigrate to the United States; in January 1987, he made it to Seattle, Washington, where he found part-time work as a medical interpreter.

In November 1997, I linked up with Rinh for the first time in over thirty years. When I asked him if he ever sent the money to the members of the Cambodian National Front, he said, "No, Donahue. I lost their address."

Hout—Assistant Machine Gunner, 3d Platoon

Hout was killed in Cambodia.

Thach—Squad Leader, 3d Platoon

Thach was fatally wounded on Blackjack-34—a July 1967 operation north of Quan Loi—and died in my arms.

Tom Horn—Senior Radio Operator, Mobile Guerrilla Force

Following Blackjack-33, Tom was reassigned to MACV-SOG's Command and Control Central at Kontum. In August 1968, he received orders to the 1st Special Forces Group (Airborne) on Okinawa where he served as a senior radio operator on an A-Team. Tom volunteered to return to Vietnam for a third tour and was assigned to MACV-SOG's Recon Team California at Kontum.

In October 1969, Tom received orders back to the 1st Group on Okinawa and a few months later again volunteered to return to Vietnam. When he arrived in Nha Trang in January 1970, he became an instructor at the MACV Recondo School. When the 5th Group returned to Fort Bragg, North Carolina, in March 1971, Tom remained in Nha Trang as an unconventional warfare instructor with the Special Missions Advisory Group.

Tom rotated back to an A-Team on Okinawa in February 1971 and, in July 1972, again volunteered to return to Vietnam. When he arrived in Da Nang, he was assigned to Forces Armées Nationales Khmeres where he trained Cambodian Border Ranger battalions at various locations.

Tom returned to Okinawa in November 1972 and, while assigned to the 1st Group, attended the NCO Academy in Korea. In December 1973, he received orders to the 5th Group at Fort Bragg, North Carolina, where he served as a member of the HALO/ SCUBA Green Light Team. As a member of the Green Light Team, Tom was trained to infiltrate enemy-controlled areas and destroy high-value targets with rucksack-portable nuclear weapons. While assigned to the 5th, Tom also attended the Senior NCO School at Fort Benning, Georgia. When he returned to Fort Bragg, he became the NCOIC of the 5th's SCUBA Locker.

In April 1980, Tom received orders to the West Virginia University ROTC where he served as the senior enlisted adviser. Tom returned to Fort Bragg and the John F. Kennedy Center for Special

Warfare in May 1983. As a member of the Detachment Officer's Committee, he taught classified subjects in unconventional warfare.

In May 1984, Tom became the NCOIC of the Special Forces Underwater Operations school at Key West, Florida, and in June 1987, he received orders to the Special Operations Command at MacDill Air Force Base, Florida. While assigned to the Special Operations Command, he served as the action officer for Special Operations Forces in the Pacific Theater and coordinated diving requalifications. During the Gulf War, Tom was a member of the Special Operations Command's Crisis Action Team.

Tom retired from the Army as a sergeant major in 1992. He and his wife have three grown children and live in Riverview, Florida, where he is a commercial fisherman.

Tom's military awards and decorations include the:

Legion of Merit
Bronze Star (3d Award)
Defense Meritorious Service Medal
Meritorious Service Medal (2d Award)
Army Commendation Medal (3d Award)
Army Achievement Medal (3d Award)
Good Conduct Medal (8th Award)
National Defense Service Medal
Armed Forces Expeditionary Medal
Vietnam Service Medal
NCO Professional Development Ribbon (3d Award)
Army Service Ribbon
Republic of Vietnam Campaign Medal
Combat Infantryman Badge
Special Forces Tab
Master Parachutist Badge
SCUBA Badge
Vietnamese Parachutist Badge
Philippine Parachutist Badge
Korean Parachutist Badge
Taiwanese Parachutist Badge

Danh—Silent Weapon Specialist, 3d Platoon

Danh was medevacked to Trang Sup and was treated at the Mobile Army Surgical Hospital in Tay Ninh. He returned to the Mobile Guerrilla Force and was later killed fighting the Khmer Rouge in Cambodia.

Tan Dara Thach—Khmer Serei Representative

From his headquarters in Cao Lanh, Tan continued to provide recruits for the Mobile Guerrilla Force, Project Rapid Fire, and the 3d Mobile Strike Force.

In October 1970, Tan was flown to Phnom Penh, Cambodia, where he became the chief of staff of the Cambodian Army's 48th Infantry Brigade. While assigned to the 48th, he attended training at the U.S. Army Intelligence School on Okinawa and, in December 1972, became the assistant director of the Khmer Republic's Foreign Aid Office in Phnom Penh. Tan graduated from the Khmer National Military Academy in September 1973, and was promoted to lieutenant colonel in early 1975. Shortly after his promotion, he received orders to attend the Command and General Staff College at Fort Leavenworth, Kansas, but his plans were interrupted when the Khmer Rouge took over in April 1975.

Following the Khmer Rouge takeover, Tan and his wife and daughter escaped from Phnom Penh and hid in the forest near the village of Bang Crum. In July 1975, he and his family again narrowly evaded capture by Khmer Rouge security forces and walked back to the village of Ke Sach in Kien Tuong Province, Vietnam. By then the Communists had also taken over in Vietnam; and to avoid arrest, Tan and his family fled to Saigon where they adopted Chinese names and hid with friends in Cholon.

In September 1975, Tan, his family, and a few friends made it to Hue where they hoped to cross the borders into Laos and Thailand. Shortly after their arrival in Hue, they were arrested, jailed, and interrogated by Vietnamese security forces. Tan convinced his captors that he was a Cambodian-born businessman who didn't speak Vietnamese. He was released from jail in November 1975 and returned to Saigon.

While in Saigon, Tan again convinced the authorities that he was a Cambodian-born businessman and obtained visas for himself and his family. In October 1978, they flew to Paris where he found work as a dispatching agent with the Renault Automobile Company.

In August 1980, they immigrated to the United States, where Tan earned a bachelor's degree in mechanical engineering and a master's in engineering. Tan is the president of the Khmer-Kampuchea-Krom Federation and devotes much of his time to promoting the interests of Khmer-Krom who live in Vietnam and abroad.

Chham—Assistant Machine Gunner, 3d Platoon

Chham was killed in Cambodia.

Bob Cole—Commander, 3d Platoon

In 1978, I decided to write *No Greater Love,* and during the years that followed located all of the surviving American members of that operation. I reestablished contact with Bob when I ran into him at the July 1979 Special Forces Association Convention in Washington, D.C. It had been more than ten years since I had seen him, and it didn't surprise me that he was still as soft-spoken as ever. Over a spaghetti dinner that night, I tried to get him to talk about the war, but it proved difficult.

When I finally got him to open up, he told me that he left Vietnam in 1968 and was assigned to the 7th Special Forces Group (Airborne) at Fort Bragg, where he taught small-unit tactics. Later that year, he was transferred to the 46th Special Forces Company (Airborne) in Thailand, where he worked with the Thai Special Forces at Nam Pung Dam.

Bob told me that he volunteered to return to Vietnam in 1969, and when he arrived in country, he was assigned to MACV-SOG's Command and Control North at Da Nang. About halfway through his tour, he took a weekend R & R and caught a flight south to visit some old Vietnamese comrades who lived in Tay Ninh. On his first night back in town, he took a couple of his friends to the Bamboo Club for grilled buffalo steaks and cold *Biere "33."* While eating dinner, he recognized a Cambodian who had fought with Bill Ferguson's 2d Platoon at Quan Loi and Ben Soi.

Bob completed what was to be his last tour in Vietnam in 1970 and returned to the 6th Group at Fort Bragg to retire as a master sergeant. As a retiree, he told me he found himself faced with a dilemma. He had grown up in Brooklyn and couldn't decide whether to return there or remain in North Carolina. He decided to flip a coin. If it turned up heads he'd go back to New York, and if it was tails, he'd stay in North Carolina. Well, New York lost, and Bob stayed in North Carolina, where he went to work for the post office. He worked for the post office for twenty-one years and retired in September 1994. Bob has five grown children and, in his spare time, enjoys surfing the net and fishing for trout and smallmouth bass.

Bob's military awards and decorations include the:

Silver Star
Bronze Star (2d Award)
Purple Heart
Army Commendation Medal
Good Conduct Medal (4th Award)
National Defense Service Medal
Vietnam Service Medal
Republic of Vietnam Campaign Medal
Vietnamese Cross of Gallantry
Combat Infantryman Badge
Special Forces Tab
Senior Parachutist Badge
Vietnamese Parachutist Badge
Thai Parachutist Badge
Thai Fourragère

Men—Rifleman, 3d Platoon
Men was killed in Cambodia.

Set—Rifleman, 3d Platoon
Set was killed in Cambodia.

Jim Battle—Deputy Commander, 2d Platoon
During a 13 August 1967 raid on a Viet Cong base complex north of Ben Soi Special Forces Camp, a rocket-propelled grenade blew much of the flesh from Jim's left arm. Jim was medevacked to the 196th Light Infantry Brigade's Mobile Army Surgical Hospital in Tay Ninh where they cleaned and dressed his wound. More than a week later, he was evacuated to a hospital in Yokohama, Japan, and then to Walter Reed Army Hospital in Washington, D.C.

Jim underwent several muscle and nerve transplant operations at Walter Reed and remained there until May 1968. At that time, he was offered the options of remaining on active duty with a medical profile or accepting a medical discharge from the army. Since a medical profile would disqualify him from serving with Special Forces, he made the difficult decision to accept a medical discharge.

Following his discharge, Jim and his wife and daughter moved to Richmond, Virginia, where he became a health and physical education teacher and a basketball and football coach with the Richmond Public School System. Jim remained with the school system for seventeen years and, in July 1985, became the athletic director at Virginia Union University in Richmond. In his spare time he enjoys hunting, fishing, and golf.

Jim's military awards and decorations include the:

Bronze Star
Purple Heart
Good Conduct Medal
National Defense Service Medal
Vietnam Service Medal
Republic of Vietnam Campaign Medal
Combat Infantryman Badge
Special Forces Tab
Parachutist Badge
Vietnamese Parachutist Badge

Kim—Rifleman, 3d Platoon

Kim was killed in Cambodia.

Roc—Rifleman, 3d Platoon

Roc was killed in Cambodia.

James "Bo" Gritz—Commander, Mobile Guerrilla Force

While attending the 1979 Special Forces Association convention in Washington, D.C., I linked up with Bo. At that time, he was staying at a friend's home in suburban Washington and invited me to stay with him while I was in town. The following morning, we were up before first light doing push-ups on the front lawn, and by the time dawn cracked, we were well into a long-distance run over the rolling suburban hills.

While working up a good sweat, he told me that he left Vietnam in 1968 to attend the army's Chinese Language School in Monterey, California. When he completed language training in 1970, he received orders to attend the Command and General Staff College at

Fort Leavenworth, Kansas. After graduating in 1972, he moved to Washington, D.C., to become an aide to Gen. William C. Westmoreland, who at that time was the chief of staff of the army. Later that year, Gen. Creighton W. Abrams replaced Westmoreland as chief of staff, and Bo received orders to enroll in a full-time graduate program at the American University in Washington.

Upon completion of his graduate studies in 1974, he became the commander of the 3d Battalion of the 7th Special Forces Group (Airborne) in Panama. In 1976, he returned to Washington and the Pentagon to become the chief of congressional relations for the office of the secretary of defense.

That night over dinner, he told me that in October 1978 he had been asked by Lt. Gen. Harold Aaron, deputy director of the Defense Intelligence Agency, to retire from the military to organize and command a civilian prisoner of war rescue operation. He explained that General Aaron and others within the military and intelligence establishments knew that American prisoners of war were being held in Southeast Asia.

Bo retired from the army in 1979 and was given a "cover" position as a program manager with the Hughes Aircraft Company in El Segundo, California. Gen. Eugene Tighe, Aaron's superior at the Defense Intelligence Agency, also made the necessary arrangements for Texas billionaire H. Ross Perot to front the "private sector" operation.

Since his retirement, Bo has organized four major prisoner of war rescue missions: Velvet Hammer in early 1981; Grand Eagle in late 1981; Lazarus in late 1982; and Lazarus Omega in early 1983.

Bo lives in Kamiah, Idaho, where he is a conservative radio-talk-show host and land developer.

Bo's military awards and decorations include the:

Silver Star (3d Award)
Legion of Merit (2d Award)
Distinguished Flying Cross
Soldier's Medal
Bronze Star (8th Award)
Purple Heart
Air Medal (26th Award)
National Defense Service Medal
Vietnam Service Medal
Republic of Vietnam Campaign Medal

Vietnamese Cross of Gallantry
Gold Star of Cambodia
Combat Infantryman Badge
Special Forces Tab
Ranger Tab
Master Parachutist Badge
SCUBA Badge
Pathfinder Badge
Vietnamese Parachutist Badge
Panamanian Parachutist Badge
Honduran Parachutist Badge
Colombian Parachutist Badge

Suol—Rifleman, 3d Platoon

Suol was wounded north of Quan Loi in July 1967. He recovered from his wounds and was later killed in Cambodia.

Huong—Rifleman, 3d Platoon

Huong was killed in Cambodia.

Dale England—Commander, Recon Platoon

In 1989, I decided to write a book on Blackjack-31—*Mobile Guerrilla Force*—and during the months that followed tracked down most of the surviving American members of that operation.

When I located Dale, he told me that, following Blackjack-33, he was medevacked to the 1st Infantry Division medical clearing station at Phuoc Vinh. From there, he was sent to the 93d Evacuation Hospital in Long Binh, a hospital in Japan, and finally to Walter Reed Army Hospital in Washington, D.C.

Following five months of medical treatment, he received orders to the 46th Special Forces Company (Airborne) in Thailand. While stationed at Nam Pung Dam and Nakhon Phanom, Dale taught light infantry tactics and weapons to Thai military personnel and members of the Village Defense Corps. Dale returned to Vietnam a year later and was assigned to MACV-SOG's Command and Control South at Ban Me Thuot. While with Command and Control South, he ran cross-border reconnaissance teams into Cambodia.

Late in 1970, Dale returned to Thailand to serve an additional three years with the 46th Company. For over two years, he served at a classified site and then was reassigned to the 46th Company Liaison Detachment in Bangkok.

In September 1973, he returned to Fort Bragg, North Carolina, to serve with Special Forces Training Group (Airborne) and later the 5th Group. While assigned to the 5th, Dale's mobile training team deployed to Liberia, Africa, where they trained Liberian army cadre that included a master sergeant by the name of Samuel K. Doe. On 12 April 1980, Sergeant Doe and a handful of enlisted men from the Peoples' Redemption Council overthrew the government of President William R. Tolbert.

Dale deployed to Saudi Arabia with the 5th Group during Operation Desert Shield and served as their operations sergeant major. During Operation Desert Storm, he was assigned to the 5th's tactical command post. Following the war in the Middle East, Dale retired and currently lives in Clarksville, Tennessee, with his wife and two grown daughters.

Dale's military awards and decorations include the:

Silver Star
Legion of Merit
Bronze Star (3d Award)
Purple Heart
Meritorious Service Medal (3d Award)
Air Medal
Army Commendation Medal (2d Award)
Good Conduct Medal (10th Award)
National Defense Service Medal with Bronze Star
Armed Forces Expeditionary Medal (Dominican Republic)
Southwest Asia Service Medal with two Bronze Stars
NCO Professional Development Ribbon (4th Award)
Army Service Ribbon
Overseas Service Ribbon with numeral 2
Vietnam Service Medal
Republic of Vietnam Campaign Medal
Saudi Arabian Liberation of Kuwait Medal
Kuwaiti Liberation of Kuwait Medal
Combat Infantryman Badge
Special Forces Tab
Master Parachutist Badge
Military Free-Fall Parachutist Badge

Thai Parachutist Badge with fourragère
Vietnamese Parachutist Badge
Cambodian Parachutist Badge
Canadian Parachutist Badge
Jordanian Parachutist Badge
Kenyan Parachutist Badge
Greek Parachutist Badge

Thinh—Squad Leader, 3d Platoon
Thinh was killed in Cambodia.

Dat—Rifleman, 3d Platoon
Dat was killed in Cambodia.

Francis "Blackjack" Kelly—Commanding Officer, 5th Special Forces Group (Airborne)

Blackjack returned to Fort Bragg in July 1967 to assume command of the Institute of Strategic and Special Operations. In June 1970, he was transferred to Denver, where he served as the senior military adviser to the state of Colorado.

The colonel retired from the army in August 1972 to become a professor of economics and political science at Loretto Heights College in Denver. Blackjack authored nine books and wrote the foreword to my second book, *Mobile Guerrilla Force*.

Colonel Kelly died on 26 December 1997 and is buried at Fort Logan National Cemetery.

Blackjack's military awards and decorations include the:

Silver Star
Legion of Merit (4th Award)
Bronze Star (2d Award)
Purple Heart
Air Medal (5th Award)
Order of Military Merit
National Defense Service Medal
European-African–Middle Eastern Campaign Medal
Army of Occupation Medal (Germany)
Armed Forces Expeditionary Medal
Vietnam Service Medal
Republic of Vietnam Campaign Medal

Combat Infantryman Badge
Special Forces Tab
Master Parachutist Badge
Vietnamese Cross of Gallantry
Vietnamese Parachutist Badge

Phone—Rifleman, 3d Platoon

Phone survived the war and is believed to be living in the state of Washington.

Nair—Rifleman, 3d Platoon

Nair was killed in Cambodia.

Glen Bevans—Commander, 4th Platoon

Glen left the Mobile Guerrilla Force in August 1967 and returned to Fort Bragg to serve as an instructor with Special Forces Training Group (Airborne). In September 1968, he became the Special Forces Recruiter at Fort Ord, California, and in January 1970, he returned to Vietnam to serve with Mike Force Detachment A-401 in Don Phuc. Later that year, he was transferred to the Forces Armées Nationales Khmeres training center at Chi Lang, where he trained Cambodians for the army of Gen. Lon Nol.

Glen rotated back to Fort Bragg in October 1971, and served as the intelligence sergeant of the 2d Brigade, 82d Airborne Division. In July 1974, he received orders to report to Special Forces Detachment A in West Berlin where he was involved in counterintelligence and site-reconnaissance operations against the Union of Soviet Socialist Republics.

In July 1976, Glen was promoted to sergeant major and was transferred to Bad Tolz, Germany, where he became the operations sergeant major of Special Forces Detachment Europe (Airborne). In July 1978, he was assigned as the sergeant major of the 1st Battalion, 10th Special Forces Group (Airborne) at Bad Tolz, and in September 1979, he returned to Special Forces Detachment Europe.

In April 1980, Glen received orders to the South Western Oklahoma State University ROTC in Weatherford, Oklahoma. Glen retired from the army in July 1982, and is currently the Immigration & Naturalization Service's assistant port director at the Dallas–Fort Worth International Airport. He and his wife live in nearby Carrollton.

Glen's military awards and decorations include the:

Silver Star
Legion of Merit
Bronze Star (2d Award)
Army Commendation Medal
Good Conduct Medal (10th Award)
National Defense Service Medal (2d Award)
European Occupation Medal
Vietnam Service Medal
Republic of Vietnam Campaign Medal
Vietnamese Cross of Gallantry
Combat Infantryman Badge
Special Forces Tab
Master Parachutist Badge
Vietnamese Parachutist Badge

Truong—Rifleman, 3d Platoon

Truong was killed in Cambodia.

James Williams—Recon Section Leader, Recon Platoon

Jim's body was evacuated to Phuoc Vinh and then back to the States. His name is listed on panel nineteen of the Vietnam Veterans' Memorial in Washington, D.C.

Hoa—Rifleman, 3d Platoon

Hoa was killed in Cambodia.

Donald "Ranger" Melvin—Commander, 1st Platoon

Following the battle on 3 May 1967, Ranger was medevacked to the 1st Infantry Division's medical clearing station at Phuoc Vinh. That night, he checked himself out of the hospital after he was caught drinking beer in his hospital bed. Ranger returned to Trang Sup; and after his stitches were removed, he became the special operations sergeant of MACV-SOG's Command and Control North at Da Nang.

In April 1968, he received orders to Furman University in Greenville, South Carolina, where he set up a Ranger training program for ROTC cadets. Ranger left for the 1st Group in June

1969 and, when he arrived on Okinawa, became the first sergeant of the Headquarters & Service Company.

Ranger returned to Fort Bragg and the 7th Group in June 1970 and served as the group's special operations NCO until he volunteered to return to Vietnam. When he arrived in Nha Trang in January 1971, he was assigned to MACV-SOG's Command and Control Central at Kontum, where he served with recon teams Arizona, California, Kentucky, New York, South Carolina, and West Virginia.

Ranger rotated back to Fort Bragg and the 7th Group in January 1972, and again served as the group's special operations NCO. In February 1976, he received orders to attend the Sergeants Major Academy at Fort Bliss, Texas, and upon graduation became the sergeant major of Training Command at Fort Jackson, South Carolina.

In June 1981, Ranger was ordered to Korea where he served as the command sergeant major of the 2d Brigade, 2d Infantry Division. In September 1981, he became the division sergeant major.

Ranger returned to Fort Jackson in June 1982 to assume the duties of command sergeant major of Troop Command and retired from the army in 1984. Ranger has three grown children and lives in Wilmington, North Carolina. In his spare time, he enjoys competitive bass fishing.

Ranger's military awards and decorations include the:

Silver Star
Bronze Star (3d Award)
Purple Heart
Air Medal
Meritorious Service Medal (3d Award)
Army Commendation Medal (3d Award)
Good Conduct Medal (8th Award)
Vietnamese Service Medal
Republic of Vietnam Campaign Medal
NCO Professional Development Ribbon (5th Award)
Korean Chief of Staff Medal
Vietnamese Cross of Gallantry
Combat Infantryman Badge
Special Forces Tab
Ranger Tab

Master Parachutist Badge
Recondo Badge
Vietnamese Parachutist Badge

Suong—Rifleman, 3d Platoon

Suong was killed in Cambodia.

Huon—Rifleman, 3d Platoon

Huon survived the war and is believed to be living in Arizona.

Roy Sparks—Deputy Commander, 4th Platoon

Roy survived the war and is believed to be living in one of the western states.

Son Thai Hien—Machine Gunner, 2d Platoon

In November 1997, I linked up with Son for the first time since September 1967. When I arrived at the Philadelphia airport, I spotted him standing in the crowd. He didn't say a word and was waiting to see if I would recognize him. Of course I did, and after an emotional reunion, he took me to a Vietnamese restaurant for lunch. Over jasmine tea and bowls of steaming Vietnamese soup, we looked at faded photographs and talked about old friends.

Son told me that as a member of the 3d Mobile Strike Force, he attended jump school in Nha Trang and that his company was airlifted to Phnom Penh in the spring of 1970. After the overthrow of Prince Sihanouk, he was assigned to the Cambodian Army's 43d Infantry Brigade at Borey Keila; and in October 1971, was selected to attend leadership training in Chi Lang. Following graduation, he rose to the rank of captain and became the commander of the 271st Battalion at Kampong Cham.

In a December 1973 battle with the Khmer Rouge at Chero, Son lost his right leg—above the knee—to a claymore mine. He was evacuated to the 701st Military Hospital in Phnom Penh and in April 1974 was fitted with an artificial leg.

On 17 April 1975, the Khmer Rouge took over in Cambodia; and to avoid execution, Son decided that he, his wife, and two children would attempt to walk back to Vietnam. It took them seventeen days, and when they arrived in Tay Ninh, he was arrested by Communist authorities and sent to Tra Vinh prison. For five years, he was beaten and interrogated on a regular basis but never admitted his involvement with Special Forces.

When Son was released from prison, he told his wife that he couldn't live under Communism and started planning his escape to Thailand on foot. In September 1981, he, his wife, and three children began their long march across Vietnam and Cambodia, and during their thirty-three-day ordeal had many close encounters with Vietnamese and Khmer Rouge security forces and bandits.

When they reached Thailand, they were sent to the Khao Y Dang Refugee Camp and remained there for almost two years. In September 1984, he, his wife, two sons, and four daughters immigrated to the United States and currently live in Philadelphia. Son is the president of the United Cambodian-American Association and devotes much of his time to helping his fellow Khmer Krom veterans.

Alvin "Cajun" Rouley—Deputy Commander, 1st Platoon

Cajun survived the war and died of a heart attack on 28 October 1989. He is buried at the Lafayette Memorial Park Cemetery in Lafayette, Louisiana.

Dung—Rifleman, 3d Platoon

Dung was killed in Cambodia.

Chem—Rifleman, 3d Platoon

Chem survived the war and is believed to be living in Texas.

Tom Johnson—Deputy Commander, Mobile Guerrilla Force

Following Blackjack-33, Tom was selected to attend the Infantry Officer's Advanced Course at Fort Benning, Georgia. Tom spoke fluent Arabic and, when he completed the course, was ordered to Saudi Arabia, where he served as an adviser to the 4th Royal Parachute Battalion in Jidda.

In July 1970, he received orders to report to Kitzingen, Germany, where he was the training officer of the 2d Brigade, 3d Infantry Division. The following year, he became the executive officer of the 1st Battalion, 15th Infantry, 3d Infantry Division.

When Tom completed his tour in Germany in August 1973, he attended the Command and General Staff College at Fort Leavenworth, Kansas. In March 1974, he was selected as the army aide to

President Richard M. Nixon and traveled to the Middle East and Russia with the Nixon entourage. When President Nixon resigned in August 1974, Tom went on to graduate school at the University of North Carolina at Chapel Hill. He completed a master's degree in organizational psychology in June 1976 and was assigned to the United States Military Academy at West Point as an instructor in the Behavioral Science and Leadership Department. While at West Point, he was promoted "below the zone" to lieutenant colonel.

In June 1978, Tom took command of the 1st Battalion, 41st Mechanized Infantry, 2d Armored Division, at Fort Hood, Texas, and under his command, the battalion set records for fitness, discipline, and effectiveness.

By 1980, the army was reeling from the effects of drugs, racial tensions, and loss of popular support. Gen. Bernard Rogers, the army chief of staff, wanted to restore the army's "fighting edge" by employing organizational effectiveness consultants as internal agents of change. When Tom heard that the general was looking for combat veterans to carry the message to a reluctant army, he volunteered.

After training at Fort Ord, California, Tom became an organizational effectiveness officer in the office of chief of staff of the army at the Pentagon. Tom was promoted to colonel in 1982, and was selected to attend the National War College at Fort McNair in Washington, D.C. Upon graduation, he stayed on at the college to teach Middle Eastern Studies.

Tom retired from the army in May 1985, and following a five-day vacation went to work as an international business marketing manager with Sikorsky Aircraft's United Technologies Corporation in Stratford, Connecticut. In March 1998, he retired from Sikorsky and is now working as a defense industry consultant in Washington, D.C. Tom also teaches at the State Department and provides assistance to Khmer-Krom veterans.

Tom and his wife have two grown children and live in Chantilly, Virginia.

Tom's military awards and decorations include the:

Legion of Merit
Soldier's Medal
Bronze Star (2d Award)
Meritorious Service Medal (2d Award)

Air Medal
Joint Service Commendation Medal
National Defense Service Medal
Vietnam Service Medal
Army Service Medal
Overseas Service Ribbon (2d Award)
Republic of Vietnam Campaign Medal
Combat Infantryman Badge
Special Forces Tab
Ranger Tab
Senior Parachutist Badge
General Staff Identification Badge
Greek Parachutist Badge

Nuong—Grenadier, 3d Platoon

Nuong was killed in Cambodia.

Binh—Squad Leader, 3d Platoon

Binh suffered a chest wound on Operation Picnic—an August 1967 raid on a Viet Cong base complex north of Ben Soi Special Forces Camp. When he recovered from his wounds, he returned to Project Rapid Fire and the 3d Mobile Strike Force. Binh was killed in Cambodia.

Ray Fratus—Commander, Recon Platoon

Dale England ran into Ray in Nha Trang in 1970. He told Dale that he was on his third tour and that, during his second tour, he had served with MACV-SOG. Ray survived the war and is believed to be living in the New England area.

Hoi—Rifleman, 3d Platoon

Hoi was killed in Cambodia.

Thang Kieng—Rifleman, 3d Platoon

In November 1997, I linked up with Thang at a Buddhist Temple in Lowell, Massachusetts. Over the years, nothing of any importance had changed. He was still as hard as woodpecker lips and retained those soldierly qualities that I had admired when we served together in the Mobile Guerrilla Force.

Over dinner that night, Thang told me that he suffered serious gunshot wounds to the head and shoulder during an October 1967 battle near Tonle Chon. When he recovered from his wounds, he returned to Long Hai to serve with Project Rapid Fire and later the 3d Mobile Strike Force.

Following the overthrow of Prince Norodom Sihanouk in the spring of 1970, Thang was assigned to the Cambodian Army's 1st Infantry Division in Phnom Penh. He soon became a company commander and was seriously wounded in a 6 February 1972 battle at Vihear Sour. Thang was evacuated to the 701st Military Hospital in Phnom Penh and returned to his unit following his recovery.

Thang's wife was murdered by the Khmer Rouge in 1975, and he and his son and daughter escaped to Pursat Province where he continued to fight as a guerrilla. He and his children made it to the Khao Y Dang refugee camp in Thailand in November 1979, and in August 1981, they immigrated to the United States. Thang and his family now live in Providence, Rhode Island.

Chote—Interpreter, 1st Platoon
Chote was killed in Cambodia.

Kenneth "Critchley" Crighton—Deputy Commander, Mobile Guerrilla Force
When Critchley recovered from his wounds, he returned to Project Rapid Fire. He survived the war and was last sighted in New Guinea.

Chon—Rifleman, 3d Platoon
Chon recovered from his arm wound and was later killed in Cambodia.

Dave Rose—Deputy Commander, 1st Platoon
When Dave completed his tour with the Mobile Guerrilla Force, he received orders to the 10th Special Forces Group (Airborne) in Bad Tolz, Germany. In 1969, he volunteered to return to Vietnam, and when he arrived in Nha Trang, he was assigned to MACV-SOG, Command and Control North at Da Nang. When he completed his second tour in Vietnam, he was assigned to the 6th Special Forces Group (Airborne) at Fort Bragg, North Carolina.

In 1973, Dave was selected to attend the army's physician assistant program at Baylor University, and in 1975, he completed the program as the honor graduate.

From 1975 to 1978, Dave was assigned to the 72d Field Artillery Brigade in Wertheim, Germany, where he served as the primary medical adviser to the brigade commander. From 1978 to 1981, he was attached to the U.S. Army Health Clinic in Wertheim, and from 1984 to 1992, he was a staff orthopedic physician assistant at the U.S. Army Hospital in Augsburg, Germany.

During Operation Desert Storm, Dave deployed to Kuwait with the 1st Armored Division. When he returned to Germany, he received orders to report to Vicenza, Italy, where he became an orthopedic physician assistant at the U.S. Army Health Clinic.

Dave retired from the army as a major in 1992, and remained in Vicenza as a civilian orthopedic physician assistant at the same clinic. He and his wife have a grown daughter and live in a villa that was occupied by Napoleon's troops during their invasion of Italy. Dave is a member of the American Academy of Physician Assistants, the Society of U.S. Army Physician Assistants, and the Society of European Physician Assistants. Dave is an avid skier and, in his spare time, enjoys skiing in the Italian Alps.

Dave's military awards and decorations include the:

Silver Star
Bronze Star (5th Award)
Meritorious Service Medal (2d Award)
Purple Heart
Air Medal (4th Award)
Army Commendation Medal (3d Award)
Good Conduct Medal
National Defense Service Medal
Vietnam Service Medal
Republic of Vietnam Campaign Medal
Southwest Asia Service Medal
Kuwait Liberation Medal
Combat Medical Badge
Parachutist Badge
Special Forces Tab
Vietnamese Parachutist Badge

Son—Machine Gunner, 3d Platoon

Son was killed in Cambodia.

Ernest "Duke" Snider—Commander, 1st Platoon

After he completed his tour with the Mobile Guerrilla Force, Duke returned to the States to serve with Special Forces Training Group (Airborne) at Fort Bragg, North Carolina. In 1970, he again left for Vietnam and was assigned to the B-Team at An Loc. Later that year, he returned to working with the Cambodians when he was assigned to Forces Armées Nationales Khmeres in Bien Hoa.

Duke told me that while he was in Bien Hoa, he ran into his old friend, Chote. The 1st Platoon Interpreter had become a captain in the Cambodian Army and, at that time, was operating out of one of the camps in the Seven Mountains area of South Vietnam. After his tour with Forces Armées Nationales Khmeres, Duke received orders to report to the 75th Rangers at Fort Hood, Texas, and in 1973 was assigned to the Joint Casualty Resolution Center in Nakhon Phanom, Thailand.

Following the war in Southeast Asia, Duke returned to the States to serve at Fort Stewart, Georgia, and to attend the Sergeants Major Academy at Fort Bliss, Texas. After graduating from the academy, he reported to Fort Lewis, Washington, and then to the 10th Special Forces Group (Airborne) at Fort Devens, Massachusetts. Duke told me that the high point of his tour with the 10th was a nine-month mission to Liberia, Africa.

Duke retired from the army in 1983 as the command sergeant major of the 10th Group's 2d Battalion. Duke and his wife live in Sumas, Washington, where he works as an immigration examiner. Duke has three grown children and, in his spare time, enjoys fishing for salmon.

Duke's military awards and decorations include:

Silver Star
Bronze Star (2d Award)
Meritorious Service Medal
Purple Heart
Joint Service Commendation Medal
Army Commendation Medal (6th Award)
Good Conduct Medal (6th Award)
National Defense Service Medal

Vietnam Service Medal
Army Service Medal
Overseas Service Ribbon
Republic of Vietnam Campaign Medal
NCO Professional Development Ribbon (5th Award)
Vietnamese Cross of Gallantry (2d Award)
Combat Infantryman Badge
Special Forces Tab
Master Parachutist Badge
Vietnamese Parachutist Badge

Dien—Headquarters Section Interpreter

Dien was last seen at a classified site in Thailand in 1972. He was a major at that time and was later killed fighting the Khmer Rouge.

Bill Ferguson—Commander, 2d Platoon

Fergy was killed in action during a Project Rapid Fire raid on a Viet Cong base complex eight kilometers north of Ben Soi Special Forces Camp on 13 August 1967. For his heroism exhibited on that fatal mission, he was posthumously awarded the Distinguished Service Cross, our nation's second-highest award for valor. The citation reads as follows:

For extraordinary heroism in connection with military operations involving conflict with an armed hostile force in the Republic of Vietnam: Sergeant First Class Ferguson distinguished himself by exceptionally valorous actions on 13 August 1967 while serving as platoon leader of a Mobile Guerrilla Task Force on a combat mission deep in hostile territory. When another company of the same unit came under attack from a numerically superior Viet Cong force, Sergeant Ferguson immediately volunteered to lead his men to their aid. Upon reaching the scene of the battle, he moved freely among his men directing their assault although exposed to withering automatic weapons fire. An enemy grenade seriously wounded him as he attacked a hostile position, but he refused medical aid and continued to press the offensive. With complete disregard for his own safety, Sergeant Ferguson directed deadly fire on the insurgents and hurled numerous grenades into their positions. He moved openly through the bullet-swept area time after time to inspire his men to greater efforts. He was mortally wounded while leading his men with dauntless courage in the face of grave danger. Sergeant First Class Ferguson's extraordinary heroism and devotion to duty, at the cost of his life, were in keeping with the highest traditions of the military service and reflect great credit upon himself, his unit, and the United States Army.

Luc—Platoon Sergeant, 3d Platoon

From Blackjack–33, Luc was medevacked to the 24th Evacuation Hospital in Bien Hoa. I caught up with him on 19 July 1967 when I was wounded and evacuated to the same hospital. Luc was killed in Cambodia.

Larry "Stik" Rader—Deputy Commander, Recon Platoon

In February 1983, I put together a team of Vietnam veterans to make a parachute jump and seven-day, one-hundred-mile run across Death Valley, California. One of the first to volunteer was Stik Rader—he was as skinny as ever and looked every inch the long-distance runner. During the run, we passed places with names like Ubehebe Crater, Hell's Gate, Furnace Creek, and Badwater, and talked about Dong Xoai, Song Be, Trang Sup, Phuoc Vinh, and Quan Loi.

As we ran, Stik told me that when he returned to the States in October 1967 he became a foreign weapons instructor at the John F. Kennedy Center for Special Warfare at Fort Bragg. In 1968, he volunteered to return to Vietnam and was assigned to MACV-SOG at Da Nang and Long Thanh. Upon completion of his tour, he volunteered for duty with the 46th Special Forces Company (Airborne) in Thailand, where he worked with the Thai Special Forces at Phitsanulok.

Stik was transferred to the 1st Group on Okinawa in 1970. In 1971, he again volunteered to return to Vietnam and was assigned to MACV-SOG's Command and Control Central as a team leader with Recon Team Texas. In 1972, he returned to working with Cambodians when he was transferred to the Forces Armées Nationales Khmeres Training Center in Phuoc Tuy Province.

After completing his last tour in Vietnam in 1973, Stik returned to the 5th Group at Fort Bragg. In 1974, he received orders to the Military Advisory Assistance Group Laos and a year later was assigned to the Thai Advisory Group in Bangkok. While in Bangkok, he ran into one of the Cambodians from the Recon Platoon at a bar on Pat Pong Road. He told Stik that some of the Bodes from the Mobile Guerrilla Force had survived the Vietnamese, Prince Sihanouk, Lon Nol, and the Khmer Rouge and that they were pressing on with guerrilla operations from camps located along the Thai-Cambodian border.

Stik completed his assignment in Thailand in 1976 and again returned to the 5th at Fort Bragg. In 1977, he became the operations sergeant of the Georgetown University ROTC in Washington, D.C., and in 1978 attended the Sergeants Major Academy at Fort Bliss, Texas. After graduating from the academy, he attended the army's Korean Language School in Monterey, California. When he completed language training, he was assigned to the 8th Army Headquarters in Korea and in 1981 became the first sergeant of the Honor Guard Company of the United Nations Command in Yongsan.

Stik left Korea in 1982 and was assigned as the sergeant major of the San Diego State College ROTC. In 1985, he asked to return to Special Forces and was assigned as the sergeant major of Company A, 3d Battalion, 1st Special Forces Group (Airborne) at Fort Lewis, Washington.

Stik retired from the army in February 1986, and was last sighted at the Maharajah Hotel in the Republic of the Philippines.

Stik's military awards and decorations include the:

Distinguished Flying Cross
Bronze Star (5th Award)
Army Commendation Medal (3d Award)
Purple Heart
Air Medal
Defense Meritorious Service Medal
Joint Service Commendation Medal
Good Conduct Medal (8th Award)
National Defense Service Medal
Vietnam Service Medal
Republic of Vietnam Campaign Medal
Vietnamese Cross of Gallantry
Combat Infantryman Badge
Special Forces Tab
Master Parachutist Badge
Vietnamese Parachutist Badge

Thai Parachutist Badge
Korean Parachutist Badge

Kien—Rifleman, 3d Platoon
Kien was killed in Cambodia.

Sarine—Grenadier, 3d Platoon
Sarine recovered from his head wound but was physically unable to return to duty with the Mobile Guerrilla Force. Sarine was killed in Cambodia.

Jim Donahue—Deputy Commander, 3d Platoon
Late in the morning on 18 July 1967, the Mobile Guerrilla Force made contact with a numerically superior, well-armed unit of the North Vietnamese Army and was immediately surrounded. During the first human-wave attack, I was shot in the left temple and after a day-long battle was medevacked to the 24th Evacuation Hospital in Long Binh.

On 10 August 1967, I was released from the hospital and returned to Trang Sup. With constant ringing in my left ear, devastating headaches, and what appeared to be a permanent partial loss of hearing, I knew that at some point I would be found unfit for Special Forces duty. It was at that time that I made the difficult decision to leave the army and return to Buffalo to attend college. I would study anthropology and one day return to Vietnam as a civilian to help the Montagnards and Cambodians.

Following a 13 August 1967 raid on a Viet Cong base complex north of Ben Soi Special Forces Camp, I returned to my home in Buffalo and registered as a student at the State University of New York at Buffalo. In September 1970, I received a bachelor's degree in anthropology and, in February 1974, a master of science degree. By the time I finished college, there were few employment opportunities in Vietnam, so I went to work for the United States Department of Labor's Veterans' Employment and Training Service.

In 1988, my first book, *No Greater Love,* was published by New American Library, Daring Books, and the Military Book Club and was awarded the Freedom Foundation's George Washington Honor Medal. My second book, *Mobile Guerrilla Force,* was published by the Naval Institute Press, Saint Martin's Press, and in Chinese by the Qunzhong Publishing Company in the People's Republic of China.

I live in Glenwood, New York, with my wife, Sandi, and have two grown children.

My military awards and decorations include the:

Silver Star
Bronze Star (3d Award)
Purple Heart
Air Medal (2d Award)
Good Conduct Medal (Army and Marine Corps)
National Defense Service Medal
Armed Forces Expeditionary Medal
Marine Corps Expeditionary Medal (Cuba)
Vietnam Service Medal
Republic of Vietnam Campaign Ribbon
Vietnamese Cross of Gallantry
Combat Medical Badge
Special Forces Tab
Parachutist Badge
Vietnamese Parachutist Badge
Cross of the Netherlands
German Performance Badge
German Sports Ribbon
German Shooting Badge
Thai Marine Amphibious Reconnaissance Badge
Thai Marine SCUBA Badge
Thai Marine Parachutist Badge
Union of Myanmar Parachutist Badge
New York State Conspicuous Service Cross
New York State Military Commendation Medal
New York Guard Service Medal

Kim Lai—Platoon Sergeant, 2d Platoon

Dale England ran into Kim at Ban Me Thuot in early 1970. At the time, Kim was a company commander with MACV-SOG's Command and Control South. In the spring of 1970, Kim returned to the 3d Mobile Strike Force at Long Hai to take part in the coup d'etat in Cambodia. Following the installation of Gen. Lon Nol, he became a captain in the Cambodian Army. When Phnom Penh fell to the Khmer Rouge on 17 April 1975, Kim was captured but escaped execution by concealing his identity. He was sent to a Khmer Rouge reeducation camp where he was beaten and tortured on a regular basis. A year after his capture, he escaped and walked back to his home in Soc Trang, Vietnam.

When Kim arrived in Soc Trang he was arrested and imprisoned by the Vietnamese Communists. He escaped from the Vietnamese prison in 1979, and after making it back to Cambodia on foot, he joined a Cambodian guerrilla group that was fighting the Khmer Rouge along the Thai-Cambodian border. In August 1982, he was wounded for the ninth time and was treated by the Thai Red Cross at a refugee camp in Thailand. Kim and his wife and two daughters immigrated to Lowell, Massachusetts, in May 1984.

A week before Thanksgiving 1997, I attended a Khmer-Kampuchea-Krom Federation meeting in Cherry Hill, New Jersey, and linked up with Kim for the first time in over thirty years. It was a reunion that I would never forget.

While enjoying a Cambodian feast at Son Thai Hien's home, we talked about Blackjack-33, and Kim reminded me of the night in War Zone D when he told me that Dale England and I wouldn't be killed because we were the special people of God. As Kim and I talked, he never let go of my hand, and I found it difficult to believe that a man who had suffered so much could retain his monklike qualities.

After dinner, Kim lay down on the couch and died.

They were Special Forces. . . .

GLOSSARY

Ace bandage   Elastic bandage that was used to cover and or add pressure to dressings and splints.

Air America   Airline operated by the Central Intelligence Agency.

AK   AK-47 rifle.

AK-47   Standard automatic infantry rifle used by Viet Cong and North Vietnamese Army.

ALO   Air liaison officer.

AO   Area of operations.

Ao dai   A traditional Vietnamese dress that was slit to the waist.

A-1E Skyraider   Single-engine, propeller-driven attack aircraft.

APC   Armored personnel carrier or aspirin, phenacetin, and caffeine.

ARVN   Army of the Republic of Vietnam.

A-team   Special Forces operational detachment that normally consisted of twelve men.

AT-892   Short antenna for PRC-25 radio.

AT-271A   Long antenna for PRC-25 radio.

Azimuth   A compass direction.

Bac-si   Doctor.

BAR Belt   Japanese-made ammunition belt and pouches intended to hold magazines for the Browning automatic rifle. The MGF used them to hold M-16 magazines. Each pouch held five magazines.

BA-386   Magnesium battery for the PRC-25 radio.

Beaucoup   French for many. Often used by Vietnamese and Cambodian troops.

Benadryl   Dyphendrydramine hydrochloride. A strong antihistamine used to counteract an allergic reaction.

Betelnut   An opiate chewed by many people in Southeast Asia. It stains the user's lips red and teeth black.

Biere la Rue   Vietnamese brewed beer.

Biere "33"   Vietnamese brewed beer.

Big Red One   1st Infantry Division (American).

Black box   Top secret electronic countermeasure (ECM) System 13A equipment carried on board U-2 spy aircraft. Unlike those ECM systems that filled enemy radar screens with clutter, the System 13A device gave no indication to the enemy that the information displayed on his radar screen was false.

Bo-chi-huy   Headquarters section of MGF.

Bode   An abbreviation for Cambodian.

Break contact   The tactic of disengaging from contact with the enemy.

B-team   Exercised operational control over subordinate Special Forces A-teams.

Bu Dop   A Special Forces Camp in Phuoc Long Province.

Bullheaded Clap   Gonorrhea.

Cam   Booby trap.

Canister round   40mm M-79 grenade launcher round that is similar to, but larger than, a buckshot round that is fired from a shotgun.

Cao-Dai   A religious sect.

CBU   Antipersonnel cluster bomb unit.

CC   Cubic centimeter.

CCC   Command & Control Central, at Kontum. Coordinated SOG missions into Cambodia and Laos.

CCN   Command & Control North, at Da Nang. Coordinated SOG missions into Laos, Vietnam's Demilitarized Zone, and North Vietnam.

CCS   Command & Control South, at Ban Me Thuot. Coordinated SOG missions into Cambodia.

C-4   High-explosive puttylike material. Small pieces would burn at a high temperature and could be used to heat water or rations.

CG   Commanding general.

Chao ba   Hello (married female).

Chao co   Hello (unmarried female).

Chao ong   Hello (male).

Charlie   Viet Cong.

Chen-Tang   Victory.

Chey-yo   Victory.

CH-47   Large American helicopter used to transport troops and equipment. Also called a Chinook.

Chicom   Chinese Communist.

Chinese Nungs   Mike Force troops who were of Chinese ancestry.

Chloroquine   Drug used to prevent and treat malaria.

Cholon   Chinese section of Saigon.

CIC   Combined Intelligence Center.

CIDG   Civilian Irregular Defense Group.

Citroen   French-made automobile.

Clap   Gonorrhea.

Claymore mine Mine packed with explosive plastique and rigged to spray hundreds of steel pellets.

Cleared hot You have correctly identified the target and are cleared to attack it.

Clyde Viet Cong.

Codeine Narcotic analgesic used to treat moderate to severe pain.

Col. Colonel.

Commo check Radio check.

Compartments The valleys between ridgelines.

COMUSMACV Commander, U.S. Military Assistance Command, Vietnam.

C-130 Four-engine medium-size combat assault aircraft capable of landing on unimproved airstrips.

C-123 Two-engine medium-size combat assault aircraft capable of landing on unimproved airstrips.

COSVN Central Office of the Communist Party of South Vietnam.

CP Command post.

CS Tear gas.

CS gas grenade Used by the MGF to assist in breaking contact with the enemy.

C-team Exercised operational control over subordinate Special Forces B-teams.

C-3 Special Forces C-team in Bien Hoa.

CTZ Corps tactical zone.

Cyclo Three-wheeled tricycle with a large seat that carried one or two passengers.

Dai uy Captain.

Danger close Calling in artillery fire within six hundred meters of friendly forces.

DASC Direct air support center.

Debride To surgically remove dead and devitalized tissue from a wound.

Demerol Analgesic used to relieve moderate to severe pain.

Dianna one-time pad Used by radio operators to encode and decode messages.

Doc-Thai Break contact.

Dong Xoai Special Forces Camp in Phuoc Long Province.

Duc Phong Special Forces Camp in Phuoc Long Province.

Duece-and-a-half Two-and-a-half-ton truck.

Dustoff Medical evacuation helicopter.

DZ Drop zone.

Eight digit fix When a forward air controller provided an MGF unit with his estimate of their location—within ten meters.

Epinephrine Injectable vasoconstrictor. Increases blood volume—and blood pressure—by constricting the blood vessels.

FAC Forward air controller.
FANK *Forces Armées Nationales Khmeres.*
Fast mover Jet aircraft.
FDC Fire direction control (or center).
F-4 Phantom Twin-engine, supersonic fighter-bomber.
5th Special Forces Group (Airborne) Headquarters Located in Nha Trang. Provided leadership and support to the four C-teams and other special operations detachments located in South Vietnam.
Fifty-one Fifty-one caliber machine gun.
Fix When a forward air controller provided an MGF unit with his estimate of their coordinates.
Fixed wing Fighter-bomber aircraft.
FOB Forward operations base.
F-105 Single-engine, supersonic fighter-bomber.

Gen. General.
Grazing fire When bullets pass through an enemy formation at a level never higher than their chests or lower than their hips—the most deadly form of fire.
Green Light Team Trained to infiltrate enemy areas and destroy high-value targets with backpack-portable nuclear weapons.
Groupment Mobile de Partisans Partisan mobile guerrilla group that fought the Viet Minh under French command.
G-2 Intelligence officer.
Gunship A Huey helicopter armed with machine guns and rockets that was used to provide close air support to troops engaged in ground combat.
GWOA Guerrilla warfare operational area.

Halazone tablet Water purification tablet.
HALO High altitude–low opening. A technique of infiltrating an enemy-controlled area by parachute.
H&I Harassment and interdiction. When artillery fires at locations where they think the enemy might be.
HE High explosive.
Hemostat clamp Surgical instrument used to stop bleeding by clamping tissue or blood vessels. Also used to hold a suture needle when sewing up a wound.
Ho Ngoc Tau Special Forces camp north of Saigon.
Hop To hitch a ride on a helicopter or airplane.
HT-1 Radio Walkie-talkie type radio used by MGF platoon sergeants and squad leaders.
Huey UH-1 helicopter.

Hustler   The forward operations base at Phuoc Vinh during operation Blackjack-33.

Immediate action drill   Practicing a preplanned reaction to contact with an enemy force.

Indig   Abbreviation for indigenous personnel—Cambodians, Chinese Nungs, Montagnards, and Vietnamese.

Instant detonation   To remove the four-second time delay section from a hand grenade so that it will explode instantly when its pin is removed and the spoon released.

Intel   Abbreviation for intelligence information. Processed information whose validity has been confirmed.

IV   Intravenous injection of blood replacements such as normal saline, or blood plasma expanders such as serum albumin.

JCRC   Joint Casualty Resolution Center.

K-Bar   Marine Corps knife.

Kampuchea   Cambodia.

Khmer   Cambodian.

Khmer Krom   Cambodians who live in what is now Vietnam.

Khmer Rouge   Cambodian Communists.

Khmer Serei   Free Cambodians.

KIA   Killed in action.

Kilometer   1000 meters.

Klick   Kilometer.

Lidocaine hydrochloride   An injectable local anesthetic.

Listening post   An outpost set up at night on the likely avenues of approach to a mission support site. Their mission was to listen and report on enemy activity.

LRP   Long-range patrol.

LRRP   Long-range reconnaissance patrol.

Luc-Luong-Dac-Biet   Vietnamese Special Forces.

LZ   Landing Zone.

MAAG-Laos   Military Advisory Assistance Group, Laos.

MACV-SOG   Military Assistance Command, Vietnam—Studies and Observations Group. Conducted reconnaissance and intelligence operations in North and South Vietnam, Cambodia, and Laos.

Mags   Short for magazines.

Maj.   Major.

"Marseillaise"   French national anthem.

MASH   Mobile army surgical hospital.

MAT-49   9mm French submachine gun.

Medevac Helicopter extraction of the sick, wounded, and dead from the battlefield.

M-5 medical kit Large medical kit carried by platoon and company medics.

MIA Missing in action.

Mike force Multipurpose reaction force whose primary mission was to come to the assistance of Special Forces units that were under attack or the threat of attack by larger enemy forces.

Mike-Mike Millimeter.

Mister Charles Viet Cong.

MK-2 British Sten gun Silencer-equipped 9mm submachine gun that the MGF used when the silent killing or wounding of an enemy soldier was required.

MM Millimeter.

Mobile Guerrilla Force A Special Forces commanded unit that conducted guerrilla operations against Viet Cong and North Vietnamese Army forces.

Montagnards Hill people of Vietnam.

Morphine Injectable high-potency narcotic pain reliever.

Morse code A communications system invented by S. F. B. Morse that was used by the MGF for transmitting encrypted radio messages.

Mot One.

M-79 40mm grenade launcher.

M. Sgt. Master sergeant.

MSS Mission support site.

M-3 medical kit Small medical kit carried by squad medics.

NCO Noncommissioned officer.

NCOIC Noncommissioned officer in charge.

Normal saline IV A sterile saltwater IV that was used to treat or prevent shock. Also used to treat serious cases of heat exhaustion and sunstroke.

Nui Ba Den Black Virgin Mountain.

Numba-one Very good.

Numba-ten Very bad.

Nung Vietnamese soldiers of Chinese ancestry.

Nuoc mam Strong-smelling fish extract used by Southeast Asians to add flavor to rice.

NVA North Vietnamese Army.

OIC Officer in charge.

O-1E Single-engine, propeller-driven aircraft flown by forward air controllers.

105 105mm artillery.

106 106mm recoilless rifle.

175 175mm artillery.

OP   Observation post.
Orange ground panel   International orange reflective panel that was used by the MGF to signal aircraft.

Pallet   A wooden platform on which fifty cases of beer or soft drinks were stacked and banded together.
Penicillin   An antibiotic made from mold that is effective against certain classes of bacteria.
PHisoHex   Surgical soap.
Piasters   Vietnamese currency.
Pith helmet   Helmet worn by some Viet Cong and North Vietnamese Army units.
POC   Point of contact.
Point   Lead man in an infantry column.
Porked   Killed.
POW   Prisoner of war.
PRC-74   Radio used by the MGF Headquarters Section to communicate by voice or Morse code with someone beyond the range of the PRC-25 radio.
Project Delta   Special Forces unit that conducted secret reconnaissance and intelligence-gathering missions.
Project Omega   Special Forces unit that conducted secret reconnaissance and intelligence-gathering missions.
Project Sigma   Special Forces unit that conducted secret reconnaissance and intelligence-gathering missions.
Pull device   A wire that, if pulled, would detonate a booby trap.
Pungi pit   A camouflaged hole containing sharpened pungi stakes.
PX   Post Exchange.

Recon   Reconnaissance.
Recondo School   Special Forces school in Nha Trang that trained personnel for long-range patrol and other special operations.
Red Haze   Aircraft-mounted infrared system.
ROTC   Reserve Officers Training Corps.
RP   A reference point on a map where two grid lines cross.
RPG   Rocket-propelled grenade.
RPM   Revolutions per minute.
RT   Recon team.
Rucksack   The backpack carried in the field by MGF troops.
Russi   Russian.
RV   Rendezvous.

Sak-sa-bai?   How are you?
Sau-lam   Not good.
SCUBA   Self-contained underwater breathing apparatus.

Serum albumin   A blood-volume expander that increases blood volume by absorbing fluids from the area surrounding the vessels.

SF   Special Forces.

SFC   Sergeant first class.

Sgt. Maj.   Sergeant major.

Shock   A state of acute circulatory insufficiency of blood. Usually caused by injury, burns, or hemorrhage.

Short round   An artillery round that explodes prematurely.

Six o'clock   Rear.

16s   M-16 rifles.

Sky Spot   Computer-controlled air strike that could be called in on known coordinates at night or during bad weather.

SLAR   Side-looking airborne radar.

Slick   Helicopter troop carrier.

SMAG   Special missions advisory group.

Soc-mow   Bloody nose.

SOG   Studies and Observations Group.

SOI   Signal operating instructions.

SOP   Standard operating procedure.

Special Forces   American soldiers trained in unconventional operations. Activated at Fort Bragg, North Carolina, on 20 June 1952 and first deployed to Vietnam in 1957.

Special operations augmentation   Cover name for MACV-SOG.

Spider hole   Enemy foxhole.

S. Sgt.   Staff sergeant.

Sterile technique   To perform a medical procedure without contaminating the wound.

S-2   Intelligence officer.

Sump   Garbage pit.

Swedish K   9mm submachine gun that was manufactured in Sweden.

Systolic pressure   A measurement of blood pressure.

TAC   Tactical Air Command.

Tail gunner   A stay-behind ambush whose mission was to booby-trap the trail left by the MGF and to ambush enemy trackers.

Tan Son Nhut   Large Vietnamese/American Air Force base located on the outskirts of Saigon.

Third Herd   The 3d Platoon.

III Corps   Third Corps Tactical Zone. Included the city of Saigon and extended from the northern Mekong Delta to the southern highlands.

Thud   F-105 jet aircraft.

Time pencil   A time-delay device that could be attached to grenades or claymore mines. Once attached, it would delay the detonation for periods ranging from four minutes to nine days.

Toe popper Small pressure-detonated booby trap intended to disable the enemy.

TOT Time on target.

Tracer A bullet with a phosphorus coating designed to burn and provide a visual indication of the bullet's trajectory.

Trung si Sergeant.

Trung si Khmao Sergeant Black.

Two by two Weak and unclear radio transmission.

Viet Cong South Vietnamese Communists.

Viet Cong Secret Zone A well-defended enemy base area about which allied forces knew little or nothing.

Viet Minh Short for Viet-Nam Doc-Lap Dong-Minh or League for the Independence of Vietnam. Organized by Communist and Nationalist forces during the Japanese occupation of Vietnam.

VT Variable time fuse.

WETSU Short for "we eat this shit up." Used as a password by the MGF.

White dot signal mirror U.S. Air Force–issued signal mirror that was used by the MGF to signal aircraft.

White phosphorous round Gave off a thick white smoke. Used by the forward air controller to pinpoint the location of enemy targets when he was directing air strikes.

WIA Wounded in action.

Willy Pete White phosphorous.

Xin loi Sorry.

Xylocaine Injectable local anesthetic.

ORGANIZATIONS

Khmers-Kampuchea-Krom Federation
c/o Kim Thong
P.O. Box 2639
Lakewood, CA 90714-6239
(562) 598-5431
E-mail: kkfed@yahoo.com

Special Forces Association
c/o Jimmy Dean
P.O. Box 41436
Fayetteville, NC 28309-1436
(910) 485-5433
FAX (910) 485-1041
www.sfahq.org
E-mail: SFAHQ@aol.com

United Cambodian-American Association
c/o Son Thai Hien
5402 B Street
Philadelphia, PA 19120
(215) 455-2216
FAX (215) 455-8794

INDEX

Follow the bloody story of
the 101st LRP/Rangers by a soldier
who was there.

SIX SILENT MEN:
BOOK ONE
by Reynel Martinez

In Vietnam, the only way to really
learn about the enemy was to put small
teams of well-armed men among
the Viet Cong and NVA to observe—
and survive any way they could.

Published by Ballantine Books.
Available in bookstores everywhere.

Find out the whole story about
Nam—from the swamp warrior
who served five tours in hell.

DEATH IN THE JUNGLE
Diary of a Navy SEAL

by Gary R. Smith
and Alan Maki

Death reigned as king in the
jungles of Vietnam. Gary R. Smith
and his teammates gave each other
the courage to attain the unattainable.

Published by Ballantine Books.
Available in bookstores everywhere.